It was 1971, her dad suggested Beth Hindle should be a lawyer. The Headteacher of her newly reformed comprehensive school replied that only boys from his school studied law. A productive and successful career in law, in public service including a judicial appointment, did follow eventually. The book is an expression of the writer's massive gratitude to her father for being the perfect inspirational and challenging role model and never taking anything for granted.

To Dad and all my ancestors who helped make me what I am.

Beth Hindle

DAD'S BOOK

AUSTIN MACAULEY PUBLISHERS™

LONDON * CAMBRIDGE * NEW YORK * SHARJAH

A CIP catalogue record for this title is available from the British Library.

ISBN 9781035805549 (Paperback)
ISBN 9781035805556 (Hardback)
ISBN 9781035805570 (ePub e-book)

www.austinmacauley.com

First Published 2024
Austin Macauley Publishers Ltd®
1 Canada Square
Canary Wharf
London
E14 5AA

Thank you to my brilliantly artistic granddaughter, Ruth Dafnis, for her painting of her great grandfather's army photo taken in 1944. It is the front cover of the book.

To Jenny Marks for her technological skills in refreshing old photographs for reproduction in the book.

To Clare Bullen, my cousin, who helped with researching the Rishton's Hindles.

To Alex for always loving and supporting.

Finally, much gratitude to all at Austin Macauley Publishers who have made the public telling of this man's life possible.

Nearly Now

It is 08 August 2017. I walk down the Market Street. I am on my way to a station to catch a train to the airport. I pass a man standing in front of three paper cups with his back against a wall. Just beyond the three cups is a pool of vomit. He is shaking his arms about and talking without meaning. Unaware, incoherent, no self-control or inhibition. He is unaware of what he is doing or saying. No one takes any notice of him though. It appears he is under the influence of drugs. I walk on, like everyone else does.

More humans are slumped with their backs against a wall or a street sign. Some ask for money. Some are catatonic, their abdomens folded over. Their bodies contorted into strange, inhuman shapes as if fried into cinder statues by an atomic bomb. All of these people are dirty and unkempt, hopelessness and weariness cloak their faces. Hair straggly and tangled, the men have stubble or beards. A few tattered belongings may be stuffed into a carrier bag. Someone has left three boxes of fruit next to a seemingly unconscious man, strawberries and plums. We who have somewhere to reach—the shoppers, the tourists, the visitors, the workers carry on walking.

This is not the back streets of some poor third-world country. This is Manchester, England, United Kingdom, Europe. One of the richest places in the world.

The same thought always occurs. How can it be? Even when growing up in the 1950s and 1960s, a decade or saw after the war, it was never like this. Born at a time when most people had lived through and with and in the war, an unshakeable conviction that life could only ever be better than before, was proudly owned and celebrated by everyone. My dad believed it and won his own personal victory, growing a family and following his dreams. He had been there in the maelstrom of global conflict. But even he with such positivity has recently been asking these questions.

Did he who fought in the war and other wars do it for this? Did the service man and woman die, suffer and lose limbs, eyes, sanity for a country that is unable and immune to this degradation of the human being?

I walk on and arrive at the station to find all trains to Sheffield and Leeds are cancelled. Not an unusual occurrence. In the last month I know of four trains cancelled and that is just the experience of two people who travel occasionally on trains. Those headed for Yorkshire are told to go to Victoria Station to catch a train to cross the Pennines. It is a Friday evening in the holiday season. People need to get places. The Northern Rail trains will be full already with the afternoon's Friday commuters' journey home to the suburbs and satellite towns. The trains will leave people on the platform; the passengers in the trains will be squeezed and uncomfortable. Hot and sweating. But nothing changes. The trains have run like this for years. But billions are being spent on a high speed train which will do nothing for the Northern Rail passenger and lots of other passengers on other lines who do not need to travel to London. They would just like a reliable, efficient train service in clean carriages which are not 30 years old. It is turning into a rant—this thinking. All we can do is rant, rant, rant. So little changes, until a pandemic comes along and the trains are empty as are the streets of the homeless—at least for a while. So many problems; so few real solutions to everything so it feels.

The suffering of the spice addicted homeless man and woman is inestimably greater than the inconvenience to a commuter that must use a third-world train service to travel to work and home. Suffering has many shapes and faces. But that term again—third world.

Trains ran on time my dad said when he was a lad. The fireman shovelling coal into the steam train's engine made sure of it. Dad had a friend who turns up later in the book explaining how trains caught up time. Nearly a century of living being the story of one man, my father is told in this book. His family history and background and his war years recounted and remembered through an account of his life, told to me. But the book aspires to be much more than a personal history. It is also a love story expressed in the letters he wrote to his future beloved wife during the four years he was stationed overseas together with her 1945 Diary. And it also asks questions of where on earth are we now given we seem to be going backwards in some ways.

But there was one question that nagged at my father again and again in our conversations. Tragically in some ways because he recalled the sacrifices and questioned whether it was all worth it. So the question again?

Did those like my father who fought Nazism—did they do it for this? Did they die, suffer, lose limbs, eyes, sanity for a country that is unable to provide basic and decent services to its populace and start the healing of so many apparent sores and pain? Did they do it for politicians who have lost public trust? Did they do it for what he have now? Have we honoured their sacrifice?

What has happened?

What has gone wrong?

What has gone right?

Let's see if there are any answers through this account of a life lived for almost 100 years.

99 Memories

This man's life came into being just five years after the last shell was fired on 11 November 1918, 99 years ago. Few remain now who were touched as infants by the grim legacy of the First World War and whose parents experienced its horrors. Parents sold the pretence that it was the war to end all wars, believed their children safe from future massacre and pain. Their father, their brother, their uncle, their husband may have fought the German foe and died, but their offspring would not, never hurt again as their menfolk had suffered. Their children had escaped the trenches, the bullets and the mud. The world would see no more cataclysmic upheavals.

We know now that it was not to be. There would be no enduring peacetime so promised by this ultimate war. How quickly it changed; how speedily effective was Hitler's power grab. The past is always nagging at us, always a gloomy light glowing in the distance, wanting to offer its uncomfortable lessons. Looking back to learn for the future feels worthless and pointless when the present is crammed full of endless opportunity, material gain and personal growth. A rosy present deters reflection on past times that are resurrected in grey, grainy photographs, newsreels and print. Contemplation of a future without the extravagant consumerist freedoms of the present is almost self-flagellation.

Worrying about maybes is fruitless, although taking action to prevent them is not. It is easier to carry on with the status quo, to stay fixed in the present without heed to the future or past. Such a focus leaves us exposed and vulnerable to when an unexpected crisis comes along to hit us in the face. Living in the opening decades of the 21st century few knew how quickly the easy, the ever available and safe can disintegrate because of never having had such a life experience. Never having lived through an overwhelming crisis that upturns daily lives—we are fortunate indeed. Wars in Iraq and Afghanistan, apart from the consequential germination of a domestic terrorist reaction, left the inhabitants of these islands untouched. Fought thousands of miles away, politicians and the populace were safely ignorant of the menacing fear of the slyly concealed explosive booby trap or the Taliban sniper. Not until the terror infiltrated our streets did we turn our heads and wonder if we could be victims. Even then it was contained and limited, not the fear generated by the sound of the bomber droning overhead or the sound of distant shellfire creeping ever closer.

A welfare state, an education system and many other institutions and creations of a civilised society have rightly protected most of the population from the poverty and destitution experienced between the wars, even accounting for the power cuts of the 1970s, the forced removal of industry in the 1980s and the 2008 economic crash. Since the 1950s life has improved for the vast majority of people. Less risk in life, more stability, security and predictability that economic growth was unstoppable, life would continue to get better. And for many in Europe this was the dreamt promise at the end of 1918.

Nothing was settled in Europe by the Great War. It laid the seeds easily germinated through the discontent of an impoverished Germany belittled by the terms imposed by the victors. No lasting peace; no settled future for millions, only cataclysmic change awaited this man when he was born into a world of uncertainty. The grim reaper was already waiting round the corner and few could escape the road that led inevitably to annihilation. Not much that an individual in the 1920s and 1930s could do to stop the Nazis gaining hold, apart from to march and protest which in Germany led to incarceration in a concentration camp or death. Or flee to a place of safety, away from ever growing fingers of evil.

Growing up with reminders and recollections of the 1914-1918 conflicts and its consequences never deterred this man and many of his compatriots from wanting to be part of the next war. It was a certainty for some years that it would happen although many avoided the unmistakable signs preferring pretence or believing other less threatening outcomes from the visible rearming and militarisation of Germany. It is difficult to accept the inevitable when the signs are unmistakable. He knew what awaited him in the years to come when he celebrated his sixteenth birthday in 1939. There was no room for wishful thinking in this household. His father had received some insider information. Repeated to his 15 year old son, it also came with a frightening prediction that Germany's war machine was so efficient, effective and ruthless that the next time war beckoned the nation's young, Britain and its Empire would fail succumbing to an overwhelming superior force.

There used to be many who could share their hard evidence of experience— of Dunkirk, the Battle of Britain, the Blitz, El Alamein, the D Day landings, the Battle of the Atlantic, the Burma Campaign and the Japanese prisoner of war camps, to name but a few of the places of war. The facts always available to be retold, to be remembered, to add to the history of Britain's collective endeavour in the Second World War and life before and beyond. This 99 year old man is a veteran, a term he hates; describing himself as an ex-soldier who spent years fighting Hitler and now nearly 80 years later sometimes wonders why he and others did and why he lost his pals. He feels that those who were not there now look back and see it as a just and noble cause. Without doubt it was, but the frustration that the present is not worth the sacrifice of so many needs answering. In recording not only his war, but how he came to that moment when he had to board a ship and leave British soil, uncertain whether he would ever return may give some answers. The telling of this story is the truth as spoken by its owner; not the second hand version of the listener. So it is his account. His experiences of yesterday may inform and advise our present and tomorrows. It may help us understand this moment of time—where we are going and where we have come from. Serving as a warning that change is a certainty and change may be devastating and horrific. The warning signs can be there but not heeded, because eyeing up the face of a future where the comforting habits and assurances of life are torn to pieces requires courage and non-conformity. But some onslaughts do seem almost undetectable. But never totally.

It was not until 2020 that many difficult changes inundated a complacent population. A new virus went viral wreaking havoc. The pandemic was an occurrence, not wholly unforeseen. Covid 19 emerged, it is reported, in a live animal market in Wuhan in China some time in 2019, or possibly it was created in a laboratory and was not kept safe and secure within that laboratory for ever more. If it was a bat passing it on to some other living thing it was an event that could not possibly be known by anyone, including the creature that passed it on. Only later when it had spread through the local population was the virus identified and the threat became manifest. Coronavirus was here in the world. It was though totally predictable that a pandemic of its destructive magnitude could descend upon the human race. Other killer viruses such as SARS, Ebola, HIV, Swine Flu and many others have originated in small mammals and stealthily mutated creeping over a species barrier to infect humans. Warnings that man has messed up nature big time and continues to do so leading to mass extinction of species, a planet that is expiring in the heat and pandemics have been around for a long time. There was little anyone of us could have done individually in 2019 to stop the jumping of this coronavirus, most likely from another creature to a human in a country thousands of miles away whose dietary choices and animal welfare practices do not align very much with those in these islands. Not much we could do either if it started life in a laboratory.

Staying though with the theory it passed over from another species to humans we have been negligent. In 2010, twenty targets to improve biodiversity and prevent further annihilation of wild life were agreed in Aichi, Japan. The targets included the cutting of pollution and the protection of coral reefs. 2020 was the year by which these targets had to be achieved. Governments have failed. Not one target has been reached. And what happens in 2020—a pandemic. A cause and effect here that has been ignored by the world's leaders and continues to be so. Failure to heal our relationship with nature threatens our continued existence. The world is changing for the worse, but much has changed for the better since this man was born.

The record of experience lived through by this man, is an opportunity to reflect and review looking back at the changes over the past one hundred years. Better or worse now—where one person finds a benefit another will see a disaster. The main aim is surely to think and ponder and not rush to swift judgements. To question ourselves; to put aside the headline for the detail. But not in any arduous way; this isn't homework. It's a story that makes the "Who dares wins" TV show contestants and their play acting masters look a little pathetic. This man did incredible things, but did not see them as such. He was just in the war, getting on with his job. Just like Captain Sir Tom got on with it, in pushing his walker up and down his garden, a distance of 50 metres, 100 times before his 100th birthday. Determination etched on that old soldier's face, every brave step an inspirational antidote to the despair brought by coronavirus. Captain Tom had been in Burma the worse of the worst places to fight in the Second World War. He never gave up in his massive NHS fund raising effort. He never relented to the obvious tiredness and pains he would have felt and suffered. He kept on walking back and forth. Just one of many from an incredible generation who never give up.

My father's history, his exploits and experiences are a collection of his stories some already family folk lore; some dormant awaiting release in their telling. Story strands woven together into a warm, loving blanket—in this case a blanket of a life lived well and to the full. His origins are explored delving deep into his family heritage that goes back as far as the ongoing struggles in the 17th century for democratic government. It exposes the suffering and injustice caused by an industrial revolution spearheaded by Lancashire in the late 18th and early

19th centuries; a never ending revolution, perpetually continuing and giving boundless technological miracles. The building blocks of scientific and engineering invention and innovation from the late 18th Century kept and keep moving ever skywards. From Crompton's Spinning Mule and Stephenson's Rocket train, the finding of electricity, the discovery of antibiotics and all the other momentous changes that have improved our lives to our current ability to communicate instantaneously with anyone anywhere in the world, we are surely blessed to be living now, at this very moment in time. Nostalgia may disagree.

Time moves, always moving, catching and incorporating those immense changes that only looking back in time reveals. Changes are only recognised by the benefit of hindsight; they are rarely accurately predicted. Some are able to sense their approach and eventual appearance, but at the start of that 99 years of life of this man there was so much that was to become that was unknown and unpredictable. The account is a recording of a life as it journeyed through many ages and places until a today that beckons as a tomorrow, finally arrives and is past in those fleeting moments of time.

Looking back over the life of an 8th Army British soldier may lead to painful dead ends, bringing no enlightenment, no hope or possibilities to help understand where we go from here. Many feel blocked in by walls of impotent frustration, disappointed at an inability to change their world in the new millennia, despite manically using Twitter, Instagram and TikTok. Experiencing an impotent rage at being unable to make their voice heard by a deaf government. Looking back to a life that has been nearly lived to its end potentially unearths from the past a hoard of golden guidance which may assist in informing choices and decisions now. Delving into memories may produce nothing more than sentimental recollections of halcyon days that never really were. Problems never run dry. They continue to abound. Even though the levels of pre-war poverty have gone, poverty still remains. Inequality persists.

The destitution on streets; the transport system; the chasm between the haves and the have nots, the feelings of exclusion of so many for so many reasons, the boiling up of the planet—just a few of the daily problems which seem unsolvable. Yet we have a world of an information web and artificial intelligence that was not dreamt possible, or maybe a dream for a genius handful, in those past glory or gory days of the first half of the 20th century. Remembering inevitably leads to the making of comparisons—the past with the present, the old with the new, the changes for the better and for the worse. Even the hardiest glass half empty is blinded by chinks of light streaming through those walls. Blessed to be living now with those brilliant life giving changes created by human imagination, ingenuity and intelligence. The wonderful human mind freed a sprint of incredible progress and betterment that are now taken too much for granted. People who seek sexual relationships with others of their own gender are no longer outlaws; women have conception within their control; difference protected—discrimination condemned; freedoms protected by human rights legislation. Despite such reforms the bad ways continue in so many ways. Human rights has done little for economic equality promoting the individual's rights over the collective rights. Racism lives on. The abuse of vulnerable children never stops. Women are still fighting for equality and freedom from fear of damage or murder. And so on and so on. But by looking back progress can be identified and tracked. But all is certainly not for the better and it is a deception to pretend it is. So much sacrifice has been betrayed. And the future holds many hesitations and doubts. The lessons of the past; have they been learnt or are they just blowing in the wind?

Memories

It starts at age 92.

"Are you writing my obituary?" dad asks. An unusual question when very much alive and with years to live. Although on reaching the 9th decade of bodily existence, you may experience a wobbly life as tenuous as the first thread of a spider's web. Ready to be broken at any moment by a not altogether unexpected gasp of deathly wind.

This forthright question was a response to a proposition and typical of this man who was approaching his own century. The proposition was a book. A record of his life story. The idea to record his memories in a book surfaced some years ago when there seemed to be a surplus of years left to gather in a crop of precious reminiscences. The thought had grown in possibility and portent with the passing days, but with the oppressive knowledge that time was running out. The opportunity was obviously finite because eventually this man would be silent for ever after. The words would no longer flow. The words would die with him. The years forever rushing onwards made certain the realisation that capturing this man's history and the world in which he lived through would not survive his passing. It had to be done now. He is one of the few remaining who experienced the 20th century in its near totality. Those like him who were there and can speak of the past as though it was the present are decreasing by the passing of the years, days and hours as one by one these heroes of the yesteryears pass on to a more glorious destiny and land, or eternal silence, depending on your point of view.

The truth of a memory—trusting what you read—no fake news here!

Accuracy and honesty and truth are important in any work of non-fiction—otherwise belief is tested. Truth is not universal—the eyes, ears, taste buds, nose and skin can lie and trick their owner. Where someone tastes pear in a Chardonnay, someone else may sense butterscotch. Opinion and description they maybe, but both may be true or false as another person may experience nothing but a sweetish white wine.

Eyewitnesses remember the same event differently and depending on personality some may be more prone to remembering what they see accurately. There are many studies that show the witness of experience and the recall of that experience is imperfect. So the stories must be authentic—the reader must have faith in that they represent the truth, or the best possible truth.

Truth is precious, yet fragile. Always being attacked and undermined and not just by the aging process or ability to recall with accuracy. Goebbels propaganda secured enough believers that Jewish people were evil thereby oiling the wheels of the holocaust. Trump shouted fake news, "it's a con", "she's a liar". Boris Johnson seems to have difficulties in distinguishing truth from lies. Liars always have a self-interested motives. There are no lies in this book because there are no self-interested motives. This man just tells it as it is and how his memory tells him to tell it.

Memories, stories and myths. Some of them already known, they became family folklore from their often repeated telling handed down as a precious legacy to the next generation, but no less true. This man's brain pathways are like the roots of a strong, secure and fearless tree impenetrable to wild storms and ferocious winds, anchoring the memories of family histories. Every so often, when the mood and time allowed, the stories inevitably rise to the surface and burst forth once again. Accounts of past deeds, happy and sad occasions became this family's narrative through their repetition, through that imperceptible tradition of the retelling, passing down through generations—treasured family heirlooms. An oral tradition always waiting to be passed on to the unborn.

A tradition dying out as memories have now become compartmentalised into Facebook and Instagram, smart phone apps, electronic photograph galleries, texts and emails. They may be lost in the swamp of indiscriminate information or deleted without a trace of the memory ever being known. Images, thoughts, experiences locked away for eternity in an invisible and inaccessible cloud. The memory still existing, but lost, unknown and unimportant. But some memories are so written on our hearts, mind and souls that they can never be lost. The major life events—birth, the first sexual encounter, the first and last love, marriage, partnering, divorce and death. Some memories get sealed away in a lead lined box. Too painful to recall, too risky to the self, too destructive. Until one day the box cracks and they come storming out to hit the core. Memories that are traumatic, that cannot be contained or rationalised. Most such memories can soften with age as other more wholesome and self-affirming recollections take

19

their place but some are resistant. They refuse being drowned out with alcohol, drugs or distractions. They infect the being and like a determined parasitic worm are resistant to coaxing out. Treatments to deaden or manage a ghastly memory worm have been developed. The problem like so many such problems has been medicalised and named Post Traumatic Stress Disorder or anxiety state or given some other label; almost as though the memory can be sanitised and anaesthetised. Some pains become cast in stone, immovable, oppressive burdens. Others as in some of the First World War shell shocked soldiers manifest their pain through a bodily tic such as a bizarre walking gait.

Some just get on with life, moving onwards helped by appropriate treatment and care. Others cannot. The memory is stuck like a thorn in the gullet.

A trigger—a television programme, driving past a particular place, a current event repeating history—a phenomenon so common when war is around, switches on that particular memory cell, somewhere in the brain, its actual location impossible to identify, allowing the memory to emerge for its retelling. Never frightened by memories, his tales are those of the witness, the one who saw, the one who heard, the one who felt and smelt and experienced.

This man's memories, in common with so many of those of advancing years recalls the past with the depth of clarity of a Bahamian sea. Memories can be simple, like this one, often repeated:

Driving down the A6 road between a stately and magnificent avenue of horse chestnut trees that had been planted in his very early years he always refers to the age of the trees as nearly equalling his. An early landscaping project aimed at shielding the first road bypass in England from the cottages and grander houses up on the hillside, he sees his own aging and growth reflected in the towering branches. He sees his own life's growth and journey and loves seeing those trees and saying they are nearly as old as him. Not the often forgetful and rambling repetition of the Alzheimer afflicted, but just the joy of knowing he has aged as these magnificent trees have done. The bypass was to allow the swifter movement of traffic avoiding the narrow lane through a village which the bin lorries and double decker buses must still squeeze through. The trees have stood testament to an example of 1920s progress and modernisation so momentous in its time that the ribbon to this one mile by pass was cut in 1927 by the Prince of Wales who lasted as King for just 326 days.

Some memories are mysterious and tempt the casual listener into inescapable commitment to hearing out the full story. Such stories may challenge the beliefs of those who have not had such experiences. No less truthful than the planting, growing and pruning of a horse chestnut tree, they can be hard to be believed. Memories can appear mysterious and perplexing, almost supernatural. Memories that tune in a sceptical and disbelieving ear of the listener in the hearing of an unexplainable, bizarre event. There are many memories retold in this book. Some of those memories have facts that are difficult to accept. One such memory is part of the family folk lore. It relates, as you will read later, to the visitation of a poltergeist to the family home in the 1960s. No historical documents exist to prove beyond reasonable doubt that it happened as told. Relying solely on the experience of the witnesses and observers to such out of the ordinary events make such memories tangible and real, even without other evidence. The world is full of the weird and inexplicable, as is the Universe.

There are more tales of strange happenings experienced from time to time through his life and by his children sometimes involving the inexplicable escape of water. Such accounts have been around for a long time, some more recent and witnessed by unbelievers and sceptics. They are not the ramblings of an old or even young man. They are not made up to provide subject matter for the book. They are true accounts even if there may be other untold and unknown explanations for their happenings. There is no self-interest to make the truth a lie.

Obvious truths such as the holocaust or the success of a vaccination programme are denied by some because for a few the truth cannot be ingested and coped with. Easier to construct different, but false worlds to overcome internal fears over an irrational terror of having a needle in an arm or that humans can commit unspeakable crimes to other humans. If they can be abominably cruel to others, it means that as a human you may have such a capability. So difficult for some to accept; easier to deny the truth.

A sound memory as a nonagenarian (being a person who is between 90 and 99 years old) is a definite blessing. 1 in 6 people over the age of 80 have dementia in the UK, an alarming statistic, even though turning it around 5 in 6 people in their 80s have a sound functioning memory. Being in the unfortunate one sixth group can be resistant to contemplation. The ravages of memory loss for those who are in that one sixth group are devastating; prevention rather than cure has the potential for escaping the disease. This man's formidable ultra-biking and walking expeditions when younger may have given him protection; recent research found that those in their 60s and 70s who could ride a bike for 100 kilometres in under 6.5 hours for a man and 60 kilometres in under 5.5 hours for a woman had the immune system of a 20 year old. His father had died 63 years old with vascular dementia from long term heavy smoking, but he had stayed free of any such disease giving his ration of fags during the war to his mates. His memory is as good as a 20 year old both long term and short term. His stories are sound, including the coming and going of the visiting poltergeist.

"Are you writing my obituary?"—What a question to ask.

Characteristic of my father, my one and only marvellous dad. He did so with a chuckle and big smile. No hint of irony, no hint of self-pity, no vulnerability—this is him. This is the man. Always teasing, gleeful and happy. The innate ability to look on that bright side of life, just as those Monty Python comedians sang, but never the fool, throughout his whole life he has shrugged off trials and tribulations. Lifelong traits where he sees light in the dark, hears the song through the noise and tastes the sweet before the bitter. He is a body boarder skimming life's icy bumps and crevasses with resignation and resilience avoiding the pitfalls and snares, possibly by luck sometimes, rather than design. His temperament and probably his cycling and love of adventure has helped him survive the undoubtedly tough and testing times of his long life. Not just survived, but flourished in facing adversity.

So how has he found these strengths and maintained positivity, always making the best of a bad situation. Where did that resilience and resourcefulness come from?

Staying Alive

Resilience is a powerful word. Cropping up regularly now in self-help books making the point that each of us needs it—from the richest to the poorest, to the youngest to the oldest. It is a crucial quality for us human beings to have if we are to make the best of our time on earth. If we can cope with the tough, surviving its barbs and cuts, then we may continue stronger going forward in the knowledge we came through hard times and the better bits hopefully lie ahead. Some people have bucket loads of misery and suffering to contend with during their lives; some have the Midas touch where life is a sunny, endless harvest of joy. Most of us suffer at some time. The rich and privileged may not need as much resilience as the homeless person on the street, but each and every one of us experiences during our lives unexpected personal crises and challenges in life. Lung cancer diagnosed in a non-smoker in her 30s, learning of an infidelity and breach of a trust you believed was eternal, losing employment as a high street business once thought rock solid closes its doors to customers who would rather purchase on line from companies that do not pay a fair share of their profits in tax, being in the wrong place at the wrong time as the driver losing consciousness cannot stop the bus ploughing into a line of waiting pedestrians. Those random accidents, those horrible health afflictions and personal ice flows of pain and trouble. A rich person can buy the best health treatment and best divorce lawyer, but the fear and hurt will be the same. Resilience is undoubtedly helped by luck. It plays a big part in our ability to overcome the suffering adversity can bring. The luck of being born with a good set of genes, of being born into a loving family able to provide secure and stable parenting, and schooling where self-esteem and personal worth and self-belief are implanted with irremovable roots. Of knowing your humanity and being able to greet each day with a wide grin and open arms—oh to be imbued with resilience, not the swagger of the arrogant or the aggressive, but the wisdom of knowledge of self and that whatever happens in life—all will be well in the end and it will continue to better futures. Dad's philosophy for life is of always looking on the bright side of life as those two great entertainers and comedians Morecambe and Wise sang.

Resourcefulness is another important word—we started off as hunter gatherers, fine-tuned for searching out food and shelter, the means to survival together with a mate to provide for the future of our homo sapiens species. Human resourcefulness for the individual is vital in our daily lives and is expressed in millions of ways—it is problem solving at its most basic. Sadly resilience and resourcefulness is gradually being removed from us bit by bit by many forces. The pandemic though has reminded us of our vulnerabilities, such that many of us have had to dig deep to adapt to and withstand the challenges of many unnerving changes caused by the pandemic. Many have found personal wells of resources they never knew they had; many have survived overwhelming hardship, some have flourished, most sadly some have withered. Testing times but nowhere near as tough as experienced during the last war. Since then life has become safer and more comfortable in welcome ways. Personal freedom has proliferated at the expense of collective and individual social responsibility. Some people see themselves entitled to have what they want, to do as they please without thought or regard to any other person. Selfish actions, witnessed at times during the pandemic, but balanced by wonderful selfless acts of caring and love especially from NHS workers and the many others who have died or been left with continuing ill health having caught the virus whilst working and serving the public. The most these people get is a clap. Most of the populace are not sufficiently moved to ensure that doctors and nurses do not have to work for free when jobs that need to be done are still outstanding at the end of their shift. Or are given a room where they can go and make a cup of tea and have a break. Or are given the right protective equipment to save their lives and health. Or are provided with free car parking as many public sector workers are. Examples of how badly health care workers are treated are multitudinous, and the poor pay of care home staff is another shocking indictment that our society does not really value those who look after the most needy in body and mind.

Resilience of the workers inside lifted the roof of every hospital and care home during the pandemic. Those at the top of an organisation do not make a difference. It is not the Prime Minister or top civil servants, it is not chief executives or managers—it is the person looking into the eyes of the sick patient, the confused and the demented, the neglected child, the vulnerable, the homeless, the forgotten. These are the ones who always make a real difference in this world.

The megalithic government cannot imitate the power of individual action. If the state does for us the actions we can do ourselves then we are lessened and disempowered. If social media and the pursuit and following of fame, celebrity and glamour distract from the real and important concerns, priorities become distorted—we sit on the couch and watch the screen, we follow meaningless tweets and postings and look at photographs instead of reading a book and learning something new, we Royal watch as if to own and be part of their lives. If we buy everything ready-made we forget how to create, if everything comes fed to us then we forget how to make things happen and work in our best interests; we forget how to think for ourselves; we forget we must protect, provide and secure for ourselves and our future.

The memories and experiences of my dad born in a different era shows the changes and challenges experienced during the 20th century where self-reliance, resilience and resourcefulness were crucial for survival. Perpetual changes, little stays static. Changes that have run away from some of us, the speed defying any ability to catch and harness them. Leaving us bewildered and confused such that we seem unable at times to control our destinies having lost the ability to control our lives and future. Many have lost control over a crucial predictor of happiness—health. For instance a healthy intake of nutrition eludes many people.

Take the example of Type 2 diabetes. It is a condition caused at its most simplistic by an inability of the body to process sugar and the reason the body can no longer process the sugar is that the person who inhabits the body may not have given their body the right food over a longish period of time. Over many years it has had too many calories. The reasons why a person overeats and puts on weight which makes them unhealthy are well known. Eating food and drink can be glorious, the variety is outstanding, its accessibility bounded only by the ability to pay for it. And the most comforting food—chips with curry sauce or an egg and sausage roll or chocolate or cake are often cheap and indulgent. Advertising and marketing, secret calorific ingredients, availability of food 24/7 all contribute to making us have more bodily fat than is good for us. Food gives comfort when there is little else to feel good about. Bodies come in different shapes and sizes with different abilities to burn up calories. Many reasons more than equal to the many books and TV programmes on diets, contribute to obesity.

But why would a person allow their overeating to such a degree that they could lose eyesight, have kidney failure or lose feeling in their feet? The temptations of food are immense but were never a problem during this man's 99 years. It was not that food was scarce, even during the war years food was always sufficient through rationing and because his family were in the business of providing food as butchers. There was not the variety of food available now— no pastas or curries or pizzas but the apple pies made by his mother with the lightest, flakiest pastry would tempt the most disciplined eater. One of the differences is that over indulgence then was seen as a failing, but now free will rules. The individual's personal needs trump the rest. The "Me" seems to be more important than the "You". My need is to eat what I want to eat regardless of the cost to my health and the cost of maintaining that health to a National Health Service free to all users regardless of how much taxes they may pay. Everyone pays taxes; when we buy anything that has Valued Added Tax (VAT) a tax is paid. But our payment of VAT is unlikely to amount to enough to pay for our health care. Unless we are a high earner such as a premier league footballer or a company executive on similar pay scales it is unlikely the tax we pay would cover the cost of all that we take back in services, including the health service?

So is it selfishness that leads me and millions of others to overeat and possibly put themselves in a position where they are going to need treatment from an overstretched health service. It's a highly charged and emotional subject.

Food is plentiful now for those in developed countries. It is relatively cheap. It provides much happiness. It is such a struggle to keep within the calorie limits that a body needs. It seems the body is programmed to keep eating. The body does not switch off its hunger messages when it has reached its calorie maximum. A big cooked breakfast in the morning probably providing enough calories until way into afternoon will not stop those pesky messages popping up in our stomachs saying "Feed Me, Feed me!", sending some of our tummies in search of a coffee and bun at 11.00 and adding a few more hundred calories to our daily total. And it is not even lunch time! So much is written about the causes of being overweight and the health problems it causes. The starting point is to say it is a daily struggle for most people to balance intake of calories with energy output. Many approaches are needed and fat shaming is not one of them. But our culture now is not only to withdraw responsibility from a person for their choices, diminishing their autonomy, but then to pretend that a problem can be solved by different solutions which may require the person to take responsibility. Catch 22 situation. Giving people a feel good reason for not eating as much as their stomach tells them to can be part of the strategy. What are the consequences to the person themselves and to other people if they over eat? They may damage themselves and they may hinder the ability of health services, social care and disability provision to provide similar services adequately for other people. Making a person feel guilty for what they do should not be the result; self-reflection on the consequences of our actions, a thinking to be learnt from birth should be encouraged and celebrated. Attitudes have changed to smoking; attitudes are changing, too slowly though, over one component of the huge mountains of waste we produce—plastic. Why can't our attitudes to other substances and activities that can damage us such as food and also drugs and alcohol and bad driving also change?

Food provides incredible pleasure. Pleasure in choosing, pleasure in anticipation, pleasure in the eating. We do live in a time of plenty. It may not always be so good. We may have to learn once again to live off and have pleasure in very little. Our food security is something we take for granted in the UK, but only about 60% of our food is produced in the UK. If for some reason the imports of food stopped or were severely reduced, we may go hungry. We may not be able to replace the shortage immediately. It takes time to grow crops or rear animals. Panic buying to hoard food, as has already been witnessed in some supermarkets following the Coronavirus outbreak, quickly empties shelves. This behaviour could be characterised in many ways—some of which are selfishness, irrationality, and farsightedness.

Self-reliance and personal responsibility are no longer in fashion, unless you are cast away on a televised desert island or having a race around the world with no phone and a limited budget. Bandwagon jumpers decry these attributes of personal resourcefulness and resilience as an attempt to minimise the duty of the state to provide for the citizen's needs. These vital human qualities for survival have become politicised. A battle ground for opposing forces that may call the other to be right or to be left. At present we have billions of public money paying for private enterprise to provide for the needs of the citizen. If the state takes over responsibility for all a person's needs what happens to that person's ability to fend for themselves? We expect the state to ensure our health and wellbeing, our homes, our travel, our food, our money. And the state has been happy to do that because it wins votes if the state promises to give something, very often for nothing. The state has provided billions of state aid during the pandemic. The debt the UK owes is in its trillions. What happens if there are other similar or worse pandemics? How will we afford it? A day of reckoning may come especially if interest rates rise and the debt to be repaid grows even bigger. We might no longer be able to afford as a nation to buy essentials from other countries—medicines, fuel and food. Now is the time to think long term, working out a new way of living, a sustainable future where less maybe more.

It has not always been like it is today with the state guaranteeing and providing so much. It may not always be so. Three days of no food deliveries and supermarket shelves are empty. Distribution chains are vulnerable to cyber-attack; food crops may be hit by a deadly disease or by climate change—drought or floods destroying land in which crops are grown or on which animals graze; other countries might out bid us for food—the Chinese or the South East Asia nations may pay more so the cost of food becomes unaffordable. We could run out of food very quickly. How would we cope? How would we adjust? Some of us might go foraging or try and catch a rabbit. The Eddie Grundys (from The Archers) of this world together with the rich would be the ones with full bellies. I expect we could quickly adjust to digging up gardens and uncovering the earth, freeing it from its covering of tarmacadam or concrete to plant grains and seeds to grow into produce to feed ourselves. And our farmers would grow and rear more. Just like they did in the war.

History tells us never to take the status quo for granted. To be able to cope with an uncertain future which may leave us fighting in lots of ways for our personal survival needs us to reconnect with resilience, resourcefulness and self-reliance—the 3 Rs. How do we do this? Easier said than done if your life is consumed with working hard to make ends meet or you have an incapacitating disability or you are abandoned, alone, homeless and feeling hopeless. The 3 Rs will not happen unless there are some radical imaginations and boldness in expressing different ways of living, becoming more individually and collectively independent from the state so that the worry of having a monetary benefit withdrawn or paying the heating bills or losing the home from inability to pay the rent are hopefully eliminated. Or perhaps we need to accept that since the world began the poor will be with us always, just as Jesus said. Don't switch off and close this book because religion has made an appearance. There should be no poor in the world given its resources, and in accordance with Christian teaching we should love our neighbours as ourselves. If we followed that commandment to love the neighbour as ourselves then poverty would be eradicated. Profound, but difficult words to follow proven to be so for the 2000 years since first uttered—a real truth followed by many good, caring and compassionate souls whether believers or not. You could stake your life on the fact that there will always be poverty in the richest of societies. Look at our own country where a bride and groom can spend millions on a wedding, but a footballer has to start a campaign for children to be fed. There may be many reasons why British children are not fed including parental neglect or parental inability to budget, but whatever the reason a child should not come to school without a breakfast. The reasons and causes for the need for food banks and free school meals need to be fully identified and remedied so that no child or their carer needs to be dependent on charity.

A better world was surely a reason those young men and women went to war. Dad said it was expected that he would fight for his country and he wanted adventure. Some young men and women seek adventure by going on reality TV shows like Big Brother or Love Island or to highly structured and controlled events such as festivals or adventure races. It is difficult to find raw adventure. Those living now know the sacrifices made to redeem Europe from Nazism and the subsequent raising of peace and prosperity from the ashes of destruction. Even if the new world we enjoy now could not have been envisaged by those who boarded the troop ships and the millions of others that lived through the war could not have one tiny second imagined there would be the homelessness and drug taking destitution seen on Manchester's main shopping street. So Jesus was right the poor are still with us despite the country having massive wealth and despite so many successive governments having programmes and policies to combat poverty. So look forwards and find humanitarian and workable solutions, if the sacrifices of war are to be honoured. The country should not be as it is. Here is one possible solution to eliminate poverty—give everyone an income above the poverty threshold. This is sort of what happened during the Covid 19 pandemic when the Government stepped in to pay 80% of the wages of those made workless by the forced closure of so many businesses. By looking backwards even by just a few months or years to this momentous time in all our lives when we came together to fight a potentially killer virus and help those who were left vulnerable and at risk we are surely given the impetus to strive for better futures.

Returning to the three R's Resilience, Resourcefulness and self-Reliance. They are often the result of birth characteristics present in body and soul from the very beginning of conception ready to be developed over the 40 or so weeks of pregnant gestation into a fully formed human being. Elements of a character and person are waiting in the raw materials of the mother's egg and the father's seed, to be unleashed at the moment the sperm bumps into the egg. The colour of eyes, the thickness of hair, the shape of the nose are obvious features inherited from parents and grandparents and other relatives in the family tree. But the constituent bits which make up a personality, produces behaviours and mannerisms, where do they come from—our ancestral DNA or our life experiences or both? Much research, many books and a megaton of debate has many and different answers on what makes a person. There is no universal easy answer. Where did dad's quick wit and phenomenal memory come from? Were they there from before the beginning destined to find life in a future body should the necessary genes be brought together in the embryo? Some of his characteristics were inherited in his genes that formed the baby, boy and man, but such characteristics were also surely encouraged and nurtured through the love and care of his family and friends and community and his childhood experiences.

Dad has come through the very thick and the very thin. His life example could be said to support Darwin's theory of evolution. "The survival of the fittest" is its populist and crudest description. The fittest who survive are not necessarily the strongest, the cleverest, the thinnest or the most beautiful. This is a really important message especially for those who worry about their appearance to others. He has survived by not being the typical Alpha male who is all muscle and brute force. He has survived for one reason—he has a happy soul, heart and mind. He shrugs off adversity and troubles. When on a family holiday in Southern Spain in 2018 he shrugged off a fall which scraped 6 square inches of skin from below and above his left elbow. 95 years old and he sat patiently and without flinching as his arm was dressed by attentive medics. Where does that resilience come from; it was present when his ship the Empire Pride was attacked in the Mediterranean and his continuing war exploits showed a similar lack of fear such as when German fighter planes—the Messerschmitt— used him as target practice.

Dad has lived a great many happy and healthy years because of his attitude and mind set. As anyone who has watched David Attenborough's many fantastic documentaries on TV, the creatures of this earth who do the best have the ability to be successfully different in difficult situations. We humans are part of that sisterhood and brotherhood of creatures. The power of evolution and adaptation to make the most out of its living place in the world enables a species to flourish and become established. It is the most adaptive that tend to survive. In humans could it be that it is the ones that are born with an ability to love life and stay positive and optimistic through the rough and the smooth are the ones that do the best? The ones that seek out adventure and change? That is a description of dad. He has always woken up every morning feeling blessed to be alive and unfazed by any dark horizon. An abundance of energy and determination to enjoy life's offerings, demands and fates have undoubtedly helped him to live a long and especially joyful 99 years. So what is the most influential the gene, or the upbringing?

Should the gene be identified, should it be harvested and shared so that it can be transferred to those with lesser courage or determination to survive? Such as the woman who has a gene that means she does not feel pain. But would giving that pain freeing gene release us from mental pain? Would it not defeat the essence of being a human which must be that we each one of us is created unique and different. All of us own our different behaviours be they objectively good or bad. The prospect of cloning is an abomination of what it is to be human; we creatures are mesmerizingly diverse.

But a helping of luck, call it what you will, also must surely contribute to a happy or not so happy life. The lottery starts even before conception; no one can choose their parents or grandparents and there have been studies which show that the lifestyle and fortunes of the grandparent, not just the parent, can affect the health of future generations. The technical word for the theory is epigenetics. An example of this science of epigenetics is those who have starved or experienced a lesser degree of inadequate nutrition may pass on their body's response to these privations to their grandchildren. Their grandchildren may be more likely to develop diabetes or heart problems. Studies have indicated those who smoke cannabis pass on to their future offspring the likelihood of becoming addicted to heroin. It is always sensible to look at such results with a healthy degree of suspicion especially as the results are following experiments on rats and mice. In the end there is nothing much you can do about your inheritance and what your grandparents or parents did in the past, but you can change your own life, with some help and a dose of good fortune, as my dad has shown over and over throughout his life, finding hope in the tough times and repeatedly escaping death by just not accepting its inevitability.

The length of life and the quality of that life can be determined by its owner to some extent providing that person has the tools to the make the right choices. In a healthy society the length and quality of a life should be determined by its owner. A person as a birth right should be given the knowledge, opportunities and motivation to choose the best options to attain their full potential whatever that may be. Contentment, health and wisdom are not available for millions in this world for a multitude of reasons. Dad was lucky. He arrived as a healthy baby and developed no disabling conditions during his childhood. Many diseases such as polio now disappeared through immunisation could have killed or maimed him in his 1920s childhood. Looking back over dad's life there have been momentous changes many for the better, some maybe not so. What are those changes? Where could dad and those born after him have done better? What is better? What is worse? What must change if we are to reach utopia? Looking at these changes through the life of one extraordinary man gives opportunity for reflection and wonderment about our own lives today.

Not born to riches or royalty. Not famous. Certainly not a celebrity. Not an Instagram influencer. He was like most people who do the extraordinary, they do it quietly without celebration and self-congratulation and promotion; even more they do not realise what they have achieved may seem miraculous to others. The pursuit of fame has become an obsession. It has infected such previously dignified and aloof institutions as the monarchy. Our late Queen has carefully avoided celebrity. She has maintained her separateness and constitutional role despite attempts to commercialise and popularise her. She comes from the era of reticence and deference like dad. Reticence is good; deference not as good. So much has changed. It is time to take stock. To start thinking about uncomfortable realities that beset this country. It is also time to start our own self-reflection and analysis. What really makes us contented, bursting with love of life, finding every sunrise the blessing of a new day and every sunset the satisfaction of a day well lived. Millions of words have advised how to find that elusive contentment, but there seem to be more depressed and anxious people now than there ever were.

Uncertainties and insecurities are ever present in human existence, but they are particularly present and persistent now. There are many causes. Many without foundation, but myths and false truths started and promoted through the media, campaign groups and factions skilled at manipulating people's ideas and beliefs. Dispassionate debate based on facts and absent of insults seems a thing of the past. The F word which once was taboo is commonplace. The tweeted insult has become the norm and a new phenomenon has emerged—Fake News. A certain President of the United States of America convinced people not to trust their own faculties of discernment. People closed their eyes and ears to the facts that were beyond any doubt. Closed their minds to truths that did not fit with their belief systems. Dishonesty, corruption and selfishness have always been present; the latter years of the 20th century and the nascent years of the 21st have given birth to self-seeking behaviours that are brazen in their unapologetic gilded nakedness. The sages and prophets of old who counselled restraint and propriety are now dust for many. Impassioned believers such as religious fundamentalists may rail against their interpretation of iniquities, but the protest itself is often the stuff of evil. So many difficult conundrums to explore for answers acceptable to all or at least the sizeable majority. The lessons of one man's life make for interesting reading and offers possible clues to finding Nirvana.

4000 Holes in Blackburn Lancashire

My dad is John Hindle, who also goes by the name of "Jack". Why "Jack" rather than "John" is a mystery which he has never been able to explain—the reason has been lost. He was born in January 1923, many years ago in Blackburn, Lancashire which in the 1920s the decade dad was born into, was still correctly described as a mill town where cotton weaving dominated along with other trades such as engineering, manufacturing and brewing beer. Blackburn continued as a cotton town for almost 50 years after dad's birth, but its future withering and demise was predictable as far back as the 1920s.

Cotton was everywhere. A skyline dominated by towering mill chimneys pumping out the smoke over Blackburn from the fires which powered the boilers which provided the energy to move the thousands of clattering looms weaving miles of cloth. Coming from Preston along the main road that linked the two towns a warning that the traveller was getting close to the Cotton Town, was heralded by whitened hedges.

Driving dad down to Blackburn along the A59 from the M6 one day the twisted hawthorns, blackthorns and pruned back trees, broken walls and fences that line the road fluttered with plastic waste. Carrier bags, hay wrappings, sandwich boxes, drinks bottles thrown out of passing vehicles had become caught and tangled in the bushes, barbed wire and ditches. An embarrassing eyesore created by people who must hate their country to so trash it. Pointing out to him the ugly littering from selfish and thoughtless drivers who use the road side as a rubbish dump, Dad was less exercised about the unsightly mess lining the road. "It looked like it had snowed," he chuckled. Seeking clarification he explained—"It used to be cotton, now it's plastic." Further enlightenment ensued. "Wagons transported the raw material of cotton to the spinning mills of East and South Lancashire from the port of Liverpool. The bales of cotton were not enclosed and bits blew off escaping to become caught up just like the plastic rubbish in the hedges and fences today." Cotton though has a much shorter biodegradable life span than plastic. It eventually disappeared from the road side as did the looms through the 20th century. Plastic and other such waste will stay around much, much longer than the cotton strands that had decorated the road sides.

Blackburn as is common with most towns and cities was shaped and moulded by powerful economic, social and political forces over which its working class and poorer inhabitants had little control. Even now though blessed with universal suffrage the disadvantaged may feel a crushing and overwhelming impotence to attain their hopes and dreams for themselves and their families through choosing or changing their Member of Parliament or local councillor. Universal suffrage where all women and men over the age of 21 could vote in parliamentary and local elections was enacted in 1928. In 1970 the voting age was lowered from 21 to 18. A lot of people do not vote, but this was a right fought for; a battle for democracy which continues to this day in many countries. But back at the beginning of the 20th Century when many women worked in the mills, vital to the prosperity of the town and the country the right to vote vested solely in men over the age of 21 who had to show certain ownership or tenancy of land or property.

Also at the beginning of the 20th Century Britain had an Emperor. Not a Roman Emperor who had come, seen and conquered nearly 2000 years previously, but a real life British Emperor. His other name was King Edward VII. He was succeeded by George V who became King-Emperor on his father's death in 1910. An Emperor has an empire—it goes with the job. His full title was King of the United Kingdom and British Dominions and Emperor of India. The British Empire including its Dominions had millions of subjects in its lands always coloured red on the World Atlases of chalk dusty classrooms. Caribbean islands, the continent of Australasia, Canada, the Indian sub-continent that now includes not only India but Pakistan, Bangladesh and Burma, huge areas of Africa and many other smaller islands and places all ultimately governed from London, the headquarters of the Empire and the Emperor's family.

The British had colonised these vast areas of the globe throughout the previous centuries. The remnants of its Empire continue today and are many and diverse. A Commonwealth is its current successor, but apart from finding expression in the Commonwealth Games a sporting event which takes place like the Olympics every four years, its reason for continuing to exist is not common knowledge to most people of the former lands of the Empire, its Dominions, Protectorates and colonies. Most residents in Great Britain would not be able to say what the point of the Commonwealth is other than to provide a periodic sporting jamboree. Its website shows that this is not actually the case.

The Empire could and would provide workers to produce goods in their own countries where not only labour could be bought cheaply, but where life itself was often cheap. The Empire provided raw goods like bananas to eat or tea to drink or rubber and cotton. Mr Fredric Wise, conservative party Member of Parliament for Ilford asked the President of the Board of Trade on 30 July 1923 which "Dominions, Crown Colonies, or Protectorates send bales of cotton to Great Britain: and the number of bales of cotton sent in each case?"

COTTON (IMPORTS FROM EMPIRE). (Hansard, 30 July 1923) (parliament.uk)

This is the answer. In 1922 the following numbers are centals, each cental weighing 100 lbs. Centals are a unit of weight equal to a hundredweight. Interestingly the reply described the imports coming from "British countries". These now independent states shown below were seen as part of the country and land that made up Britain in the year dad was born.

Imports from:

	Centals of 100 lbs.
British India and Ceylon	441,737
Anglo-Egyptian Sudan	80,525
Nigeria	62,067
Kenya and Uganda Protectorate	93,587
Nyasaland Protectorate	11,901
British West Indies	16,509
South Africa	14,903
Australia	12,309
Other British Countries	9,144

A massive amount of raw materials was sourced from overseas' "British Countries". Costing very little to produce because of low labour costs, the country gained immense riches from its ability to exploit the natural resources of many foods, timber, and other goods. After 1945, the rebuilding of Britain and its economy needed cheap labour. The Empire which was soon to disintegrate and become the Commonwealth as the successor to the Empire provided the workers for the mother country of the United Kingdom, the immigrants often accepting much lower wages or more menial jobs than the British worker would accept. It was a familiar situation known to many before Brexit. European workers would often undertake work shunned by British people because of low wages or arduous working conditions. People move to where the work is, if it pays more than in their home country, so keeping the wheels of capitalism turning. Capitalism brought economic benefits to billions; it has helped countries to industrialise, a process which is never without painful costs. Britain underwent massive change when it industrialised.

Such change from the rural to the urban did not come without costs. Dad's ancestors faced immense struggles but they had to strive, they had to work, they had to persevere because to do otherwise would result in the death or being sent to the dreadful workhouse. Dad's family history as you will see is probably that of your family moving from the rural to the town—or across many countries to the shores of United Kingdom or sailing over the dark depths of Dublin Bay— or a long ocean journey across the Atlantic or Indian Oceans—or flight, both air and biblical. For some a short journey in distance, as in dad's great grandparent's case. But for everyone who leaves their place of birth, their home in search of something new, something better, there is often, if not always a persistent melancholy, a yearning to return to the soil of one's birth. And a huge cost can be paid in leaving. Death. Death from drowning whether it be as a Chinese cockle picker on the sands of Morecambe Bay or in the journey from Africa, north to Italy or from Calais across the English Channel or in countless other unnamed places on a desperate and lonely journey of personal salvation.

Blackburn is also known, apart from producing cotton, for a number of surprising facts. Brewing is one and being the birthplace of a number of semi famous persons is another and for having once had 4,000 holes. The holes were in the roads. According to the Beatles' Lennon and McCartney in their song "A Day in the Life" on their truly and this is an overused word—ICONIC—album, Sgt Pepper's Lonely Hearts Club Band, someone in the Highways Department of Blackburn Borough Council is said to have counted all those holes in 1968. This was the year of revolutions, cowbells, long hair and the Rolling Stones' Beggars Banquet album. Dad did not like the long hair that had become fashionable amongst young men in the late '60s, as he always had been brought up to have a "short back and sides", a haircut that was mandatory when he was in the Army, but which he chose to continue right up until his ninth decade always insisting his hair should all be sheared off. He described the early Beatles as scruffy, but eventually became accustomed to some of the changes brought about by the massive cultural changes of the 1960s. His life has been full of changes spanning the upheavals of the 20th century, being born only five years after the end of the ghastly First World War he has seen so much shifting of what were once certainties particularly in where he grew up.

Nowadays with craft breweries in fashion it may not be unusual for a town like Blackburn to have three breweries, but they will be small affairs, not the largescale mechanisation of producing ale for thirsty throats. The clock has gone full circle. Before conglomerate companies gobbled up small breweries subsuming them into big brand names, a town, like Blackburn may have had three breweries. These were the three that inhabited Blackburn.

1. Thwaites which continued until 2015 as an independent brewery;
2. Lion Brewery owned by Matthew Brown and Company Limited bought out by Scottish and Newcastle Brewery in 1986 for many, many millions;
3. Dutton, where Dad's wife Peggy and mother of his children, worked. Dutton was taken over by Whitbread in 1964. They owned Costa Coffee before selling it off to Coca-Cola. The barmaid or man has been replaced by the barista.

Some of Thwaites' Ales such as Wainwright, named after another famous child of Blackburn Alfred Wainwright, continues to be brewed, by Marstons in Burton upon Trent, nowhere near Alfred's birthplace or last resting place. Like the brewing of beer, the manufacturing and engineering businesses have also mainly disappeared, their products and goods often now made abroad.

If you know the name of Alfred Wainwright then you will be a walker. Not just any walker but a walker of the Lake District fells. He is famous for the pictorial walking guide books he wrote and drew containing detailed descriptions of the ascent and descent of Lakeland fells, mountains and other high points, he called tops. A bit of a curmudgeon (in colloquial speech—a miserable git); he would avoid other walkers on fell tops and left none of his considerable wealth to his child giving it all to his second wife. But perhaps that is unfair; he probably preferred animals to people as he gave a lot of money to a cats and dogs' rescue centre in Kendal and having to give endless greetings and sign books when on his walks, probably led him to prefer animals that would not pester or communicate with him, at least not in any spoken language. He would detour away from the main paths to avoid human contact.

Blackburn named a bridge after him in 2008, some considerable time after his death in 1991. There are 214 tops described by Wainwright in his books and it is something of a challenge to have visited all of the tops. Finding some of them can be a challenge such as Rest Dodd set high above glorious Angle Tarn in the hills that finally ascend up to a street—High Street. Not the usual main street found running through the centre of most towns which used to be full of shops—butchers, green grocers, bakers, ironmongers, haberdasheries, post offices, newsagents. Now High Streets are full of charity shops, pound shops, phone shops, tat shops depending on the prosperity of the local economy, delicatessens may be found in well off places, cafes selling their own roasted coffee and tray bakes, posh tat shops. But you will find no commercial activities along the High Street that runs from Askham to Kentmere reaching a height of 828 metres or 2717 feet. It is a fine example of the Roman's realisation that the quickest way to get from A to B is to go in a straight line, as many mountain bikers, walkers and mountain runners confirm when travelling along High Street's bridleway.

To touch all the 214 Wainwright fell tops described in Alfred's books in less than 7 days sounds highly unlikely. But it has been done and more than once, testament to the ability of human beings to get on with the job and see it through despite exhaustion, pain and discomfort. Paul Tierney was the record holder when he summited every one of the 214 of Alfred Wainwright's Lake District peaks in one go stopping only for food, occasional naps and gear changes. He took 6 days, 6 hours and 5mins to cover 318 miles and 118,000 feet of climbing. Steve Birkinshaw's equally monumental five-year-old record of 6 days and 13 hours was broken by almost 7 hours by Paul Tierney. But there is a new record holder. Not a man, but a woman. On a 17 June 2021 Sabrina Verjee from Ambleside completed finished the 325-mile (525km) route in five days, 23 hours and 49 minutes, at 06:52 BST. 36,000 metres of ascent, which is the equivalent of climbing Everest from sea level four and a half times. She had broken the record by over 6 hours. The statistics are mind-boggling—over 50 miles each 24 hour of day and night running over rough, rocky, boggy terrain.

A survival instinct, an insatiable desire to do the impossible, to push and keep on pushing. Not to give in or give up. All qualities that mark out the great explorers and adventurers, and hundreds who during the Covid summer of 2020 used their fitness to achieve fastest known times for such feats as running all of the Scottish Munroe mountains or from Lands' End to John O'Groats. In lots of way this spirit to cover vast distances, just like our ancestor hunter/gathers did is my dad. He just believes he is indestructible and that there is too much to enjoy about this life to move onto the next, this restless spirit always urging and prodding him up the next hill to see what land lies beyond. So is it his DNA? His upbringing?

Nothing about dad suggests he is descended from the Vikings. He is not tall, not stocky and not a blonde. His family name has no hint of the Roman Empire. There is no recent Irish in him. By recent I mean from the 19th Century onwards, when a movement of people started and gathered momentum driven by starvation to escape the potato famine, but has continued ever since. Transfer of peoples between Ireland and Britain started in at least Roman times, so it is possible dad is descended from an earlier settler from Ireland, but it is also possible that he has a bit of Pict, or Anglo-Saxon or Norman or Huguenot. Like most of us he will be a mongrel—a mixture of races with diverse ancestors—the product of hundreds of years of migrating, conquering armies, different tribes and peoples, wanderers, settlers and transients. And so it continues to this day and will do so forever more as people seek better futures or simply a safer place to be.

Despite the scepticism of some as to the reliability of a DNA test it seemed a more entertaining Christmas present than more socks to fill an already overflowing hosiery drawer. Inner mouth swabbed, the test was despatched to Texas for analysis. It produced results suggesting that dad was of predominately French and German descent. Dad was amused that he may have Teutonic and Gallic origins. His heritage may be located in an auxiliary soldier and his wife brought over from Gaul with the Roman invasion. Possibly some of him came over from Northern Germany—Saxony after the Romans had given up on Britain. We are all a hotchpot and all Africans originally. Remembering we are all related however distantly may help us to accept we humans have more in common with each other than difference. It is culture, national, continental and global political systems, religion and philosophies that engender difference and ultimately separateness.

Dad's ancestors have been traced back to the 17th Century and this is where the story of his personal history starts mired in violent, politically inspired conflicts in a small village that lies on the most famous river in Lancashire. Read on.

A Long Time Ago in Ribchester

The Hindles have lived for centuries in Lancashire, in the area to the east of Preston and the valleys south of the Bowland Fells, one of which is the valley through which the bonny river of the Ribble runs. The Hindles have resided at least from the 16th Century in that part of Lancashire and probably centuries before. Dad's DNA result showing him as having French blood may indicate Norman heritage following their 1066 invasion. The Hindle dynasty has some interesting characters. One of these was Christopher Hindle, also recorded in historical records by the name of Hindley. He was the vicar of St Wilfrid's church in Ribchester, Lancashire for many years. He was a man of principle which often landed him in trouble with those who did not share his love of Royalty. He had eggs thrown at him in church for supporting a King who was subsequently executed. He was made to preach from the top step of the pulpit because another vicar had pushed him out of his pulpit and violently replaced him as vicar of St Wilfrid's. He suffered further attacks being knocked off his horse by some ruffians.

Ribchester as the name suggests sits adjacent to the River Ribble. People have lived there for a long time as far back as Roman times when it was a sizeable Roman fort called Bremetennacum first built approximately 70 years after the birth of Christ. Around 100 years later the fort was made more permanent by replacing its turf and wood buildings with stone. The fort accommodated Roman forces who patrolled the surrounding countryside often on horseback as a number of cavalry units were stationed in Bremetennacum. One of these mounted squadrons came from present day Asturias Northern Spain. Other soldiers came from Sarmartia, a region in Eastern Europe. Around the fort grew a civilian settlement, providing various services to the fort and its activities. Keeping the local Brigantes, Ancient Britains who lived in the north of England was the main reason for the presence and location of the fort.

John Leland (also spelt Leyland) was Henry VIII's chaplain and librarian. King Henry assigned him the task of searching for interesting historical manuscripts that might have been kept in the country's monasteries. Henry VIII had dissolved the monasteries, for many reasons, one of which was to seize their wealth and riches in the form of land, property and possessions. Ribchester did not have a monastery, but the then hamlet of Whalley that lay close by, did. John Leland arrived in Ribchester in 1540 at the command of Henry VIII to carry out his mission. He would have travelled through Ribchester to Whalley, now a large village built a few miles upriver, but also connected by the roads, lanes and tracks that linked settlements in the Ribble Valley. No doubt Leland's task was to not only unearth historical manuscripts, but to see if there were any remaining rich pickings to be had in the old monastic houses after their initial closure. Whalley Abbey, home to a Cistercian community of monks had been disbanded in 1537. Its valuables such as gold plates, crosses, chalices, bells and jewels would have been seized by the Church Commissioners acting on the orders of the King's chief minister and adviser, Thomas Cromwell. Abbot Paslew of Whalley Abbey had refused to hand over his abbey for ransacking by the King's men and had been part of an opposition movement that fought the King's cessation from Roman Catholicism, Henry VIII supplanting the Pope as the head of the Church in England and Wales. Like many who were part of this movement opposing the reforms, Abbot Paslew was killed by the King's forces three years before Leland's arrival.

In 1540 he came to Ribchester. Leland described the place as follows, *Ribchester is a seven miles above Preston on the further ripe* (river bank) *of Ribble as Preston is. Ribchester is now a poor thing; it hath been an ancient town. Great squared stones, vaults, and antique coins be found there: and there is a place where that the people fable that the Jews had a temple.*

So the poor villagers told John Leland that they believed there had been a Jewish temple in Ribchester. Possibly there was. Jews lived throughout the Roman Empire. Maybe it was a Roman temple built in honour of some pagan god and goddesses such as Jupiter or Diana.

There is a Roman museum and the visible remains of the Roman settlement in Ribchester following extensive archaeological excavations including the remains of a Roman bath house. The Jewish or Roman temple, if it did indeed exist, is long gone.

St Wilfrid's Church dates from the 13th Century lying next to the museum. On 10 March 1592 one of its future vicars who was dad's ancestor was baptised not at St Wilfrid's Church but at Harwood Church. There were then, as now, two

Harwoods in the vicinity of Cowhill, Rishton where Christopher was born— Great Harwood and Little Harwood. A 1610 map shows both places in existence at that time. Christopher was born on a farm which is still a working farm run by a Hindle. The farm has been in the same family for generations. Following a University education in February 1617 or 1618 Christopher was made vicar at St Wilfrid's by the Bishop of Chester. He married. The lack of birth control or natural fecundity produced at least five children from the union—Andrew, Rhoda, Elizabeth, Anne and Jane in a space of about 10 years from 1622 to 1633. He may have had more who died before baptism. It is the Baptism records from the church which have identified five children.

The English Civil War raged at various times and in different forms from 1642 to 1651 between the Royalists (those who supported the monarch King Charles 1 sometimes called the Cavaliers) and the Parliamentarians (who believed in the rule of the country by parliament rather than an autocratic regal ruler). The Parliamentarians were called Roundheads and came to be led by Oliver Cromwell, distantly related to Thomas who served Henry VIII. Every subject of the King or Parliament's rule was affected by the conflict between those seeking democracy and those wanting regal dictatorship. Christopher Hindle was very much in the middle of the turmoil.

During this power struggle "The Long Parliament" as it was termed made many laws defying the King. King Charles wanted the country's religious life to be dominated by a Church of England modelled on the Roman Catholic Church where Bishops wielded power. Many of the Parliamentarians followed Presbyterian theology which put the power of a person's relationship with God in the hands of that person without the need for the intervention of priests or bishops. It was radical and revolutionary to say to any citizen that they could ask directly for God's forgiveness, intercession and involvement in their lives. Scotland had a Presbyterian system and so as to secure the help of Scotland against the King, the Long Parliament agreed to pass legislation in March 1646 which brought in a form of Presbyterianism into a reformed Church of England.

Christopher Hindle was a dedicated Royalist and continued to support the King from the start of hostilities between Parliament and Charles. He refused to join the Lancashire Presbytery which was quickly established in 1646 after the Parliament enacted the order to change some of the practices and beliefs of the Church of England. He was not initially thrown out of his church, but was subject to a ruthless and at times physically violent campaign against him orchestrated by some of his parishioners.

Incredibly the story of what happened to this Hindle ancestor has been written by the Reverend John Walker in his book called "Sufferings of the Clergy and Church of England Responses to the ejections of 1660—1662." The Rev Walker's account of Christopher Hindle's treatment by the church authorities needs to be read with a touch of scepticism because it may be biased as the author wrote it in response to a list of nonconformist ministers thrown out from their Anglican (Church of England) vicarages and churches under the Act of Uniformity of 1662. In the 17th century there was much infighting in the Anglican Church between those who sought more radical forms of Protestantism and those who clung to more traditional expressions of their Christian faith. Edmund Calamy wrote an "Account of the Ministers and others Ejected and Silenced, 1660—1662." Both the reports of the Rev Walker and Edmund Calamy have been more recently revised and published by AG Matthews in the mid-20th century.

Much of the account of the Reverend Christopher Hindle's staunch opposition to the takeover of his church by puritan Christians is also provided in much more detail by another man of the cloth—the Reverend George Ogden who succeeded the Reverend Ingram who had usurped Christopher Hindle from his position as vicar at St Wilfrid's.

The Reverend George Ogden must have had the same political and religious views and sympathies as the Reverend Christopher Hindle for this is what he wrote on 23 November 1705:

"I have lately been at Ribchester and have here enclosed you a certificate or some remarks upon ye life of Mr Hindle and Mr Ingham, my Predecessors, both vicars of Ribchester, in Lancashire. Mr Ingham was an inferior, ignorant man in comparison of Mr Hindle, and a religious nave. I need give but this one instance among one thousand. Ignorant Ingram ingratiating himself with some fiery, rebellious zealots in this Parish, procured a Certificate or Letter Commendatory under their hands, and also about £30 in money, make them believe he would only be minister of Longridge Chapel in the parish of Ribchester, but away goes Ingham to London and procure some authority to be vicar or minister of Ribchester church and to eject Mr Hindle because he was an honest, sober, loyal, Episcopal clergyman. Thus he was forced to quit his place. But Mr Christopher

Hindle was a man whose fame will never die till virtue and Learning shall become so useless as not be regarded."

So Mr Ingham was meant to be the minister of a chapel in Longridge which lies a few miles to the north of Ribchester, but following his visit to London obtained authority to become the vicar at Ribchester being a much more prestigious and well paid position.

The account goes on to report that in Cromwell's time (the date is not known) the Reverend Hindle was summoned to appear before some form of religious assembly at Whalley probably to be questioned about his failure to follow the new nonconformist teachings and services. Reverend Hindle brought his Hebrew Bible, other Hebrew books and by speaking in Hebrew, Greek and Latin "confuted and confounded them all." The conclusion of the assembly was that the Reverend Hindle's courage and learning was very great.

Dad has a highly intelligent ancestor in the Rev. Christopher Hindle because his forefather could speak two ancient languages, as well as Hebrew and English. Impressive in his ability to speak cogently and passionately of his beliefs. A man with integrity who was not cowed by bullies who threw him out of his church.

The Reverend Hindle was ejected from St Wilfred's one Sunday morning for criticising the execution of the King. It was when he was preaching a sermon from the top step, the pulpit itself being occupied by the man who had come to take his place, none other than the rival who had obtained the authority to take over the church and parish by going to London—it was Mr Ingham. Thomas Cutler, a Sexton (a caretaker whose duties would extend to digging graves) of the church was present when Mr Ingham took over the church. The Sexton was no fan of Mr Ingham. He saw him as a criminal because he described his supporters as Mr Ingham's "wicked crew."

Mr Ingham and his accomplices had occupied the pulpit before Mr Hindle arrived in the church to preach. Mr Ingham refused to leave the pulpit refusing the Reverend Hindle access. The Reverend Hindle was not deterred by these antics. He did not give up and go home, but delivered his sermon standing on the "high step", presumably the top of the steps leading into the pulpit.

This is a transcript of that sermon. It is quite difficult to make sense as it uses outlandish language at times:

"My dear Friends and Parishioners

First to begin with that which should be most dear unto a nation our Holy Mother, the Church and the Establishment of Religion in its purity, and lustre, who is not sensible how far the Arc of God, namely our Religion, the glory of our English Israel, and the Christian worlds, has been profaned by sacrilegious hands? Whilst the name of the Gospel, and Reformation, has been used as a stalking horse to cloak the blackest designs, the sun has ever looked upon; insomuch as the Church of England, may complain and cry out as once the church of Israel did."

Verse 16 of chapter 24 of the book of Isaiah in the Old Testament of the Bible is then quoted before he continues with a reference to Satan himself.

"The Prince of Darkness is never so perniciously fortunate in his mischief is when he transforms himself into an Angel of Light: How well our Religion is reformed and secured yourselves may judge by the present complexion of our dear mother stripped, mangled and wounded to death by the sons of her own bowels, her Government dissolved, her Doctrine trampled into a puddle, the extracted purely from the Fountain of living water; her Discipline threatened nor daring to appear against professed Heresies and Blasphemies; her sacred forms of worship vilified and scorned; her Ambassadors of Christ for Peace and reconciliation imprisoned, disturbed in their own churches, impoverished and reputed as the filth and off scouring of the world; her Temples either defaced or demolished or else locked up by a wicked Military Power, and lastly the true Protestant Religion is now squeezed into such a narrow room, that few or none their own profession of it that we are obliged to make solemn protestation."

A rant indeed from a very disgruntled clergyman unhappy with the changes that have been forced upon him and his church by the introduction of Presbyterianism into the Church of England. He then goes on to damn all those who have been instrumental in the execution of King Charles I on 30 January 1649.

"But, as if all this was not guilt enough to weigh them down to the bottomless Pit, there have been added to that Scarlet Sin of murder, the Blood of one Sacred Person, (the King) of more value, then 10,000 of the best of his subjects, the light of our eyes and the Breath of our Nostrils, in whose life and Government all the Thousands that reside within these three kingdoms (being England, Wales and Scotland) are really concerned, and nearly concerned, as in the life of their Common Parent (the King). An Act so horrid and prodigious, that no language can express it: so no History can parallel it. It is no slight contribution that some of you have given to the miseries we complain of but know not how to remedy. And maybe accessory to the guilt of Blood—adding more ways than perhaps you are aware of. To only I shall name, first the contributing assistance to the Fact before it is committed; secondly by approbation, and justification of the fact, after it is committed.

"I would to God it was in the Power of My prayers, to clear those who sit at Westminster of this deep guilt; and some of you of your assistance, and adherence to them in contracting it; and yet we may not incur the divine wrath as the people of Israel did when they send themselves out of the Blessing of a King; See how God threatens them, with a severe punishment."

A further reference to the Old Testament is made, this time to Isaiah chapter 5 verse 3. So his sermon has blamed Parliament, being those who sit at Westminster and also some of his parishioners for supporting Parliament in its execution of King Charles 1. His words now seem extreme and offensive suggesting that one man—the king—was better than the best of his subjects. Even then such words were inflammatory and insulting to the Parliamentarians who believed in rule by a commonwealth where values of equality, democracy and fairness should influence the government of the country. Christopher's indignation at the killing of the King boiled over into a furious condemnation of those who had brought about the beginning of democratic government. His words are difficult to understand to the modern ear, but following his intemperate diatribe he was thrown out of his church and assaulted.

The eyewitness account from the Sexton identified a Richard Hayhurst as the ringleader of the "Rude Rabble against Mr Hindle." These may have been soldiers in Oliver Cromwell's army. Richard Hayhurst had many sons—seven or eight in number but four of them—William, John, Benjamin and Jonathan under their father's order attacked Reverend Hindle. Jonathan was described as the Captain, Benjamin was the Lieutenant and John described as "purse bearer" who paid the "wicked crew". Following the end of the sermon eyewitness accounts tells of the egging and assault where the Rev. Hindle was pushed onto his face by Jonathan Hayhurst. During the assault Hayhurst accused the Priest of drunkenness saying "There, ye Vicar! Is this man fit to preach, and is drunk?" The eyewitness says it was Jonathan who had been drinking all day. Jonathon was the one who was drunk which seems more plausible if he had egged and pushed the vicar so that he fell on his face. Worse was yet to come according to this written record of the treatment of Christopher Hindle. When he was riding his horse between Preston and Ribchester he was chased by another Hayhurst brother. He was John Hayhurst described as a follower of Oliver Cromwell. He was the one who knocked the Reverend Christopher Hindle off his horse.

Dad's ancestor was in the middle of a violent power struggle which reflected the opposing political allegiances of a divided nation after a civil war 350 years ago which had caused the death and destruction of people and property. Many have died since fighting for their rights not just in this country but throughout the world when the oppressed have risen up against autocracy and tyranny. It will continue until all peoples are treated fairly, equally and justly. Without doubt it is a work still in progress.

The story does not end with Christopher Hindle lying in the mud after coming off his steed. Being deposed from his parish proved to be financially beneficial. After he was forcibly evicted from St Wilfrid's Church in Ribchester Christopher Hindle sued those who had evicted him for loss of his livelihood. He also sought financial recovery of wages he had not received prior to the introduction of Presbyterianism in 1646. The Court found in his favour referring the assessment of his loss of income to the Committee for Plundered Ministers. He was awarded arrears by an order dated 04 May 1649 up until 1646, payment of his stipend wages from 1646 until the date of the order and then an amount of 40 marks a year, an annual sum much more that a working skilled tradesman would receive in 1649. He returned to live with his brother at the family farm at Cowell near Rishton, Blackburn. He died three years before the return of King Charles II in 1660 to the throne of England and Wales. Not living to see the return and survival of the monarchy his humiliation at being thrown out of his priestly vocation was softened by the pension and compensation he received from the Committee for Plundered Ministers.

One more interesting fact—Christopher Hindle was admitted as a Fellow of St John's College, Cambridge on 07 April 1647. A Roman altar dedicated "To the holy god Apollo" dug up at Ribchester 1678 was donated to St John's College. This was 21 years after Christopher's death. Possibly his son made sure that this precious archaeological find was sent to his father's Cambridge' college for safe keeping. It seems too much of a coincidence that it should find its way to the actual college of a vicar of Ribchester, there being unlikely to be another connection.

Inside St Wilfrid's Church is a board with the names and dates of the vicars of Ribchester. Christopher Hindle is there, but his name has been spelt wrong as "Hendley". He was an important benefactor gifting a magnificently carved wooden pulpit, no doubt the one he was evicted from, to the church. In the written notes of the history of the church available for all to read on entering the church is the following extract:

17th Century

The carved pulpit of 1636, from which preachers still teach, was the gift of Christopher Hindle the Vicar then. Later Mr Hindle was criticised by some for his support of King rather than Parliament in the Civil War, and as in many communities there was friction. A local faction ejected him from the pulpit in 1649 and he was replaced with someone of different views.

Dad will have had many more ancestors, like everyone, whose stories and lives are forever forgotten. Digging up past relatives often brings surprises which sometimes redefine who we are. A trail can go frustratingly cold if Baptism and other records of a long lost family member cannot be identified and found. Dad's family on both his mother and father's side are well documented in the 19th Century as the first population census took place in 1801.

19ᵗʰ Century Waterloo

Dad's first memories of relatives are of his great grandfather. His great grandfather James Hindle worked in the quarries on a ridge of open countryside above the valleys that bisect this part of East Lancashire where Blackburn snuggles down in a valley. The ridge is called the Yellow Hills. A name inspired by the gorse bushes that every spring still cover the hills with their golden blooms. His great grandfather was a hand loom weaver and later worked as a quarryman. He, with his wife, also a handloom weaver lived and wove cloth in a cottage almost opposite to the Clog and Billycock Inn. It used to be called the Bay Horse Inn but it changed its name in the early 20ᵗʰ century as the landlord always wore clogs and a billycock—the latter looks like a hard bowler hat. The Clog and Billycock has survived the difficult trading environments which has resulted in the closure of many public houses; it continues to this day and has a web site—an invention beyond the imagination 200 years ago. It also hosted a running road race every year.

One of dad's great grandfather Hindle's brothers had fought at Waterloo. He shares the same name as dad's father—William Hindle. His nick name was "Waterloo Willie" and he was dad's great, great uncle. His army great coat became a revered family possession, evidence of the bravery and daring of the Hindle family, one of whose sons had helped to consign Napoleon to exile—forever following the Battle of Waterloo. The coat became an object of awe, always praised for its warmth and the protection it gave to its wearer against bitterly cold European nights. The coat was eventually donated to Blackburn Corporation museum.

William Hindle was injured as the of his compensation shows by an "adverse affection of the head." Put simply he had a head injury, possibly when loading the cannon or was hit by an enemy cannonball. Or perhaps more accurately because the word used is "affection", he had a psychological or psychiatric condition such as would now be described as Post Traumatic Stress Disorder. If he had received damage of a physical nature to his skull or other head bones or structure then it is more likely the Certificate would have described the injury as

51

a gunshot wound or broken bone. Or perhaps he had become deaf from the damage to his ears from the constant firing of the canons over 12 years' service. He would not have had the ear protection given to soldiers today to protect his hearing. He may have tied a scarf around his head to muffle the sounds made by the booming guns.

Willie had served as a soldier in the Third Battalion of the Royal Regiment of Artillery, so his job was to fire cannons. The Certificate shows he was discharged aged 28 years and two months which meant that he was only 15 when he joined up. He had served for 12 years and 213 days when he was discharged from service on the 1st of May 1816. His occupation was stated as a weaver at discharge which means he must have worked before he joined up in 1803. Child labour was common, children starting work as infants. Industrialisation of textile manufacture had not moved into large mills by 1803 so his work as a weaver must have been as a handloom weaver—the same occupation as dad's great grandfather James Hindle. James and William were brothers. Working and living in a small space possibly led William to seek an escape by joining the Gunners' Battalion at the very young age of 15. Only 5 feet 7 inches tall with a light hair, grey eyes and a fair complexion, not even fully grown, he went off to serve his country leaving his home town of Blackburn.

The Napoleonic Wars started in 1803 with Napoleon finally defeated at Waterloo in 1815. Waterloo Willies's service therefore spanned the whole Napoleonic Wars period. He must have served in many places other than on the Waterloo battlefields, located in modern day Belgium. Much of Britain's campaign against Napoleon took place in Spain and Portugal. Called the Peninsular War it lasted from 1807—1814 on the Iberian Peninsula where the United Kingdom aided Spain and Portugal to fight a French invasion and occupation. Willie would have travelled across the Bay of Biscay with his Battalion to reach Spain and Portugal a journey other Hindle men would be destined to take more than a century later in the two World War armed conflicts of the 20th Century.

There is a reference in the Certificate to Her Majesty's Royal Hospital at Chelsea becoming responsible for paying William his 9d a day pension. This does not mean he was living in that hospital as a Chelsea Pensioner. The Army (Artillery &c.) Pensions Act 1833 transferred the responsibility for payment of pensions from a "master general and board of ordnance" to the Chelsea hospital.

Here is the first paragraph of the Act—note the word controul has since lost its "u".

"The whole of the said pensions, allowances, and relief payable to soldiers and others discharged from the royal artillery, engineers, and other military corps which have been heretofore granted and paid by the said master general and board of ordnance, shall be granted and paid by and be under the power, management, controul, direction, and authority of the said commissioners of Chelsea hospital."

William certainly survived until 1833, receiving a pension since discharge. Soldiers, Sailors and Aviators (the term given to people who serve in the Royal Air Force) are entitled to similar financial recompense for any damage experienced during their service. Previously called a War Pension, now Armed Forces Compensation, for some the money will never mend the damage caused by an injury or so much worse—bring back a life. Injured he may have returned home to Blackburn to join his brother and wife whom he had left working as self-employed hand loom weavers in 1801. He would have found much changed. His brother and wife would now be described as self-employed, working as hand loom weavers. Such a term had not come into existence in the early 19th century. People resorted to all types of enterprise, some illegal, to get food in their stomachs. Most people worked on the land in some capacity. The Industrial Revolution had emerged in the dying decades of the previous century—the 18th century. People worked as farm labourers or in small artisan trades and workshops as James Hindle and his wife did in their cottage up on Billinge End Road, Blackburn. Unless a member of the aristocracy, the landed gentry or the clergy you laboured in hard physical toil to keep a roof over your head and food on the table.

Every week James and his wife walked the two miles journey into Blackburn to sell the cloth they had woven and to buy their raw material for the week's work ahead. Shopping was done in the market with some of the profit from their trading when in the town. With their full first year's profit they were able to buy a cow as the Yellow Hills was then common land where locals could keep and graze their animals. From the milk they made cheese and butter. They prospered and life was good. They had an income from a number of sources, dairy products to supplement food they bought and independence in their working lives.

But it was not to last. Fieldings the local landowner enclosed the common land where the cottagers kept their livestock. The landowners stole the land for themselves and little could be done about it. Land has been stolen from common use and ownership in this country and Ireland for centuries. Fences were put up to keep out the commoners from grazing their animals on the Yellow Hills. The Fieldings had the wealth to do that; money gives power. Such a land grab could not be challenged. The cottagers were without the resources and power that the landowner enjoyed. They had no Member of Parliament they could complain to—they did not have the vote. They were poor, powerless and dispossessed of the land on which they kept their cows and other livestock.

But that was not the only cause of dad's great grandfather and mother having to leave their cottage. They could no longer compete with the cheaper mass manufactured cloth. The loom had become mechanised; the steam engine powered not one, but many looms all housed in a mill. The industrial revolution had arrived. Their products were priced out. It could be made cheaper elsewhere in the factories of East Lancashire. And just as they lost out because the goods could be made cheaper, so in the latter half of the 20th century mass unemployment hit industries such as textile manufacture in Blackburn as cheaper products could be woven in places such as Bangladesh and India. As Lancashire and Yorkshire lost its textile mills, Stoke lost its potteries, Northampton its shoe making, Glasgow and Newcastle its ship building, Corby its steel works. These were just a few of the industries in a few of the working class communities that were strangled by foreign competition.

So many products which were the bedrock of British manufacturing industry are now made abroad. If produced cheaper elsewhere then sales are guaranteed in a market eager to have the more affordable option, especially if the quality is the same or not much different. Such savings to the British consumer can come at a cost to a poorly paid worker who will not have the protection from health and safety legislation as do British workers. There may be no compensation if a worker is injured at work or contracts an industrial disease. The environment may be trashed if factories have no limitations on the pollution discharged into the air or untreated effluents into water courses. A large amount of non-food and clothes items in any household are now to be produced in China. Look at the labels or packaging. It is so difficult to buy British made goods, because they are not made here anymore. Deindustrialisation of the British economy over the decades since the end of the Second World War reached its zenith in the 1980s.

The result has been a continuing catastrophe for the inhabitants of these former mill, steel, coal mining, ship building, engineering towns and cities. There was nowhere for the redundant workers to go other than to claim a welfare benefit or seek retraining to work in the emerging economy of information technology or go and find a job in the "service" economy. Working class community devastation was the consequence. In many places the resulting poverty continues, the escape from dependence on the state and charity to provide all life's needs is barred by so many factors.

In dad's great grandpas and great grandma's time the barrier was physical. The right to graze on the common land opposite their cottage was stopped by a rich magnate who had a big house nearby. He decided to enclose the common land where their cow grazed. Enclosing land is the polite and possibly politically correct term for theft. He took the land for himself and his heirs so the hand looming Hindles could no longer keep their cow because the cow had nowhere to eat grass. No cow meant no produce to sell and milk, cheese and butter to feed themselves. James was forced to become an employee digging out the stone from the Yellow Hills' quarries for buildings that were colonising the valley below. They became dependent on their employer to keep them in work.

Black Lives Matter

Cotton was king in Blackburn as in many other Lancashire towns. It was predominately a weaving town; other towns such as Oldham were towns where spinning mills dominated the skyline. The bales of raw cotton shipped over from the southern states of the USA were spun into threads. The Industrial Revolution relied on a number of coinciding factors. It started as a revolution in the making of cloth and that cloth was predominately cotton or a mixture of cotton with other raw materials such as flax. But it needed capital—money—cash from investors. The slave trade produced vast profits which provided plenty of money for capital investment. Mills were built, machines bought, coal mines sunk, engines constructed from the profits of the slave trade. Words cannot describe the abomination of slavery. Slavery was abolished in 1833 by Great Britain in that most of its colonies no longer used slaves. But slavery continued in the USA. Most of the cotton spun and woven in Lancashire mills was grown by slave labour. 75% of all raw cotton came from the southern states of America—called the Confederacy once the American Civil War started in 1861. Due to a blockade of exports from the southern states that formed the Confederacy raw cotton supplies dried up by 1862. Mill workers supported President Lincoln in his war to a abolish slavery; there was a meeting in the Manchester Free Trade Hall on 30 December 1862 and the following proclamation was made and sent to the President of the United States of America:

To His Excellency Abraham Lincoln, President of the United States if America

"As citizens of Manchester, assembled at the Free-trade Hall, we beg to express our fraternal sentiments towards you and your country. We rejoice in your greatness, as an outgrowth of England, whose blood and language you share, whose orderly and legal freedom you have applied to new circumstances, over a region immeasurably greater than our own. We honour your Free States, as a singularly happy abode for the working millions, where industry is honoured. One thing alone has, in the past, lessened our sympathy with your country and our confidence in it—we meant, the ascendancy of politicians who not merely maintained negro slavery, but desired to extend and root in more firmly. Since we have discerned, however, that the victory of the Free North in the war which has so sorely distressed us, as well as afflicted you, will strike off the fetters of the slave, you have attracted our warm and earnest sympathy. We joyfully honour you, as the President, and the Congress with you, for many decisive steps towards practically exemplifying your belief in the words of your great founders, "All men are created free and equal." You have procured the liberation of the slaves in the district around Washington, and thereby made the centre of your Federation visibly free. You have enforced the laws against the slave trade, and kept up your fleet against it, even while every ship was wanted for service in your terrible war. You have nobly decided to received ambassadors from the negro republics of Haiti and Liberia, thus for ever renouncing that unworthy prejudice which refuses the rights of humanity to men and women, on account of their colour. In order more effectually to stop the slave trade, you have made with our Queen a treaty, which your senate has ratified, for the right of mutual search. Your congress has decreed freedom, as the law for ever, in the vast unoccupied or half-settled territories which are directly subject to its legislative power. It has offered pecuniary aid to all states which will enact emancipation locally, and has forbidden your general to restore fugitive slaves who seek their protection. You have entreated the slave masters to accept these moderate offers; and, after long and patient waiting, you, as Commander in Chief of the army, have appointed tomorrow, the 1st of January 1863, as the day of unconditional freedom for the slaves of the rebel states. Heartily we do congratulate you and your country on this humane and righteous course. We assume that you cannot now stop short of a complete uprooting of slavery. It would not become us to dictate any details, but there are broad principles of humanity which must guide you. If complete emancipation in some states be deferred, though only to a predetermined day, still, in the interval, human beings should not be counted as chattels. Women must have rights of chastity and maternity, man the rights of husbands, masters the liberty of manumission. Justice demands for the black, no less that for the white, the protection of law— that his voice be heard in your courts. Nor must any such abomination be tolerated as slave breeding states and a slave market—if you are to earn the high reward of all your sacrifices in the approval of the universal brotherhood and of the Divine Father. It is for your free country to decide whether anything but immediate and total emancipation can secure the most indispensable rights of humanity against the inveterate wickedness of local laws and local executives. We implore you, for your own honour and welfare, not to faint in your providential mission. While your enthusiasm is aflame, and the tide of events runs high, let the work be finished effectually. Leave no root of bitterness to spring up and work fresh misery to your children. It is a mighty task, indeed, to reorganise the industry not only of four millions of the coloured race, but of five millions of whites. Nevertheless, the vast progress you have made in the short space of twenty months fills us with hope that every stain on your freedom will shortly be removed, and that the erasure of that foul blot upon civilisation and Christianity—chattel slavery—during your Presidency will cause the name of Abraham Lincoln to be honoured and revered by posterity. We are certain that such a glorious consummation will cement Great Britain to the United States in close and enduring regards. Our interests, moreover, are identified with yours. We are truly one people, though locally separate. And if you have any ill-wishers here, be assured they are chiefly those who oppose liberty at home, and that they will be powerless to stir up quarrels between us, from the very day in which your country becomes, undeniably and without exception, the home of the free. Accept our high admiration of your firmness in upholding the proclamation of freedom."

Mr Lincoln, in a letter dated 19 January 1863, replied with the words that are inscribed on his statue which stands in Lincoln Square, between Brasenose Street and Queen Street, Manchester:

"I know and deeply deplore the sufferings which the working people of Manchester and in all Europe are called to endure in this crisis. It has been often and studiously represented that the attempt to overthrow this Government which was built on the foundation of human rights, and to substitute for it one which should rest exclusively on the basis of slavery, was unlikely to obtain the favour of Europe.

"Through the action of disloyal citizens, the working people of Europe have been subjected to a severe trial for the purpose of forcing their sanction to that attempt. Under the circumstances I cannot but regard your decisive utterances on the question as an instance of sublime Christian heroism which has not been surpassed in any age or in any country. It is indeed an energetic and re-inspiring assurance of the inherent truth and of the ultimate and universal triumph of justice, humanity and freedom.

"I hail this interchange of sentiments, therefore, as an augury that, whatever else may happen, whatever misfortune may befall your country or my own, the peace and friendship which now exists between the two nations will be, as it shall be my desire to make them, perpetual."

His letter was read out at another large gathering in Manchester. Relief aid for the starving mill workers was gathered by the Northern States led by Lincoln. It arrived in Liverpool with his message of support.

The workers had shown immense solidarity with President Lincoln. The mill workers of Lancashire asserted much more than Black Lives Matter. They showed their solidarity doing something real and costly. It was an act of self-sacrifice. They were willing to suffer to save the lives of black men, women and children—all slaves, all possessions of their masters and mistresses. With no supply of the raw material the looms became silent. No work meant no pay. There was no unemployment benefit or redundancy pay. The only option was to go to the workhouse, begging for a hand out from the Poor Law Commissioners—a shameful and ghastly option as proud working women and men recoiled from asking for help. They wished to work for their daily bread. The workhouse was the last resort as the conditions were appalling.

The Blackburn workhouse was opened in 1864 in time for those who could not withstand the crushing poverty brought on by the absence of work through the cotton famine brought on by the American civil war. The workhouse lived on for many years as Queens Park Hospital where many babies were born including both of dad's daughters. Not much is left of the old workhouse buildings; a new NHS hospital was built on the site just off the road that goes over the moors to Haslingden.

Not all British men and women supported the blockade of cotton. Those that suffered most—the mill workers did, but some of the upper middle classes and the aristocracy arranged their own campaigns to support the Confederacy and by implication slavery. On 18 October 1864 a Grand Bazaar was held in St George's Hall Liverpool to raise money for Confederate prisoners held by the Union, being those northern states of America. Liverpool was the most pro-Confederate city in the UK. It had built its wealth on the evil of slavery and retained a misplaced sympathy and support for its continuation in the States.

James Hindle and his wife lived through the cotton famine. So did their children. Henry is dad's grandfather and as a very young child having been born on 12 October 1856, lived for weeks on oatmeal porridge made with water. Mills were silent, their chimneys empty of smoke. No new mills or houses were needed, so the quarrying of stone ceased. Porridge was all Henry had to eat. If they had been able to keep a cow his diet and that of other starving unemployed families would have had milk, butter and cheese. But Henry did not suffer from his simple diet. He thrived, growing tall, was fit and healthy during his life and lived well into old age, never having a problem with being overweight during all his years. In 1857 the Corporation Park in Blackburn opened and during the Cotton famine a job creation scheme was devised for unemployed workers so that they could earn some money and prevent destitution and starvation. The Broad Walk and surrounding terracing was completed through this scheme. The Broad Walk is exactly what it says—a long and wide path on which the residents of Blackburn would saunter enjoying the trees planted on either side of the wide boulevard. A place for future lovers to meet or the old to sit and watch the time and strollers pass by.

Porridge

Dad's grandfather—Henry Hindle the one who lived off porridge as a child, worked as a tattler in a mill. A tattler maintained the looms; keeping the machines working, the shuttle driving backwards and forwards across the threads. He worked in a mill on Whalley New Road, near Brownhill in Blackburn. He saved money from his wages to start a horse and cart coal delivery round. He had 11 children—he earned the equivalent of £1.50 a week as a tattler, but £2 per week from his coal round. It made a big difference to the family finances as he was able to ensure his wife and 11 children were able to live well—they were never hungry. Driven by his own knowledge of starvation, Henry was determined his children would never experience what he had known—an empty belly. He was careful with his money and ensured his children would never have no food to eat.

Today we feel secure we will never go hungry as supermarket shelves are full and we feel so confident that we throw away tons of food. In 2015 52% of the food we consumed came from the UK, the other 48% was imported from various countries, mainly the European Union. If those food supplies dry up because they become too scarce through demand from other countries, or crops or animal production fails because of diseases or land becomes desert through climate change we may have to make do with the 52% that is grown or reared in the UK. We would all find ways of growing or producing food, the flowers and shrubs in gardens and parks being substituted with vegetables and fruit bushes. Foraging for food might spread beyond the fashion to prettify a 3 star Michelin meal.

As we throw away £13 billion food waste every year it is unlikely that we would starve if we have to rely on locally sourced produce. It may also encourage a resolution of other problems such as ill health through over eating disorders or unsound nutrition, global warming through damaging, exploitative agricultural practices and by sharing any surplus with those have no food. If we all have less there will be more to go around and the pressure on the planet will be eased. In the war rationing meant everyone had enough to eat. As you will read later one of dad's letters, written to his future wife after the end of the war, but whilst he was still serving abroad in the army, bemoans the continuation of rationing as food supplies had to be diverted to feed the starving peoples of occupied countries. The diet was simpler from war rationing but no one's health suffered, although hunger pangs could not always be satisfied by a rush to the cupboard, because what was in the cupboard had to last for a number of days.

Henry Hindle with his wife Mary Ellen had 11 children—Margaret shortened to Maggie, Hannah, James, John who like dad was called Jack, Sarah Ellen shortened to Sally, William, Rebecca but called Beck, Henry who was called Harry, Fred, Bessie and Tom.

Here is the whole family showing their ages and occupations at the time of the 1911 Census.

So many children born in the space of about 15 years, Margaret being the eldest at age 28 and Tom the youngest at age 13. Mary Ellen had obviously decided she had given birth to enough children by the time she reached the age of 40. Evidently a close knit and cohesive family, none had left the household at 7 Saunders Road, Blackburn. None had married. Their home must have been overcrowded with nine of the children being aged 16 or over. Only one of them Tom was at school. The rest were employed or self-employed. Henry the patriarch, a coal merchant and carter worked for himself and the first of his children to join him in the business was John (Jack) whose occupation is described as Carter in a Coal Business under Column 11 of the Census form. The women of the family, Maggie, Hannah, Sarah Ellen, Beck and Bessie at age 15 years old are all cotton weavers. Lancashire women have always been a financially independent breed often continuing to work after growing their own family. James was the intellectual of the brood—a sub-librarian at age 26. A middle-class job reserved for grammar school boys. Only the most forceful and persistent woman would secure such employment, James eventually became head librarian in 1939 when he was 54, retiring at age 60 at the end of the war. Harry was a clerk working in the office of a washing machine manufacturer. This machine was not the electric motored type of machine used today, but a hand operated tub with a gas boiler to heat the water. Fred was a shop assistant selling incandescent lights—we know them simply as electric light bulbs. The use of electricity for lighting buildings and public spaces was still in its infancy in 1911. Only the wealthy could afford the wiring of their homes with electricity. Most homes and streets were lit by gas.

One left—William Hindle—a butcher aged 21 in 1911 working for the firm of Harrisons. William is dad's dad and could have been a vet if Maggie, his eldest sibling had paid for him to study and train at Liverpool University. He was the youngest in the country to qualify as a meat inspector and sanitary inspector. He rode his bike to Bacup, a fair journey, where he studied to obtain his certificates. Following the award of these qualifications, all that was needed was for him to attend a 12 month course in Liverpool but he could not afford it, unless he worked there and attempted to undertake the course part time.

A meat inspector job in Liverpool came up. He applied but was not appointed. The reason being was that he was told that he must join the Freemasons to get a job. He refused saying that "I am not calling so and so my brother". He would not wish to compromise his independent judgement by being beholden to the fraternity of Freemasonry whose practices were secret and aimed at furthering the fortunes of its members. It would have been an interesting place to work as a meat inspector checking imports in the Liverpool docks. He had a detailed knowledge of animal anatomy, and all other expertise to qualify him admirably for the job. He was though not going to compromise his own ethical standards and values; he was not going to turn a blind eye to some disease or poor quality product in order to do a freemason crony a favour. Diseased meat could make people ill, even lead to death. His knowledge as will be seen protected British troops stationed in India where his expertise and experience were held in high regard by his commanding officer.

Dad remembers a time when working with his father in the butcher's shop after the war when a visit was made by a public health officer from Blackburn Council. The man was officious and bombastic, but was soon put in his place as William's knowledge of law of public hygiene was more detailed than that of the official. His father had a remarkable memory, being able to memorise long and complicated meat orders without putting them to paper.

Maggie was short sighted in not tipping up the money to enable William to qualify as a vet. His prosperity and future would have been secured which would have cascaded down to the rest of the family. He would have escaped service as an infantry soldier. William built a sound and profitable business nevertheless in the years to come, and future generations have benefited from inheriting their ancestor's brain power.

William had reached the age of majority of 21 years when he became an adult in law, could drink alcohol and marry without the need for parental permission, by the date of the 1911 census. Standing at the beginning of his life, the future looked promising. His brothers and sisters with the exception of Tom, were working, the family enjoyed the opportunities that working and living in a booming cotton town offered.

How quickly it changed—within three years of the 1911 census—those hopes and dreams were stopped by the onset of a world war. Born at an unfortunate time in world history—in the closing decades of the 19th Century meant these young men were of a ripe age to join up to go and fight on the many battlefields of the First World War. For the women whose loved ones would not return from Flanders; they had to turn their skills and energy to making ammunitions and taking over jobs previously carried out by men. On 02 April 1911 when Henry Hindle signed the census form he could not see into the future. He could not know that he would be saying good bye to some of his sons as they went off to war and would lose one who forever after would be buried in a foreign War Cemetery. There are thousands and thousands whose deaths and grave locations are listed. Everyone just one amongst many, but each one always remembered and commemorated.

In 1912 Blackburn had literally thousands who worked for themselves in small businesses. The town thrived through small and large scale entrepreneurship. A lot of cake was eaten as there was over 330 confectioners. There were 200 shops selling cloth, 130 tailors and dress shops. 38 Tea Dealers, 57 Tripe Dressers and Dealers and 50 Tobacconists all sold their wares within the boundary of Blackburn Corporation. There were nearly 500 Hotels, Inns and Taverns, but only 2 Temperance Bars. Clearly as now alcohol was the favoured drink.

Many worked in a variety of industries in addition to cotton manufacture. What is startling is the variety of businesses, economic activities and enterprises which occupied Blackburnians. If there was a slump in cotton manufacture then the repercussions would be felt in all the small businesses that relied on the factory and mill workers spending their hard earned wages in their shops or pubs. As now if people have surplus income it helps to keep the consumerist economy going. But what is different today is that so many small traders and businesses, the corner grocery shop, the butchers, the dress shop, the shoe shop, the hat shop, the bakers have been swallowed up by supermarkets and shopping centres very often based out of town and only accessible by car or an infrequent bus service. Shops have closed, gone from our streets. The replacement jobs in supermarkets and out of town shopping centres, and distribution centres, do not match the numbers in 1912 who made a living from running a small business. Supermarkets have maintained cheap food supplies, but the community that would shop locally, chatting to neighbours and shopkeepers alike, sharing sad stories and happy times, has gone. Similarly out of town shopping centres have destroyed once vibrant town centres. But such consumerist palaces as The Trafford Centre or the Metro Centre may have had their day as lockdown changed so many of us into online shoppers. 1912 was a good year for Blackburn. It was not to last.

In life we never know when the long, lazy days of contentment and pleasure will change and be snatched away with little warning. Coronavirus descended upon us—a plague marching around the world, only stoppable by a retreat into isolation and physical distancing from other humans. We must be more awake to threats to our lives and livelihoods. The world never stays the same and is at this very moment cataclysmic changes are happening. If the warnings of the inevitable chaotic and destructive upheavals from global warming are not heeded, Armageddon really will reign supreme.

Visualise Henry Hindle in his unpreparedness for the loss of his son and all those others signing the census form in 1911 and remember our unpreparedness for the Covid pandemic as we ate our Christmas Day 2019 feast or drank a toast on New Years' Eve of that year. Individually there was little we could have done to change the virus's course. To protect ourselves we could have perhaps started taking vitamin D, avoided closed, crowded, poorly ventilated places such as trains, tube, sports stadiums, shops, restaurants and night clubs, started to lose excess weight, wear face masks when the risk factors started to emerge. We could though not change our age as this virus seemed to single out the elderly for infection and often death. Some of us made life giving choices for ourselves when we saw the nightly scenes of health services in Italy and Spain being overwhelmed by the virus. Those with the knowledge and understanding of viral pandemics knew what public and personal health measures and actions were needed to combat or avoid the virus. Most of us were ignorant and relied on the government for information. Others unable to accept the implications and consequences of a pandemic denied its existence or invented conspiracy theories to suppress their inner fears of the unknown.

Denying something exists when it does in fact, removes the fear of its consequences. Many in Britain denied the inevitability of Germany's rearming and persecution of Jews and other groups. Those in Germany who recognised what was to come and had the financial or other means to leave did so, saving not only their lives but those of their children and future generations. Those with little resources could not escape. Poverty is so much more than not having a sufficient income to meet basic needs; poverty denies knowledge, opportunities and options. Freedom and choice of action are suffocated. Before the Great War, belief in the superiority and invincible might of Britain and its Empire led to a misplaced enthusiasm of many young men from the home countries and its dominions to volunteer on the outbreak of war in 1914. War would not soon be over; there would be no glorious swift victory, just four long years of suffering in trench warfare.

The Great War

Such sadness, mourning and desolation more than a century later is evoked by reading the names and lives of those who died in the First World War. Whether it be on a memorial or on a grave inscription or written record the effect is the same—a quietening of the spirit and a search for understanding and reconciliation to the death of so many young men and some women. Such is the effect of war—it kills and destroys. Since the guns fell silent on 11 November 1918 the destruction of lives has continued in many conflicts most notably the Second World War, followed by regional wars in places such as the Korea, the Congo in Africa, Vietnam and the Middle East to name but a few.

So many wars can seem senseless with the hindsight of history. The First World War seems to fit into that category whereas the Second we were fighting for survival and against the diabolical evil of Nazism. There was justification in that war. But not so the First is a shared feeling more than a hundred years later. Times were definitely different and it is difficult to understand the willingness of men to volunteer, or that the Government could send so many to their certain death or maiming. But not much changes. What was the point of the Iraqi and Afghan invasions? Isis was a product of the Iraqi war and the Taliban have returned to power in Afghanistan. Politicians who made these decisions should hold their heads forever in shame.

There is no need to travel to distant places to read the graves and memorials of British service men and women who have died in so many conflicts. The Commonwealth War Graves Commission web site meticulously contains records of every death, grave inscriptions, memorials and cemetery plans showing the exact location of every grave and much more. Some of the grave stones have been photographed. Looking through these pages induces a melancholy, but we must always remember, because without doing we will never prevent such pain in the future.

Dad took his family to visit the war graves of two family members buried in France—one from his side who rests in Dantzig Alley and one from his wife's side. James Catlow was mum's maternal uncle, the brother of her mother. He was a driver with the Royal Field Artillery who on 15 July 1916 died of his wounds. A victim of the Battle of the Somme, like so many, he was just 25 when he met his maker, probably quite old compared to many who died in that war and wars since. He is buried at the cemetery in Corbie, a few miles to the east of Amiens. Harry Hindle, dad's uncle, was also killed at the Battle of the Somme. He was a corporal in the East Surrey Regiment—a long way from Lancashire, but had joined up in 1914 so had been changed regiments at the dictates of some general. He was one of 58,000 British troops killed on the first day of the battle of the Somme on 01 July 1916. He is buried in grave Q.9, Row 4 at the Dantzig Alley, British War Graves Cemetery at Mametz. On his grave are the words "FOR EVER WITH THE LORD". Let it be so.

It was a June day. The mud had gone from the fields which were full of ripening wheat. But nothing could remove the melancholy of the graveyards. Since then some of his grandchildren have also visited these graves and many children as part of history studies have also travelled to the battlefields to see the trenches and ponder on the huge memorials such as the Thiepval or the Menin Gate.

The Hindle family lost one of its sons, but the rest who volunteered to fight for the Empire survived coming home to live on.

Tom was the youngest child of the Hindle brood. He had bad eyesight and could not see well enough to shoot a rifle, but the army was so desperate for men to join up that they took him anyway. He was also small so joined a Bantam Regiment who took men below the prescribed minimum height of 5 foot 3 inches. So short in stature and in sight Tom was cannon fodder, like so many whether tall or small, fat or thin. The bullet does not discriminate.

But Tom survived. He was lucky to have sustained an injury to his leg preventing him from staying in the army and returning to the trenches. His injury entitled him to a war pension. Initially he refused his rightful compensation because he said the country could not afford it; his father wisely told him to accept his due entitlement. He certainly deserved it as all do who are maimed or otherwise damaged from serving in the forces.

Then claiming the compensation was tempered by consideration of the cost to the public purse, and probably the shame of relying on "handouts" because people were fiercely self—reliant and yes resourceful and resilient. Now such thoughts are unlikely to influence the decision to claim rightful entitlement to compensation for such injuries. It could have been a misplaced deference on Tom's part, or possibly survivor's guilt. He went home to live on albeit with a bad leg, when many of his pals did not. He would have seen the killing of his comrades in arms; their death. Having such experiences can cause immense feelings of guilt as the survivor wonders why they continued to live when so many did not.

Jack (another John like dad nicknamed Jack) was even more fortunate—he was found not fit enough to join up and go to war. Jack went for his medical and was found to have a fast heart rate. No more is known about this heart which beat quickly that saved him from Flanders. It could have been normal for Jack. Different people had different heart rates. There were no Electro Cardiograms, ultra sound scans or other such tests to indicate whether Jack had a problem with the functioning of his heart. Like his father he too was a coalman following his dad into the business. He was instructed not to lift the shafts of his wagon by doctors as it might cause a strain to his heart, but he carried on regardless ignoring their advice. It did him no harm as he lived into his 80s. The doctors were wrong. His heart beat was probably normal for Jack, or maybe he was anxious during the medical and his heart rate increased as a response to such emotions. Such an arbitrary finding meant he escaped call up to France or to another posting. He survived because of the lack of medical knowledge in the early part of the 20th Century. Medicine and science have moved on massively since 1914 and the detection, diagnosis and treatment of heart disease is now routine and well informed by science. Jack probably did not have anything wrong with his heart.

Dantzig Alley where Harry lies buried is a long way from his home in Blackburn and it was never possible for his parents or brothers and sisters to visit his grave. Travel to France was inconceivable for the working classes.

Harry's family grieved; no body to bury, no grave that could be visited. Desolation in so many homes throughout the land. So much sorrow. Relieved through a Christian faith of belief in a resurrection and everlasting life. On Sundays most attended a church or chapel, either through conviction or convention, or both. Religious belief has withered through the 20th Century as other unsustainable and worldly gods fill a quest for contentment, purpose and distraction. The cult of fame and the search for its fools' gold has supplanted simple satisfactions. An obsession with knowing the personalities and lives of the rich and famous has become fed by their easier access. Such fascinations stoked by the so called celebrities themselves posting pictures and inane comments on Instagram, Facebook, Twitter, and selling the sanctity of their home, lives and sometimes their children in posted selfies, blogs, vlogs and glossy magazines. Reticence, humility, restraint, self-control and self-respect often disappear in this desire to be a somebody.

Many religions already teach that everybody is a valued and valuable somebody. Some belief systems have imploded, losing followers, because of the behaviour of their adherents or priests who have committed terrible offences of abuse against children, women and the vulnerable. Many churches and other places of worship flourish, their mission trying to heal, comfort, bring peace and change that will benefit all, not the few. How many now turn to their maker when death is imminent or following the loss of a loved one? Following the war there was a big upsurge in spiritualism as the grieving bereaved sought confirmation that their loved one was at rest and living a beautiful afterlife.

After a big battle the fear of the postman bringing bad news of death or wounding affected all the roads, street and byways of Britain as mothers and wives looked anxiously out from behind their net curtains to see whether the postman passed them by or whether the dreaded knock brought the news they feared most. And so the knock came for so many including the sad news for Henry and Mary Ellen Hindle that their dear son Harold had been killed after fighting and staying unharmed for two years. Harry had been home on leave in those two years, but he could not cross his doorstep without first ridding himself of his uniform. It was so full of dirt and lice from the trenches and their insanitary hell that he had lived in. Like many soldiers returning home from the front Harry had to strip off in the coal shed or back yard before he could enter his home. How terrible for him having travelled all the way from the battle field to Calais to get a boat over the English Channel and then a train to Blackburn from Dover that he was not able to walk over the doorstep into the loving arms of his family and the sanctuary of home. Soldiers felt contaminated physically and often mentally with their dreadful experiences. Dumping the clothes at the doorstep could decontaminate the body; it was harder to do the same with the mind.

Two other brothers, one of whom was dad's dad went to fight in countries where nearly 100 years later British troops were again deployed to die and suffer injury. History repeats itself. Politicians, those men and women in power making the decisions to send our troops to war never seem to heed the lessons of history. Fred was in Mesopotamia. Mesopotamia is now part of Iraq. Fred was in what is now modern day Iraq. Uncle Fred Hindle joined up late as he was next to the youngest in his family. Like his older brother William he was not sent to France.

His war was fighting the Red Army following the Bolshevik revolution of 1918. He was in Mesopotamia fighting with the White Army Russians. Uncle Fred told a story of the workers and peasants overthrowing their former masters and taking possession of their property. Uncle Fred and his fellow soldiers had come across a large country mansion. The previous Lord and Lady of the manor in Russia had been evicted. Their big house had been taken over by the previous gardener who had since become an official of the Communist Party. He was now living in the house where he was once a servant. Fred must have been on the northern edges of Mesopotamia near Armenia where thousands were exterminated in a genocide perpetrated by the Ottoman (Turkish) Empire who was an ally of Germany. Fred was fighting in a far off land, Empire against Empire, carrying out his duty opposing a regime, a colonial power just like Britain, but solving nothing in the long term.

We have experienced two wars with Iraq in recent times. The first Iraq war started on 02 August 1990 when Saddam Hussein, President of Iraq decided to invade Kuwait, a major oil producing country. The thirty five nations led by the United States who opposed the invasion quickly expelled the Iraqi troops from Kuwait. It was all over in a matter of months, the armistice being signed on 11 April 1991. Saddam Hussein stayed in power. His days were numbered.

Following the attack on New York's Twin Towers and the Pentagon in Washington on 11 September 2001 by al-Qaeda, a war on terror was pursued by the US government. This so called war on terror and the suggestion that Iraq had weapons of mass destruction were used as pretexts to start the war with Iraq on 20 March 2003 by the British and US governments. Forces from a number of countries, not just the USA and the UK invaded Iraq and deposed Saddam Hussein. No weapons of mass destruction were ever found. 600,000 Iraqi citizens died. The removal of this dictator who had kept the many factions of his country quiet by vicious suppression of anyone who opposed him, gave way to a vacuum. A big empty space grabbed by Isis for one. More death, more destruction, more than that wielded by Saddam himself. Was it worth it? Is it ever worth it? An evaluation of the pros and cons of this war is beyond this book; but it is a recurrent theme for reflection. Are lessons of history really learnt? As many have asked was the First World War worth such a loss of life and damage to the ones who did survive? One persuasive analysis says that it led to the Second World War. It was certainly never the war to end all wars. War gives birth to wars. This certainly happened following the second Iraqi war. War breeding continues to this day.

William who is dad's dad, my paternal grandfather, was the other Hindle son who travelled to a distant part of the British Empire. He went to India to patrol the border which runs alongside Afghanistan.

William was on the border of Afghanistan another country where once again British service men and women have fought, died or been injured before and since 1916 when William was deployed there.

William joined the Border Regiment which had its headquarters in Carlisle Castle some distance north of Blackburn. The castle now houses the Regimental museum. Dad donated his father's medals to the museum and they are there for anyone to see. Carefully stored in a cabinet, the museum curators will show you the medals of William Hindle if you care to visit and ask. There is much more than one man's medals to keep a visitor interested in the museum as the Border Regiment can trace its origins back to the Cumberland and Westmoreland foot regiments all the way back to 1702. These hardy hill men made up the only Regiment in the British army fighting Napoleon's armies on 28 October 1811 at the non-existent place now on Google Maps of Arroyo Dos Molinos in central Spain. They captured part of the French 34th Regiment along with their drums. No more beating the march out. The name Arroyo Dos Molinos is emblazoned upon the Regiment's cap badge.

William's training with the other new recruits to the Border Regiment took place in the Isle of Man. It seems a complicated journey to travel from the north west of England across the Irish Sea to the Isle of Man, but ferries sailed as now from Heysham and Liverpool to the port of Douglas. William had to make this journey but he was to make a much longer one at the end of his training. Training to be a soldier demands learning to take orders. Not questioning whether the order makes sense or not. No rationalising or evaluation of it, even if given by a fool and clearly going to lead to your destruction. Orders had to be obeyed. If not then you faced the firing squad.

Such was the disregard for the human life of thousands of young British men—a disregard exercised by, as always, it seems those in power and influence, especially those who stay safe and sound at home, who never hear the screaming sound of a shell heading straight towards the soldier or sailor, who never live in water drenched, rat runs. Here were some more men who having practised marching, rifle firing, bayonet thrusting and all the other skills needed to fight the Germans or their allies were lined up on the parade ground ready to hear their fate. But not all were destined to fight the Germans. Some were destined for a different conflict, to be sent to much more distant conflict zones. Their Colonel in Chief standing high above them drew an imaginary line down the middle of the regiment splitting the men into two equal halves. One half was destined to fight the war in Flanders France and the other half; they were off to India.

William was standing in the half assigned to India. He was relieved. Fate had favoured him. He knew from his brother Harry about the horrendous conditions of soldier life in France. Others in William's half did not see themselves as being endowed with the good fortune to have escaped the killing mud baths of France. To them India was a distant unknown country, a long, long way from their English homeland. So without the benefit of hindsight, that utterly useless commodity, some of those who were in the half going to India swapped with some of those recognising an escape route to improved chances of survival in India. This simple choice believing it to be in their best interests to go to France had the effect of giving some a virtually guaranteed death sentence. They were destined for the Somme.

Understandably India must have seemed to us now almost the equivalent of going to the moon. There was no air travel, no internet connection, and no international telephones. A remote distant place far away from family and friends. It is understandable such a choice was made. But it feels so unfair that the choice was not the right one probably for lots of reasons—a desire to be closer to home, not knowing of the horror of the trenches, a fear of the foreign and exotic. Never a real choice as many did not have the necessary information to make the right decision. So many factors contributed to whether a right or wrong decision was made as is always the case.

William sailed off to India and survived. Most of those who went to France died in the Battle of the Somme as did his brother Harry. Their parents could have lost two sons if William had been picked to go to France.

On arriving in India, William was posted to the North West Frontier. This is the area that lies on the borders of India, present day Pakistan and Afghanistan, a country to which British troops would return 90 years later with a similar futility. All politicians and those in power who commit our country and the fighting lives and bodies of our service men and women should have mandatory history lessons so that the mistakes and experiences of previous invasions and interventions in other countries are learnt in the hope, they would never occur again. So William fought the great grandfathers of the Taliban whose great grandsons learnt how to make bombs and bury them in the Afghan earth, known as IEDs—Improvised Explosive Devices. These hidden weapons killed and maimed our service men and women nearly a century after soldiers of the British Army had suffered similar losses and injuries.

Will we ever learn? The Taliban of 1916 were not defeated and the Taliban of a century later is again in power. So despite all the sacrifice by British armed forces and the millions of pounds of money that was spent in trying to defeat the Taliban, it now rules Afghanistan.

Stationed on the Khyber Pass in one of the forts keeping a vital trade route open between India and China to the north, one of the branches of routes known collectively as the Silk Road, William's job was to keep this vital trade passage protected. The Silk Road had to be kept open for commerce and safe for travellers. Compared to the French trenches it was a relatively easy posting, but not without its own challenges. William found the Afghan tribesmen to be fierce and dedicated to their clan. He admired their fighting spirit and refusal to capitulate. As in every war since and definitely before, the local militia as guerrilla fighters easily disappeared and merged into the landscape or local village communities. Identifying a fighter was difficult. One moment they could be an innocent shepherd, the next a deadly foe. Pursuing them into their territories was risky and dangerous as the opposition knew their lands, its humps and bumps, its hiding places perfect for an ambush on unsuspecting British fighters.

William always supported Indian independence as he was sickened with the way the British government, its Civil Service and what he called "do-gooders" treated the indigenous Indian people. For the rest of his life he refused to give any money or otherwise support the Church Missionary Societies because he had seen how they lived in luxury and treated their Indian servants with condescension and contempt when out in India converting what the missionaries saw as uneducated and unenlightened natives. A superior, ignorant and racist attitude was common in those colonialists who governed India for the Empire. William knew these Missionaries would never succeed in converting the local populace as they were all committed Muslims devoted to their faith. Until the Afghan war and the Khyber Pass was threatened the civilian English white skinned residents had ignored and shunned the British soldiers, disdainful of the Army. Once the fighting started and their lives and livelihoods were threatened the British Army squaddie all of a sudden became wanted and congratulated. They changed their behaviours and outward attitudes because the white settlers needed the army to protect them.

William did donate money in later life to support medical missionaries as he had witnessed their commitment and practical help given to poor Indians and Afghans. His disgust with the Church Missionary societies upset his sisters because they would knit clothes for this organisation which were then sold to raise money. Their missionary efforts were seen by William as useless and patronising. Little changes—Paul Theroux in his book The Dark Star Continent repeatedly expresses his frustration with some of the charities working in Africa who have engendered dependence, in the communities who were meant to be helped, whilst travelling around in expensive 4x4 vehicles. Contrast this with the work of Medicin Sans Frontier and other organisations whose doctors, nurses and other staff risk their lives to deliver treatment and care to civilians caught up in wars in dangerous, conflict torn places.

William spent 3 years in India guarding the Empire with no leave home. Such separation from family would not be tolerated by today's army. Transportation home from foreign deployments are given regularly, but in 1916 there were no aeroplanes to transport soldiers home. It was a long sea journey back to the UK.

William would often share his memories of his time supporting the continued existence of the British Empire with his two children. Such memories being passed down orally to future generations adding to the family's collection of stories. Valuable observations and insights adding to a personal family history, and also a national and international one. A story often told related to the pragmatism of the Afghan fighter. The local Afghan tribesmen would silence their guns during the harvest. Making sure that the grain was gathered in, took precedence over trying to kill the British colonialist. The British Army did not take advantage of this temporary cease fire and shell the villages and their meadows. They too kept their guns silent. It was an unwritten truce to ensure the locals did not starve. At that time the sole reason for the presence of British forces was to keep the vital trade route open. All hostilities resumed after the grain had been gathered in. Once carefully stored away the local tribesmen would attack the British forces once again, guaranteeing retaliation in kind. Sensitivity to local trade was also demonstrated by having a weekly one day cease fire to allow the local traders on their camels, carts and horses to pass through the Khyber Pass.

William's meat inspector training proved vital in preventing the Border Regiment from mass food poisoning. He saved his mates from hours of running to the lavatory, or worse, by detecting the meat they were being fed was diseased. Their Colonel walking around the soldier's mess one day asked his men if the food was adequate. William stood up and said it was not, saying the meat was bad according to the training he had received as a meat inspector. The Colonel came from a Cumbrian North Pennine farming background and took notice when William spoke up to say the meat was inedible respecting his knowledge and expertise. To ensure that his men were sold uncontaminated, healthy meat he promoted William to the rank of Staff Sergeant so he could oversee the food quality. William was put in charge of buying food supplies. One local supplier who tried to sell William meat offered a bribe of silver slippers saying he could take these back to England to his fiancé. William refused point blank and ensured that this supplier was banned from offering his products to the British Army ever again. William though did make sure he brought back some slippers from his time on the Khyber Pass as a present for the girl he hoped to marry. But because of his high moral standards, refusing to be bribed and wanting to ensure his fellow soldiers ate the best quality meat, the sandals were not silver, but cloth ones. He had bought them in the local bazar.

The first mail from home that reached the Border Regiment in India conveyed the dreadful news that 600 of their comrades had been killed on the Somme. William had been lucky; he was in the 50% allocated originally to India, most importantly he did not swap the lottery ticket he had been given to escape the bloodied fields of Flanders.

William liked India; he admired the fortitude of the people. He always wanted to return one day and always supported Indian independence. There was no glorious future for those who survived Flanders and came home. Such work that there was soon dwindled into mass unemployment as the global economic disaster of the 1930s unfolded. Those who had stayed at home in a protected occupation or had managed to escape the societal pressure or order to join up often had a job and prospered. They were in settled employment and did not have the horrific scenes and experiences of a deathly war lodged in their brains. William returned home to a job as a butcher and marriage to Elizabeth Jefferson, Dad's mother. His life continued believing his children would be safe from any more wars, how wrong could he be.

So two brothers were despatched to countries which nearly 100 years later British forces would occupy, suffer losses and burden the country with millions of pounds of more debt. Meddling in other countries seems to be a British obsession—dangerous and costly with apparently nil benefit. One other family member, not a Hindle, but mum's father was also sent to another country which the British had occupied for many centuries despite not being particularly loved by the locals who unsurprisingly given the history, particularly the widespread famine that devastated the country and its peoples, wanted the right to govern themselves.

Frank Stratford was dad's wife's father. My maternal grandfather. He was a kind, gentle man and a Cockney too. He was born in London within the sound of Bow Bells. His father was a gardener at Salmesbury Hall, so like most men at the beginning of the First World War came from a working class family, used to weathering hardships and poverty when work was scarce, or other troubles such as when illness or injury came along. Frank volunteered on the day war broke out. For some inexplicable reason he joined the Royal Welsh Fusiliers—not a London or Lancashire regiment. Understandably Frank had a difficult time as did not speak Welsh and was treated as an outsider. He had a rough time of it and was given all the difficult jobs to do in the trenches. Fighting at the Battle of Mons, the first significant fire fight, he was awarded the Mons Star and Clasp. Frank kept himself alive whilst in France, but was then sent to Dublin after the Easter uprising 1916. He hated it there as did not know who the enemy was. Could it be a man walking down the street towards him looking innocent but carrying a concealed gun? Such is urban guerrilla war fare. The Irish freedom fighters would now be called terrorists. Frank could never relax, he avoided going to pubs. Even though his posting in Dublin was much less likely to lead to being killed he still wanted to go back to France where he knew from which directions the bullets and shells were coming from. A kind, gentle man who never had a bad word to say about anyone his good nature was taken advantage of. He was placed on 24 hour guard duty. After that 24 hours stint, he was placed on yet another 24 hour guard duty. He could no longer cope. It had made him ill and he knew he needed go off sick. Presenting himself before the battalion medic with an inability to undertake another 24 hour duty because of what now would be categorised as a mental health problem was not an option. Ridiculed and belittled with no respite from the terrors of a further 24 hour guard duty. There was no way back to France and he hated being on the Dublin streets amongst people who he did not see or experience as his enemy. He knew he needed a reason that would convince the examining doctor that he was no longer fit to serve as a soldier. He came up with the idea of making himself physically exhausted and present for medical examination with a high pulse rate. A quickly beating heart was the sure way to obtain a medical discharge as was the case in dad's uncle. By running around the block a few times Frank pushed his heart rate up to its very maximum. Quickly going into see the Medical Officer, before his heart rate returned to normal, he was examined. His plan worked. He was medically discharged. It should have been an honourable discharge as he had given 3 years of his life fighting bravely for his country. Sadly he was refused a war pension after the war. A colonel wrote "malingerer" across his record. Nothing could have been further from than the truth. But a lowly foot soldier has no power against the rank and standing of a colonel.

Such injustices rarely happen today. Those that look back to first half of the last century with fondness need to look closer and deeper. Injustice was rampant. After the First World War, there was a peace and dad's childhood was happy. He was fortunate that his parents survived the 1918 Spanish Flu pandemic and was born to a family that did not experience the dreadful unemployment of the 1920s. The worldwide economic depression hit the Germans who were paying reparations (financial compensation) to the victors of the war. Widespread discontent bred extreme politics and the Fascists won out over the Communists in Germany. Even when dad was born in 1923 the first sparks of a future world conflagration were starting. He was destined to follow his father and uncles fighting for Great Britain in yet another war.

Birth and Place

John Hindle was born in a terraced house at 79 Leamington Road Blackburn on 14 January 1923. In that day and age, it could be described as an upper working class area. Lying between Preston New Road and Revidge Road, the house had a front parlour, a living room, a small kitchen and a back yard housing a toilet, coal shed and wash house. Upstairs were two bedrooms and a box room. It had a garden at the front. It was a house that those who lived in the streets under the smoking mill chimneys that clung to the steep hillsides of Blackburn, would envy and aspire to.

Dad's parents were Elizabeth Hindle, formerly Elizabeth Jefferson. His father was William Hindle the one posted to the Khyber Pass, escaping the Flanders's slaughter. Only two of William's sisters married—Maggie and Beck, because so many of the potential eligible young men were dead. Their broken bodies long since decayed and eventually merged with the dirt and soil of the Flanders' mud and other foreign lands in which they had fought and died.

His parent's courtship had undergone some tests. Jack and William looked like twins and were often mistaken for each other. Jack was a practical joker and after the war often played some tricks on his brother. Jack put his brother through many a practical jokes by pretending to be his brother William. One of his many audacious teases was that he passed himself off as William to a local farmer. He bought a herd of sheep, the seller believing he was selling them to William. William did not know anything about this transaction until he was passing a pen at the Blackburn abattoir. Surprised to see the notice on the side of the pen saying that the sheep belonged to him, he was even more surprised that Jack had not paid for the sheep and that he would have to pay for stock that he had not actually bought from the farmer. Jack though had made a good deal and William forgave him.

People mistook Jack for William on many occasions which caused problems for his relationship with his fiancé and future wife, Elizabeth. Communities were tight knit, extended family members and friends living within short walking distance in one of the many terraced houses which characterises Blackburn. Gossip travelled by word of mouth, not in the written messages of texts now sent at incredible speeds through the cables or digital signals of today. It was impossible to get away with anything as there was always someone watching or listening possibly through a net curtain or behind a closed door. Life was public. There was nowhere to hide. No cars to drive off to some secluded spot to enjoy an adulterous relationship. No anonymous hotel bedrooms. No after dark fumble after leaving a drinking club or pub, because such places were not visited by so called "respectable" women either alone or in company. Life was lived in the home or by the phenomena of "walking out". A man and woman going for a walk was how relationships between the opposite sex were formed and either withered, or blossomed. Finding privacy indoors was impossible in either the Hindle or Jefferson households as there were always so many siblings or parents around.

Jack was seen one day courting a young woman by walking out together. They had chosen to escape their tightly drawn streets and the prying eyes of neighbours and relatives by venturing to the rural outskirts of Blackburn. This was within a mile or so of where Jack lived. Walking down leafy Meins Road they were not alone probably because many Blackburn folk escaped the smoky skies of the town in search of the cleaner air offered by countryside. Jack who was arm and arm with his young lady was mistaken for William. Somebody thought he was William. William already had a girlfriend—his future wife Elizabeth. The busy body spread the false rumour that William had been seen walking out with another woman whilst still in a relationship with Elizabeth. The gossip spread quickly landing on Elizabeth's ears. Elizabeth, a beauty with a mane of red hair and a feisty temperament and independence of mind had no patience with gossips. Putting her faith in William's trustworthiness she saw off the gossipers with her fiery tongue, but did still check that it was a case of mistaken identity. She was a typical Lancashire lass—fearless, feisty and fun.

In 1923 babies were born at home with a midwife present. Obviously no National Health Service existed, doctors were expensive. I say the word "obviously" because I would expect most people in the United Kingdom to know the fact that the NHS came into being at the end of the Second World War with many other social reforms that were enacted after the defeat of Germany and Japan. I am not so sure having watched an episode of a BBC reality programme The Apprentice. The show is hosted by the businessman Alan Sugar. Over a number of weeks contestants are set tasks in teams of two to supposedly test their entrepreneurial skills and business acumen. One week the teams had been tasked with having to find certain items including a pre Second World War edition of The Alice in Wonderland Collection. Most of the contestants were clueless as to the date the war started, one asking whether it was 1945 and another saying it only lasted for two or three years.

This is shameful. Millions of men, women and children died in the war with millions sacrificing their life so that these privileged men and women can enjoy the freedom to go on a TV show and make a fool of themselves. It is an example of complacency in the extreme; a lack of touch with reality and the lessons of history. Learn from the past so that you can prepare for the future. Understanding the history of a society enhances future prediction of the direction of that society and the risks and benefits it is likely to face. It helps the individual prepare for both the worst and best outcomes. Essential knowledge to develop an ability to react and cope with change—a vital building block of resilience.

The world may not always be as seemingly comfortable as it is today for the UK's Apprentice' contestants and others like them. It is practically guaranteed not to be. The four horsemen of apocalyptic 21st century climate change are already mounting their devastating steeds ready to start their unstoppable and unremitting gallop towards irretrievable destruction.

What's this got to do with life in Blackburn in 1923? Why this reference to the heating of our global home here? No reason other than in 1923 the biggest threat to an unborn baby reaching old age would have been disease and a war which was not predicted or imagined only 16 years before its start. Time has already run out. Carbon dioxide emissions were supposed to reduce, but they are increasing. Methane, another greenhouse gas, is erupting from the earth. Tipping points may have already been reached. Thunderbolt changes of droughts leading to vast wild fires disgorging more carbon into the atmosphere; floods that destroy all in their path; oceanic toxicity; desertification, extinction of many species. All being experienced and witnessed now. Just as the pandemic was foreseen as a certain eventuality, climate change has also been predicted for many years but little globally has been done to really stop it. Continuing with a hedonistic exploitation of the planet will lead to future pandemics and devastation of our earthly home. The tipping point must be reversed by us all climbing aboard the non-carbon part of the see saw.

Football and Strong Women

Dad grew up on a sporting diet of football in the winter and cricket in the summer. For nearly every working class male and some females following the game of football was a passion from 1870s onwards. Even more so for dad as one of his ancestors was his footballing hero as he had played for Blackburn Rovers when in its infancy. Blackburn Rovers Football Club are presently in a Football Association league called the Championship. Being in the Championship league does not mean that Rovers are in the highest league as that is called the Premier League. Unless you are a football fan and know this fact, it is impossible to know what being in the Championship league means. Some years ago there was a simpler and clearer way of ranking football clubs. The best teams would be in the First Division and below were three other Divisions. Being in the Championship is equivalent to being in the Second Division. In football, change is a certainty; the winners become the losers and the losers the winners; the top tumble to the bottom and the bottom sometimes ascend to the top. Well it used to be a certainty until football clubs, like most nearly everything else in Great Britain, were bought up by foreign money. Manchester United succumbed to the USA dollar, Chelsea to the Russian rouble and Blackburn Rovers to the Indian chicken food processing conglomerate chain of Venky's.

Blackburn Rovers were at the top, or towards the top for many years in the First Division when the town buzzed with men and a few women who having finished work after five and half days' hard graft left the factory gate at midday to make their way to Ewood Park if there was a home game or onto coaches or trains if the Rovers were playing away.

People walked to the game from their homes in the town of Blackburn itself and its neighbouring smaller towns and villages, from places such as Darwen, Belthorn and Guide. Having a car was not as usual as it is now. In the 1950s and 60s dad's two brothers in law Ron and Frank, mum's brothers, walked over through Corporation Park to meet with dad at our house and then walk on with him the three miles or so down to Ewood Park, all three wearing their blue and white woolly striped scarves. People thought nothing of walking a few miles to get somewhere—it meant they did not put on weight so easily and kept themselves fit. Like little streams in groups of two or three from all parts of the Borough, joining with more and more fans they became a river of chattering supporters eagerly looking forward to the match and a win from their Rovers. Mum never went to the match; she would go shopping to Blackburn town centre or catch up with chores although dad would always wake us up early on Saturday morning with the sound of the vacuum cleaner as he made his way up the stairs to our bedrooms. Household tasks were shared between them, with dad keeping the Rayburn fire going in the kitchen throughout the winter and mum lighting the fire in the sitting room until a gas fire was installed followed by the heavenly warmth of a central heating installation.

If you lived in a town then you supported your home town's team. A fan was not bought by any glamour or prestige of a club. The top clubs are now international "brands" and rich young men (and they are mostly rich to afford the air fare and mostly male) fly into Manchester Airport from all over the world to visit Old Trafford and the same applies to the other major clubs like Manchester City, Liverpool, Arsenal or Chelsea. Manchester United, until it won the European Cup in 1968 mostly drew its fan base not from Manchester but from the Salford side of the Manchester metropolis. It then started attracting supporters from further away from cities which provided players to clubs. One such was George Best a son of Belfast who was spotted by a scout when playing for Cregagh Boys and brought over Irish Sea at the age of 15. Manchester City was always the club which drew its support from traditional Manchester boundaries, particularly the south and east of Manchester. Growing up in the pre-war years it would be almost inconceivable to support an out of town club. There was no television and supporters had no money to follow far away clubs. If a father moved from Preston to Blackburn then his allegiance to Preston North End would remain, and it is possible he passed on his passion to his sons and daughters. But Blackburn, not Manchester was where dad was born and grew up in the 1920s and 1930s. He supported Blackburn because it was his town.

Blackburn Rovers was his club for a number of reasons. Firstly he was given complementary tickets that were handed out to the pupils of St Silas's Primary School when aged 9 years old. Tickets were given only to the boys, not the girls. These school boys, as tickets were not given to girls, watched the match from a designated space in the Riverside Stand side of the ground. The Club gave these free tickets to schools to be handed out by their teachers. It meant that the boys would be likely to grow up to be committed fans and so guarantee a following in the future. Dad went to watch the match as a child with pals from school. The walk to Ewood Park went past the school church and down Buncer Lane to eventually go under the Leeds—Liverpool Canal at the Aqueduct bridge. This is a fine piece of engineering bridge building which takes the canal above the road. There were always some wild escapades on the way to the match. Dad remembers how one dare devil climbed up onto the aqueduct and walked along an 18 inch foot ledge 60 foot up stopping half way across as the football crowds looked up at him. He then walked to the other end and climbed down. This risk taker passed for the Grammar School and eventually became the Bank Manager at Darwen Trustee Savings Bank. He was one of dad's pals, who hopefully changed his risky ways on taking up work.

It seems astonishing that girls were considered to be unworthy or unsuitable or uninterested to be given such an opportune gift. Impossible now to know their reactions or feelings at seeing the boys being given free access to a match or the lasting message it left. Each may have reacted differently, some would simply not be bothered, not being interested in football, although maybe having been given the opportunity to attend a match, a spark of interest may have been lit which could have grown into a lifelong love of the team and the game. Others might have felt irritated that they had been excluded from the opportunity to experience a football match. Others might have just accepted it and felt nothing—the lot of a 9 year old school girl—girls and women simply did not go to football matches, they did not play the game. Perhaps that is what some of them thought, but it was far from reality. The English Ladies Football Association formed and held its very first meeting in Blackburn on 10 December 1921 following the banning by the Football Association of women's matches that year. Around 150 women's football clubs existed in 1921. Women had been playing competitive football for some time. Ladies' matches really took off during the First World War years with Preston Ladies being the foremost club in the country, often raising money for charity. There was even an international match played against a team from France.

The second reason dad supported Blackburn Rovers is that it had been a family tradition; a family member had played for the team. This was dad's grandad, his mother's father. Thomas Jefferson the footballer like many professional players today was an exceptional athlete. He could run 100 yards in 10 seconds. Dad claimed he could jump the Leeds—Liverpool Canal.

In the last few decades of the 19th Century there were two prominent teams in Blackburn—Blackburn Rovers and Blackburn Olympic. Olympic played at Hole i'th wall football ground. The team would change into their kit in the nearby Hole i'th wall pub. The ground near Leamington Road was eventually sold for house building, but this was many years later. The first team his grandad played for was Blackburn Olympic.

Blackburn Olympic was formed out of two clubs—Black Star and James Street. Their players came from the working class, weavers in the main, but also included some who worked for themselves such as a pub landlord. Sidney Yates who owned an iron foundry sponsored the team. Blackburn Rovers, in contrast, were made up of players who had attended public schools and were independently wealthy. The first time Blackburn Rovers were finalists in the FA cup was in 1882 when they played the Old Etonians at Kennington Oval. The Rovers lost by one goal.

Blackburn Olympic had better success, deciding to enter the competition in the 1882/1883 season. Beating the Old Carthusians who were former pupils of Charterhouse Public School, Godalming, Surrey, Olympic reached the final in 1883 to play the Cup holders—the Old Etonians. The team had enough money to pay a one way fare to London, hoping that the gate money would be sufficient to pay their fare home. Fortunately, it was. Over 7000 people watched the match. Olympic beat the Old Etonians after extra time. The score was 2-1 and they arrived back as the first Northern winners of the FA cup. Heroes in every sense. The establishment moaned. They had been beaten by men who they saw as beneath them and lacking in stature and status. They complained saying that the tactic of their trainer to take them away for a week's coaching at Blackpool before the match was unfair.

Hypocrisy from a highly fortunate team whose members came from privileged and wealthy families who would have had servants to look after their every need and would never have experienced factory work or any type of labouring to say that a week's pre match training was unfair. The Old Etonian had a massive head start going into the match. They would have always had the best nourishment; a joint of meat would not just be for Sundays. Food was plentiful and varied for the wealthy, unlike the working class where if there was no work or too ill to work, there would be little or no money on the table to buy food. The Old Etonians' players and supporters would not have to worry about how they would pay the fare home. Most would have lived down in the south east where Eton School is based, their riches able to pay for their own horse and carriage or a first class compartment on the train. They saw themselves as superior when compared to a bunch of Northern, Lancashire lads who were the workers they would order about in their personal and daily lives. It was a sign of the emergence of changing times.

Blackburn Olympic were the first provincial team to play at the Football Association Cup final. Sadly no medals were given out when they won in 1883. Their win heralded the beginning of a change in many walks of life, not just on the soccer pitch. People whose lives had been consigned to a narrow experience of hard toil with little control over their personal destiny would over the next century as opportunities broadened, explore and fulfil their potential as a human being. For many though the way to exploring, never mind achieving personal growth, is still barred.

A talent goes a long way if people know they have such a talent and can develop and reveal it to the world. Everyone has many talents; most do not know it or have not been able, through no fault of their own to find, grow and share it. Thomas Jefferson, joiner, footballer, mischief maker and dad's grandad had many talents. His great running speed and footballing talents secured what would be called a transfer to the more wealthy and prestigious Blackburn Rovers Club.

This is what dad said; a story told to him by his maternal grandfather. "At one match he played a blinder for Olympic against the Rovers. Rovers' management approached him and asked if he would play for them. Rovers offered him more money than Olympic so he signed to play for the Rovers in 1882."

Thomas Jefferson showed little loyalty to his local club, deciding instead to follow the money. He cannot be criticised. Having a large family to support he made a rational and sensible choice. After all it is only a game.

Surprising as it sounds but football matches were played on Christmas Day up until after the Second World War. The word surprising has been chosen with care because football matches are now played on any day of the week and almost at any time to suit the broadcasters who have paid millions of pounds to have the rights to show the matches at a time of their choosing through their channels. So why are matches not played on Christmas Day now? The family ructions caused by relatives wanting to see live football at home or in the stadium rather than watch the King's Speech or settle down for a turkey dinner would be huge. So how did families cope when football matches were played on Christmas Day?

Not very well according to dad. On Christmas Day Rovers would play and Grandma Hindle would get cross as her husband would be watching the clock knowing that the turkey and Christmas Pudding had to be on the dinner table by a certain time for him to walk down to Ewood for the start of the match at 3.00pm.

Dad described how his mother would become more and more cross as her husband's impatience became more and more apparent. William was eager to set off to Ewood in good time for the start of the match. Grandma H. became more irritable as her husband's impatience became more visible. Would the Turkey be cooked on time? It did not promote a happy celebration of Christ's birthday.

William was an enthusiastic supporter of the Rovers and his mischievous father in law (Thomas Jefferson the one who played once for the Rovers) knew this very well. Lizzie, his wife, wanted a door changing in her home so it would open out a different way. She naturally asked her father, a joiner, to undertake the job for her. He turned up on a Saturday just as William was getting ready to leave for Ewood Park to watch the Rovers. Knowing William would be anxious to get on his way he asked him to help him move the door around. William naturally agreed; he was a generous, kind man who would never refuse his father in law's request for help. William watched the clock ticking slowly round to the point that he must leave or miss the match. Just before it arrived at that point, his father in law knowing the latest time he would have to leave to arrive at Ewood said "You get on your way lad, you don't want to miss the match. I can finish door off,". A relieved William rushed off to watch his beloved team.

Traditionally football games were played on Christmas Day from well before the First World War and the tradition continued in the trenches when the opposing sides famously had a football game on Christmas Day 1914. It was not until 1965 that the last English football league fixture took place on Christmas Day when Blackpool beat Blackburn 4-2. Some Scottish league fixtures continued to be played for some years after 1965.

By then family leisure time was becoming more established and diversifying. Increased incomes led to car ownership which gave greater freedom to travel for days or afternoon drives out and to visit friends and relatives. There was more money to buy gifts and presents, and marketing to children of games and toys started to appear. Women's aspirations for self-determination were growing; making a Christmas dinner for quick consumption to permit a 3.00 pm attendance by usually just the man of the house at a football match with his male footballing mates was demeaning drudgery by today's standards. Without a shadow of doubt most women's lives have been transformed for the better through the last century. There is still a long way to go. Domestic and other violence, income inequality, and child care responsibilities to name a few of the heavy burdens women have to withstand continue to this day.

Lancashire women have always been independent, working for themselves and making their own way in life. The play Hindle Wakes written by Stanley Houghton in 1910 was ahead of its time in dealing with the subject of extra marital sex and the determination of the central character in the play—Fanny Hawthorn to choose her own destiny. Becoming pregnant in Llandudno when Fanny enjoyed a weekend with the son of the local mill owner for "a bit of fun" as she described it. She actively chose to bring up the child conceived in that North Wales seaside town as a single parent. Refusing to marry the father of the child she was expecting, she came under the combined persistent pressure from her own parents and the parents of her lover who both demanded she should wed. Fanny sees no reason to commit to her weekend lover. She is not interested in a life determined largely by a man. She is an independent woman, earning her own money as a weaver in a mill in East Lancashire as many did. She does not need a man to support her and her child. She can do it herself. She is assertive, self-confident and knows her own mind which could also describe many women who worked in Lancashire in the cotton industry.

Grandma Hindle—Elizabeth Jefferson spoke her mind on any topic just like Fanny Hawthorn. So did her sister my Great Aunt Florrie, but her tongue was less abrasive than my grandmother's. Elizabeth, born of Jefferson stock, was proud, dynamic, hard-working and made the best food ever. Born into a liberal household towards the end of Queen Victoria's rule, all the family were adventurous, Fred going off to Canada in 1929 to seek his fortune. Thomas Jefferson the footballer, carpenter and joiner worked for one of the town's brewing companies. He had been born in Accrington. He, his wife Alice and 6 children lived in Albany Road, Blackburn in 1911 in a good sized terraced house with a stone bay window, small front garden and in one of the most desirable areas of Blackburn, near Corporation Park and open countryside. Like the Hindle family, children aged over 14 were in full time employment so there was a substantial income coming into the household. Pre 1914 working class families prospered in Lancashire from its cotton industry; war put an end to the improvement in living standards.

Grandma Hindle always spoke her mind, sometimes upsetting those who were the object of her criticism. Political debate and the exchange and sharing of ideas was an often constant feature of working class households. No television, no radio, no internet to distract. None of these media existed. These often aimless media serve as time fillers for empty lives or escapes from the humdrum, but are also the source of fabulous, limitless information. So reading, reflection and discussion had time and space to fill any empty moments after long working days both in the work place and in the home where there was no labour saving equipment. Think of living in a house without any electricity—any lighting came from gas lamps or candles. Think of living in a house without central heating—all heating came from coal fires. Think of having to prepare every meal—no microwaves or take away other than the fish and chip or pie shop. This was the reality in working class and many middle class households.

Self-improvement through Workers Education classes and night schools was eagerly sought out by many wanting to improve their understanding of the world. Society was too rigid in its imposition of the class system to allow aspiring workers to move up into the middle classes, but that did not mean the working classes were supine and moribund in their quest for improvement. It is perhaps because the suffragette movement was not born out of the experience of the conditions of mill and shop workers, that Grandma H. as a working class woman disliked its objectives. There were many agitating for change as there is now and always will be. Political consciousness among the working classes grew slowly and mainly among men. The reason for that is simple. Women, once married and with child care responsibilities were at home away from other workers who might talk to them about unfair and very poor (compared to now) working conditions or other inequalities which abounded in Victorian and Edwardian societies and it can be said, still do. People do not become politically aware and involved when cut off from the work place. Even though Grandma Hindle grew up in a vibrant, adventurous, free thinking household she was not bothered about winning the vote for herself. She was critical of a family friend, a single woman, a Miss Parker, the sister of her future husband's good friend. Miss Parker lived in Barrow in Furness and supported Votes for Women. Grandma Hindle or Lizzie Jefferson as she was then called criticised this courageous woman. Like Lizzie she was a spinster not dominated or subservient to her husband, not that Grandma H was ever subservient to anyone even when she moved from spinsterhood to wedlock on marriage to William. Grandma H. even though she had a controversial streak outspoken and opinionated was torn between her working class roots and her aspiring upper working class living that came from a profitable butcher's business. Always busy, there were times when she would work in one of the shops serving or mopping down the counters and floors. A job at home was to wash the dirty aprons in the wash house which had been built specially to hold a clothes boiler. Boiling them obviously killed all the germs.

Corsets have always been a both sexy and unsexy item of clothing. It depends on the wearer and the corset. A corset was an integral part of a woman's attire in the 1920s unless embracing the new flapper craze where the corset was ditched together with a cropping of the hair. Dad's mum did neither and always wore a Spirella corset to keep her lumps and bumps controlled. In her retirement she always wore the best quality clothes when out and about; at home where she would be invariably constantly baking pies and bread, cooking, washing and cleaning she would have on old clothes with a wraparound apron (like they wore in Victoria Wood's Dinner Ladies series) and a knotted scarf on her head. She was a confirmed member of the Church of England, but frequently attended the Baptist Church where the preaching spoke little of God's love and forgiveness but of hell and its interminable fires. She sought out these warnings of damnation as an antidote to her belief that she was a sinner. She felt she needed the good telling off and warnings given by the Baptist Pastor's Sunday evening service.

Grandma H. was never afraid to an express an opinion. She did so about the Boer Wars, the major one fought by the descendants of mainly Dutch settlors at the turn of the 20th Century. Against them from the start she recognised that the aim of the wars like most wars was to get hold of and exploit a country's resources, stealing it from its rightful, historical owners, in this case the indigenous Africans. Under South Africa's grass lands lay massive resources of diamonds and gold—lots of it to be dug out by the victorious country—the British or the Boer. The British destroyed the Boer's homes, crops and interned men, women and children in concentration camps where they were starved, kept in unsanitary diseased conditions resulting in many deaths. 50% of the total Boer population of children died—24,074. No wonder my grandmother spoke out about this British policy of genocide as she was growing up, probably conscious that that same absence of British mercy could in future war times descend on the British people.

Sister Lilian

Grandma and grandpa Hindle had another child after dad—a daughter. Dad's first memory is indistinct, but he remembers being taken into his parents' bedroom at the age of 3 years, 3 months to be introduced to his new baby sister Lilian on 10 April 1926.

Grandfather Henry Hindle the one who lived off porridge during the cotton famine was a coal merchant and lived with his many children who we have already met on Saunders Road in Blackburn, a steep street that climbs up the side of the valley to Preston New Road. He was a quiet hardworking man whose sound and profitable business provided for all his family. Lilian's memories have also been gathered. She remembers her Grandpa Hindle's lounge. It had a horse hair sofa that scratched her legs and even though she was given a cushion to sit on, it did not prevent the horse hairs prickling the inside of her knee. At age 95 she can still remember the sensation and the scratches from sitting on that sofa. The room had an iron fire place with an oven to one side and on top of the mantelpiece was a green velvet cover fringed with bobbles that dangled over the side.

She also remembers her great aunts on the Hindle side. A stern bunch of women, each had what would now be termed a "signature bake or dish". Vanilla slices were Lilian's favourites. Fashioned out of flaky pastry, topped with icing and filled with a creamy, golden crème patisserie known as custard by plain speaking Lancashire folk, its creator, the great aunt Sally refused to yield up the recipe—it was a secret known only to her.

In Saunders Road when visiting her grandfather Hindle, Lilian was always frightened of the big washer tub with what seemed to her as a small child terrifyingly large wooden rollers to squeeze out the water from the wet clothes and other laundry. There was a big tank on the side of the washer tub and a posser. A posser is an implement for washing the clothes. It had a copper dome full of holes attached to a wooden handle. The handle was plunged down into the tank to agitate and pummel the dirty washing. The water was pushed up and out of the holes. Many homes did not have electricity so used gas to give light and for all other activities needing energy. The gas lights had a fragile mantle that would crumble if touched once it was lit.

Lilian was also frightened by the gas iron which Grandma Jefferson used. The iron contained a gas jet and as she ironed, flames could be seen coming out the side of the iron. Clothes must have been easily burnt, if not the flesh of the woman using the iron. Women did the ironing in the 1920s and for many decades after. Liberation from domestic chores came not only with advent of mechanisation and the invention of wondrous machines that we now take for granted. Feeding electricity to a motor located in a metal box that moves a stainless steel drum with holes in it constitutes our present day washing machines. It does the work that the posser did, but without any of the effort and drudgery. It was not as though the clothes were made of fabrics—such as nylon, polyester, lycra—plastic fabrics which are easy to dry. The materials used were wool, cotton, linen, canvas, fustian. All heavy fabrics that hold water. Clothes were multi layered and voluminous, serving the need for warmth and adherence to fashion which in the 1920s was slowly raising hem lines. Washing for 11 children and 2 adults as in the Hindle household before the Great War must have been a mammoth task; even with today's most efficient washer/dryer such vast amounts of laundry would be laborious. To do it all by hand is difficult to comprehend. Obviously clothes would be worn for longer than now and there were different outfits allocated to different activities. Sunday best only worn for church on Sunday and other high days and holidays. These clothes would not readily become unclean. Hot water was not on tap. It had to be boiled. Showers were unknown and baths rarely taken by the working classes, not because they did not want to keep clean but because it cost money to heat a large amount of water for a bath. Simple washing with a flannel or piece of cloth with water in a bowl sufficed.

Grandma and Grandpa Jefferson did not have electricity but dad's home did. But it was no safer than the open gas flame that heated irons and lighted lamps as the plugs were two pin and not earthed. Gas could not power a radio. Without electricity an accumulator was used to power the radio so it could receive the BBC broadcasts. There was no other broadcaster. Compare that to now when we have hundreds of radio stations that we can tune into. The accumulator was a battery and every week it was taken to the hardware store in New Bank Road near where dad lived as a boy to be exchanged for a replacement battery. It was large and heavy and had to be carried in a holder to prevent spillage of acid and consequential skin burns. One of dad's jobs was to carry the battery to the shop for changing. He was told never to take the battery out of its holder. Ever inquisitive, one day he decided to investigate the workings of the battery, ignoring his parents' advice. He did not get far as having lifted out the battery from its holder he found that the battery acid had touched his finger. Wondering what to do as the acid was stinging his finger he scratched his head. He screwed the anode back and even though his finger and scalp were stinging dared not mention his accident to his parents. His finger eventually recovered but not the spot where he touched his head. A small patch of baldness appeared. His parents alarmed to see him losing his hair took him to the doctors for examination. The doctor looked at the bald patch through a magnifying glass, but was baffled by its cause. Dad never uttered a word about the real reason.

Central heating only warmed the houses of the wealthy. Coal fires warmed dad's home but he denies ever feeling cold even though he can remember ice forming on the inside of the windows. Double glazing was invented in 1930 in the States. It never became a commonplace installation in the United Kingdom until 40 years later when Everest salesmen, and they were men, always white with perfect skin and hair, made regular appearances on TV adverts. The sash windows that froze up became a relic of the past in many houses with the arrival of two panes of glass to keep out the cold.

Undoubtedly we have benefitted from fantastic inventions that have freed our lives from many laborious household tasks and given us the ability to experience our global home through the internet and travel. Our use of electronics comes with an energy cost in terms of carbon generation in the manufacturing of appliances and gadgets, and their use.

A Total Eclipse of the Sun

Dad's memory is remarkable. He recalls his father taking him into the front bedroom to watch an eclipse of the sun when he was four years old. On 29 June 1927 there was a total solar eclipse in the early morning. It lasted only 23 seconds. The weather conditions were poor with clouds high in the sky, but dad saw the sun disappear and then come back. He has always had a fascination with the unusual.

William, dad's father had started as a butcher's lad. He became a successful small business man having a shop at 8 Limefield, at 5 Arthur Street and another on Shear Brow. Dad's parents were never short of money, but did not have any spare. Every Saturday dad was given a penny which he split and bought two lots of sweets costing half a penny each from the sweet shop on New Bank Road round the corner from where he lived. The Saturday penny was the later equivalent of pocket money. Nowadays a parent may pay their child's mobile phone bill and provide a free endless supply of unhealthy snacks and sweets. There was a parade of shops on New Bank Road with two butchers, Eccles bakery, a Co-op store on the corner, a newspaper shop, a tripe shop, a haberdashery , another bakers—Kenyon's, a shoe shop, a hardware store, a chip shop and a Post Office. The chip shop sold just chips, battered fish and peas, and suet savoury puddings, but no chicken. Chicken was not mass produced as it is today. 2.2 million Chickens are eaten EVERY DAY in the United Kingdom. That's an awful lot of chickens and makes us questions how such chickens come into being, how and where they grow and whether they can be a healthy food source.

Dad used to have take-away fish and chips, but not often. As a boy he loved eating what he describes as "just good grub". Sunday dinner would be a roast and rice pudding. His favourite day for food was Monday lunch because of scallops (scallops are round slices of potatoes deep fried in batter and sometimes with a slice of onion sandwiched between two rounds of potatoes) and rice pudding especially as by Monday the surface of the rice pudding had congealed into a thick, creamy skin. He loved apple pies and custard.

As a child he would help his parents in many ways. He would be sent to the grocers to buy 5lb of flour and 3 halpeth of barm which was yeast, all brought back in a basket after being weighed out by the grocer. His mother would then be able to make the daily bread. On Christmas Day, a turkey was always the centrepiece dish. Christmas was a very busy time in the butchery business just as now, with orders for different types of meat, poultry and game. Christmases were great fun dad recalls.

Dad's Aunty Lucy, sister to his mother had the best party at New Year. She lived on Logwood Street before moving up in the world to York Crescent at Brownhill. Aunt Lucy married Jim Hunter. She was a weaver and had two children Margaret and Hilda. She loved her weaving work, but was not accomplished, whereas her sister Lizzie hated her job, but was a skilful weaver. Lucy's husband died during the second world war of cancer. But before the tragedy of losing her husband and father to her girls she was guaranteed to put on the best party. Lots of games were played at the parties. One game involved each player in turn reciting from memory a short verse of nonsense. It was not a tongue twister, but it was easy to miss a word or say it wrong in some way. If an error was made by a player their forehead was marked with a blue spot. The blue spot came from the "dolly bag". A dolly bag is not a receptacle in which to place dolls. It was used to brighten white clothes and other laundry that needed whitening. The laundry was placed in the bag together with the dolly blue which then went into the hot water in the dolly tub. The water was heated by a gas boiler called a copper. The dolly blue works were at Underbarrow, near Newby Bridge in the Lake District, The works were replaced by an upmarket hotel called The Whitewater Hotel. Every so often the old dolly blue works have a good washing—it rains a lot in Cumbria and sadly the floods from the River Leven which flows out of the south end of Lake Windermere have inundated the hotel in November 2015 from storm Desmond and on other recent times.

Back to the daft and possibly dangerous party game. The blue mark would be put on the player's head when they got a word wrong. A new dimension was added to the game. As the turn came round not only would the verse have to be recited by the player, but she or he would have to say how many blue spots on their head they had. If either answer was wrong another blue spot would be added to the head. In our Health and Safety world the marking with a blue spot on the forehead would probably be prohibited and seen as risky because the blue was a chemical, an acid. It was the Dolly Blue added to the Dolly wash tub. Dad remembers the sensation of his skin stinging as the blue spot was applied. The winner of the game was the one who had the fewest blue spots when the winner could remember how many spots they had on their forehead and could recite the verse accurately. A bizarre past-time but no more than some of the similarly crazy competitions featured in reality shows such as "I'm a celebrity—get me out of here" and "Love Island". The blue spot game played at Aunty Lucy's is definitely the "ibble dibble" game featured in Episode 4 of Season 4 of the Netflix production—"The Crown." A fictitious portrayal of the party games enjoyed by the Royal Family whilst on holiday at Balmoral relatively recently, it is certainly a game that has fallen into disuse in the Hindle/Jefferson family.

Other games enjoyed at such celebratory occasions were the standard children's party games of Pin the tail on the donkey, Musical chairs, and "Murder" but that was a game for the adults so dad could not describe it, but he believes no one was actually hurt, let alone murdered. Another game needed players to be blindfolded so that they could not see the masquerade of various everyday items as pretend bits of body parts taken out after some surgical procedure. Warning—these were not actual body parts, but a shrivelled carrot that was described to the unseeing party goer as an appendix. Some thick blancmange would be described as a diseased liver and the narrator would take pleasure in pushing the fingers of the player into the gooey substance. This game definitely passed down through the generations as it was a favourite and still is at birthday and other parties. Games are often still an essential part of any family get together—Charades are a usual post-Christmas meal must and board gaming provides many hours of enjoyment unless the family members all have a competitive nature and must win.

Aunty Lucy's Christmas Party was the first time that dad met his future wonderful wife—Margaret Annie Stratford as she was called then.

Food was plentiful and delicious, but a potato pie was often the centrepiece at the party. Potato pie which is very much a Lancashire creation actually contains some meat. It is the most delicious concoction of potatoes, onions, shin beef and butter. The meat adds depth of flavour but vegetarians could substitute tofu, lentils or Quorn and flavour with miso, and vegans similarly substitute an oil for the butter.

Butter and cream predominated in pre-war cooking. A trick of any chef or cook trying to impress—make the food full of fat. You are probably wondering how a potato pie was the most looked forward to meal. In days when products such as Pomegranate Molasses and other exotic foods, often difficult if not impossible to source outside the hip quarters of the large metropolises regularly featured in the recipe offerings of some weekend magazines and newspapers, how is potato pie special food. Pie is the most wondrous food. Much depends on the filling and the pastry, but as with most food the experience depends on context. Pies, like stews, tickle the taste buds best when the nights are long. The dank winter greyness when cold seeps in through the skin is the time when such food provides comfort and necessary sustenance. Vegetarianism was unknown in working and middle class households. It is a sign of great wealth when a consumer has the ability to make such choices. Wealth in the variety of plant products available, wealth in the time and energy it takes to combine such products in recipes or where time is short wealth in the ability to purchase ready meals and take away products.

Sadly, if you are starving you are likely to eat anything, as the last crew members alive may have done when marooned and lost on islands in the far north west of Canada. Archaeologists and other scientists searched and found the wrecks of an ill-fated expedition to find whether a North West Passage was possible. The story has recently been turned into a television play, embellished by fictitious side plots. In 1845 two Royal Navy ships HMS Erebus and HMS Terror set sail to find a short cut between Europe and Asia by sea in the waters to the north of Canada and Alaska. To find such a navigable passage would take months off a journey to the Pacific Ocean as the journey required a ship to sail the whole way down into the Southern Hemisphere rounding the dangerous and notorious Cape Horn at the bottom of the South American continent. Finding a speedier way to potential markets in countries bordering the Pacific would facilitate British trade, with the prospect of Empire expansion. The story of the two ships was gradually pieced together by various researchers who not only located the ships but found other remains from the expedition including human bones in 1981 with cut marks indicating cannibalism. A very sad and frightening ending that no human should have to contemplate. In Cormac McCarthy's book "The Road" the world is turned to ash by an event which is not described in the book, but which results in no food or water other than what may have survived the apocalypse in tins or other forms of storage. Most of the food has been eaten or destroyed. There is nothing left other than humans who are seen by some as a source of food. It is a searing, difficult story to read as it totally reminds us— there is only one planet we live on—we cannot catch a space ship to another one if it starts to burn, as it is in parts already doing. A film has also been made of the book. Reading the book is difficult enough to cope with; watching the story on screen requires some courage and fortitude. But perhaps it should now be essential reading for all of us as fires the size of Wales burn in the Russian tundra. Unstoppable conflagrations rage in Australia, California, Brazil and many other countries including Greenland. Yes Greenland—a country mostly covered in permanent ice way up above the Arctic Circle. The alarm bells have been ringing for many years now but hardly anyone is putting the fire out as our home burns, creating more heating, causing more fires as land once damp and sodden dries out.

In the 1930s global warning was not a worry for anyone, even though it was happening. For most working people it was the often eternal worry about how to feed, house, clothe and keep warm. The British unemployed during the '30s were often under nourished and went hungry, even those in work had a weekly battle to pay all the bills and put food on the table. Very few were overweight between the wars because even when working, wages were low. No spare money and basic, but essential foods such as bread and potatoes formed most meals. Relatively cheap compared to proteins such as meat and fish. Energy rich meals filled up empty bellies, giving important calories needed to cope with demands of the long working week. Mass unemployment in the 1930s led to great hardships and suffering. Working hours extended to Saturday morning—a five and half day week. The work itself was usually physical and walking was how most people got around supplemented as necessary by public transport. Dad would walk the mile or so into Blackburn town centre even though a tram ran straight down Preston New Road. He might catch the tram going back home. He was skinny as were all his pals. The word "diet" was unknown to the working man and woman. Diets have been around for a long time, but only for those who were privileged enough to afford to eat what they wanted, when they wanted. Possibly a left over instinct or gene from the evolution of homo sapiens which used to ensure the potential for starvation was reduced when food was scare, because fat stores had been laid down when food was plentiful.

The Hindles were relatively prosperous and owning a three outlet butcher's business meant meat was always available, but not necessarily the best cuts. Dad's mum could make brawn out of a pig's head; often all of the animal was used to make tasty dishes. Now meat and poultry is marketed in such a way that the buyer may have little understanding of which part of the animal is being eaten, how it was fed and how it had been treated. The cow, pig or lamb or chicken is chopped up into certain recognisable pieces. A slice being called a steak, or a chop if it has bone running down the side of the meat. Meat and poultry is often chopped up into smaller pieces or put through a mincer, but most people will be clueless as to what happens to the rest of the animal such as the brain and the organs. Such packaging of animal products removes the consumer from the real source of meat, poultry and even fish produce resulting in a lack of awareness of the birth, growth, slaughtering and dissection of the creature which eventually arrives in a form ready for a recipe—such as chicken fillets for stir fries or beef mince for spaghetti Bolognese or chilli con carne. A butcher knows or should know the farmer who tended the animal. S/he should know how the animal was looked after and how it was fed. S/he should know about the animal's rearing and slaughter. Dad and his father knew exactly how the meat they bought had been reared. Meat would never have been bought from a farmer who did not care for his animals. Meat was bought locally, slaughtered humanely and locally, reducing any stress to the animal. Cattle ate the grass growing in the pasture, not grains and other food grown to feed them.

Undoubtedly this was the case in the pre-war years and for the years after until the arrival of the supermarket. The mass packaged sale of meat divorced the consumer from the origin of the product other than, if lucky, knowledge of the producer country. Given that beef or any other food stuff produced from grazing in the burnt Amazon lands must be avoided at all costs it is astonishing that people do not ask where the meat or chicken they eat comes from. An awareness of where the food eaten comes from is vital. It is also essential to know how it is reared. Cattle fed on food such as grains and beans, like soya, and not grass lying under their hooves, are eating food that humans could eat. Cows produce a lot of methane, a very effective earth heating gas. It would be better if the human can eat the nutrition provided by the grains and beans rather than it being fed to a cow who will turn it into meat polluting the environment in the process by its methane belching and farting. It is not efficient. But meat is good and tasty and for some an essential part of their diet. The amount of meat eaten by those who refused vegetarianism or veganism needs to be drastically reduced to about 200 grams a week. Cattle and sheep grazing on grass on the high moorlands or on the pasturelands of the plains and the valleys especially where such land cannot be used for growing any other food crop, should be our food source. The whole of the animal should be eaten.

At a visit to a fancy Manchester restaurant who had on the menu a dish using "Swaledale beef", it took some time to elicit that the beef did not actually come from Swaledale, not a surprising fact as sheep predominate in the stone walled enclosures and higher open fells above Muker, Keld and Reeth. The beef came from a supplier in Skipton calling itself "Swaledale". The meat was a sound, excellent product—the supplier ensured it lived up to its marketing leaflet. What is surprising is that the fancy restaurant did not know where the meat came from other than from its supplier in Skipton. More worrying was that fellow diners did not ask. Did not enquire. The meat could have come from cleared land which were previously Brazilian rain forests. It could have come from a cow fed on a feed that uses the earth's precious resources; food that humans could eat with less damage to the planet. It could have come from a cow that is eating fish caught from seas off Cape Town. So how has a cow become a fish eater? The fish are ground up into a meal for the cow. How strange. There is a consequence, there always is when man exploits nature. The fish are being taken out of the ocean food chain. Something will undoubtedly suffer the most. The African Penguin, robbed of its major food source has become hungry and consequentially its numbers are declining. The human being robs the penguin of its food source so the human can gorge on steaks and burgers. All done for profit which could lead to the extinction of the African Penguin just like the loss of so many other species through humans' selfish activities. Countless species have been lost in the Amazonian rain forest and many other places because of their destruction to find space for cattle to grow meat for humans to eat. Removing the habitat of wildlife pushes these creatures nearer to humans with inevitable consequences—one of which maybe a pandemic.

Animals manufactured, not reared, to feed a highly profitable production line is a dreadful change for the worse since dad was a lad working in his parent's butcher's shops. Meat eating in the form of cheap burgers or chicken products has taken over our diet. Recently there has been a surge in interest in veganism and some are reducing their meat consumption. Until each and every one of us knows how our food is sourced and cares about how it has come into being and arrived in the shop or on our table, the ridiculous waste of food resources continues. Fish which could feed humans or their rightful hunters—African Penguins goes into the mouths and bellies of cows. Less meat eating and reduced dairy consumption will contribute to reducing carbon emissions. Although the tipping point where the earth is in a cycle of ever self-heating has probably been reached. The burning of Australia in their 2019/2020 summer is an indicator that it has. It may already be too late to stop the warming in time to save the planet; it is already too late for many species which have been made extinct.

Dad said that no one however poor would go without meat if they visited one of their shops. Some meat was given away. So though the viciousness of inequality through poverty meant then that the cheaper cuts were only available to the poorest, as now, the meat was produced in a way that caused vastly less damage to the planet. Animals can be needed to graze the land because their natural fertiliser can ensure healthy soil without the application of man-made chemicals. In dad's youth the land was healthier, the meat was healthier, the slaughtering of animals more humane as the stress of travelling in a lorry long distance was eliminated. The most awful cruelty is when sheep are packed in the bowels of freight ships as is the case of the transport of live sheep from Australia to the Arabian Peninsula. This is so that the sheep can be killed whilst alive the Halal way, but it causes great stress and suffering to the animal.

Our meat production in some regions and countries has gone backward. Some will argue that the availability of more meat, more consumer choice and cheaper products are beneficial to human kind. We should not be stealing a penguin's food or destroying the home of millions of creatures in the rain forest to satisfy our meat greed. It is leading and has led to the destruction of our planet. Protein needs of a particular individual vary according to body weight, sex, activity level and age. The nutritional needs for protein can be quite substantial. The average need for a sedentary woman is 45 grams a day and for a man is 56 grams a day if aged 19 to 50 years. A tiny amount of protein. Clearly we do not need a lot of meat; eating a steak or chop or burger is way over our needs. We can cut our meat consumption so that we all have a small amount from an animal reared on areas which have no other use, such as upland moorland or other non-productive pasturelands.

Dad though was brought up in a time when the staple plate of food consisted of meat and two veg—with fish on Friday. As already mentioned all the animal was used—tripe the lining of a cow's stomach was sold from the tripe stall on Blackburn market and was eaten on Saturday. Dad though has moved on from traditional English and Lancastrian dishes.

Dad was and still is an amazingly accomplished cook—a hearty stew or his own take on pizza making have to be tasted to experience his talent for producing fantastic dishes. For a meat stew he finely chops up skirt beef then marinates it for a good 12 or more hours in red wine, usually a Rioja, before cooking it with finely chopped onions, garlic and carrots. He adds raisons too. It works as delicious mix of sweet and savoury. His chocolate brownies and shortbread are legendary in the prize winning halls of local produce competitions. Dad was irritated one day after watching a TV programme about families who were having difficulty putting food on the table. The woman being interviewed said that she could not afford lamb chops—she meant the loin chops that are grilled, or roasted.

"Neck end is the tastiest and cheapest cut—makes a wonderful hot pot with some sliced potatoes and onions." Dad's point in saying this was that there were ways to put delicious and nutritious food on the table with the benefit of the knowledge of how to cook that food. Working class food was based on a knowledge of where to buy ingredients or to grow them, how to cook them and how to value them. Markets provided locally grown root vegetables. Potatoes, swede, carrot, cabbage cut up and combined with stock made out of bones or lamb neck end for a bit of meat together with barley , some red lentils and marrowfat peas added with a bunch of fresh herbs made a fantastic nutritious broth that would feed a large family for a couple of days. It just needed bread to mop up the gravy. A meal at the fraction of the price of take away or ready meals. Even today with expensive food prices cooked meals can be extraordinarily delicious, nutritious and inexpensive. Convenience foods have displaced foods made from scratch with a consequential loss of the cooking skills needed to provide such food. Poor people historically knew how to make delicious food out of ingredients sometimes declined by the rich. If driven by hunger then previously perceived unpalatable nourishment is consumed. Dad's own family had known starvation in the Cotton Famine years; dad grew up in a time of massive economic depression—visible signs of poverty as now were conspicuous. The techniques and knowledge used to provide sustenance at a low cost have withered, replaced by often cheap high calorie and fat junk food having little valuable nutrition. The production of such food has often damaged the planet. No one can live without food, but it is taken for granted in so many ways. Just like meeting friends and family without restriction, not wearing a face mask in a public indoor space, being able to holiday abroad—all taken for granted until coronavirus. From the time when our ancestors first walked on this earth the one lesson that should be known by us all is that our lives can change quickly and disastrously. Because we live in an age of bounty in the western world, in a society where individual need takes priority over a greater common good and where politicians have captured our votes based on outlandish promises of a better life, we are unable to accept unpalatable truths and change our behaviour. We carry on regardless of the need to look ahead, to plan to save ourselves and our loved ones, especially our children and grandchildren. It is human nature to deny, closing eyes and ears to a potential dystopian future. Easier to believe in a fiction that all will be well because it always has been and the government will make sure it is, rather than to look ahead into possible abysses and devise bridges to cross them or otherwise neutralise their destructive depths.

Easy to say that the individual can make a difference, for instance can make plans to withstand a pandemic and even flourish through such strange times. No one can act alone; it requires humans to do what they are particularly good at. Getting together with others to find solutions, new ways of working, new ways of rejoicing and keeping resolute in the face of such uncertainty.

When dad was playing the games at Aunty Lucy's New Year's Eve party in 1932 few knew that 1933 would witness the rapid intensification of German government persecution of its Jewish citizens. Some reacted and knew they were doomed and started plans to get out. Others stayed believing life would return to some previous kind of normality where they would be free to go to school, pursue careers as other non-Jewish Germans and discrimination would disappear, perhaps also thinking their lives could get no worse. Others may have perceived the threat, but were too poor or unskilled to be able to emigrate and escape their doomed future. Reality is often blanked out by wishful thinking. Certainly, as dad enjoyed his 10th birthday any thoughts of another war in his head were far off.

Before the war parties abounded. A celebration of the love and companionship between family and friends, stuffed full with chuckling and silliness, as testified by the daft "Blue Spot" game. Christmas, birthdays, christenings, anniversaries and timely deaths of those who have lived long lives provided many opportunities for a get together. Family and friends lived locally in one town—in Blackburn. Not spread out all over the country or even the world, as is the case now with children often having to leave the destitute places of previous industrial hubs such as Blackburn for South East England or further afield, to find jobs or pursue promising careers.

The New Year, after the long awaited light brought in by Christmas feasts and fun, was celebrated with gusto. To bring in the New Year someone went

103

outside the party as the clock stuck 12 midnight with a piece of coal. At the beginning of the New Year that person brought in the coal as a symbol of delivering warmth and heat into the home. They sang the usual New Year song of "Auld Lang Syne". Some traditions are indestructible to the pressures of modernisation and material progress.

Apart from an occasional sherry or glass of port there was no other alcohol drunk at any other social gathering or occasion. It did not feature as a part of daily life for a family that knew hard work and the saving of any money, however meagre, left over after payment for the essentials, would provide some rainy day money. Rather than spending it on alcohol or other temporary pleasures families knew that they had to safeguard their future if at all possible. Putting aside money was essential as the welfare state hardly existed. People had to work to survive, but there was not always work to be had. Buying alcohol was seen as a waste of money particularly by the Hindle side of the family. They knew how to enjoy themselves without alcohol, but there were other reasons. Alcohol was drunk mainly in pubs in the form of beer and predominately by men. Drinking at home was not something working class families did. Downton Abbey and other such dramatic portrayals of the lives of the rich elite show large quantities of wine and port being served at nightly dinners where all the participants dress up in long gowns or black-tie dinner suits depending on their gender. The social drinking of wine so prevalent today has developed since the 1960s when the sight of bottles of Blue Nun and Mateus Rose on the table was considered a mark of sophistication and suaveness. So much has changed; the range and qualities of wine available to the consumer is now vast, especially as more and more regions of the world have developed vineyards. As in the case of most products bought by consumers, new brands have spawned so that the exercising a choice from anything as apparently simple a product as baked beans to the purchase of a car or holiday can be mesmerizingly complex. Just checking out the contents of the beans tin, looking for its sugar and salt content, its weight, product sourcing and manufacture can make a supermarket shop turn into a lengthy expedition. Complexity in life has increased since dad was a child in some ways. Anxieties should be lessened as living standards have greatly improved. We have a mass of support unknown to pre-war society and to many billions in poor countries today. Yet social and other anxieties seem more prevalent than ever now in post industrialised countries. The more we have in the material, the more anxious we seem to become. Or have anxieties always been present, a characteristic of being a human—that we feel, that we fear, that we always want more. Less stuff being possessed is good for our planetary survival; no habitable planet—no us.

The Other Side of the Family

The Jefferson's were different from the Hindle clan. Canny people who enjoyed themselves, finding ways to amuse themselves; teasing each other—they all had twinkling eyes. His grandad Thomas Jefferson had 6 children one of whom we have already mentioned in some detail—Elizabeth, known as Lizzie (William Hindle's wife and dad's mum). The other five are Florence, Fred, Herbert, Lucy, and Tom. Dad's grandad Jefferson had helped set up a trade union for joiners. He was a proud supporter of trade unionism and had an illuminated poster on the wall publicising and promoting the benefits of unionisation to the working man. It niggled one of his sons. Uncle Bert (Herbert) had wanted to train and work as an electrician, but his father would not allow him because the electricians were not unionised. Most joiners were in the union, but dad remembers one of his grandad Jefferson's friends who refusing to join the Union went to work in Ireland as a black leg when the General Strike was on.

Dad would call in to see his grandad Jefferson after school. Thursday afternoons was when his grandad would meet with three old chaps to play card games, all of whom had worked as joiners, but were now retired. It was a serious game played for money. Dad coming into the room could always tell if his grandad was winning or losing by his mood. So, impressed by his grandfather's dedication to winning and the seriousness he applied to playing his cards, dad thought it would be an interesting subject for an essay he had to write at school. He wrote an account of his grandfather's card games explaining that he always knew when his grandad was winning at cards because he would be greeted with a big grin when he entered the room, asked how he was doing and given a penny. But if he was losing then his grandfather Jefferson was morose and grumpy, asking dad why he had come to visit. Dad's acute perceptions of his grandfather's moods whilst playing cards featured in the essay. Being so well written and entertaining, dad's teacher showed it to his mother who then showed it to her father, to Grandad Jefferson. He must have won at cards as he was in a good mood when he read it, laughing at his grandson's description of him.

The Hindles (dad's dad's family) in contrast were stern and disliked unbridled gaiety. At Christmas dad got a 10-bob note, which is 10 shillings in old money, 50p in new, from granddad Henry Hindle as did all his grandchildren. The 10-shilling note was put in the home safe after its receipt on Christmas Day and then dad walked down to town to put his money in the safety of his bank account when banks opened once again after the holiday. Saving and investing money was a dedicated pursuit of the Hindle clan. A habit that has undoubtable benefits. Money grows over time if wisely invested. Saving has gone out of fashion, not only because of the obvious reason that people spend more than their income allows for them to spend, but because much is provided by the state. Rainy days still pour on many people's heads and people often have little or nothing to tide them over. In the 1920s benefits were not as numerous and as well paid as they are today. People had to put by for times when work was not available through unemployment, infirmity, and old age. Many had no spare cash and when hard times hit, reliance on neighbours, friends, family, and charity was the only help available. Poverty especially during the Great Depression was extreme and terrible. But many survived, sometimes only to be killed in the Blitz or on a faraway battlefield. Those born post 1945 are indeed blessed, compared to those born in the pre-war years. They had a welfare state, universal education, a national health service, scientific developments such as penicillin to kill dangerous bacteria which in former times would have been a near death sentence. Most of all they did not have to face war or global conflict.

Dad's Grandad Jefferson was always up to some mischief. One of his favourite pastimes was walking with his small dog on the public footpath through a golf course. There was often another purpose to this walk. Grandad Jefferson particularly liked walking his Jack Russell dog down the footpath which descends from Revidge Road across fields eventually arriving in Mellor. The footpath cut across Blackburn Golf Club located in the area where the rich and professional and business elite of the town lived—Billinge and Beardwood. Dad as a young boy would accompany his grandad on his walks and walking down past the golf course provided entertainment for grandad, grandson and dog alike. Whenever a golf ball ended up in the rough Grandad's little dog would be sent to fetch it, but not with any public-spirited intention. The dog would bring the ball back and his grandad would reach down quietly as if to adjust his shoelaces taking the ball from the dog's mouth. He would then pocket the ball whispering to my dad in his Lancashire dialect, "Say now't lad". As the golfers thrashed around with their golf clubs in their plus fours trying to locate their ball Grandad Jefferson would say quietly to his grandson, laughing at them "They'll nay find the ball there". Subversive behaviour; theft of a golf ball—a bad example to his grandson. But to dad and his grandad—they were empty swanky men, jumped up, riddled with a false class superiority, looking down on the working classes. It did not turn dad into a delinquent, but there has always been a streak of the rebel in dad. Not a resident of Scotland he has been known to display a vote SNP poster in his window and pays a yearly membership fee. It was intended as a challenge to his centenarian neighbour who lived above him and was a lifelong Liberal and then Liberal Democrat supporter. Dad's reason was that he liked Nicola Sturgeon. He also thought Ruth Davidson leader of the Scottish Conservatives was an excellent politician. He always favoured plain speaking dynamic female politicians—a fan of Barbara Castle, Blackburn's legendary MP until Jack Straw took over. Barbara Castle should have been the country's first female Prime Minister, but the Labour Party has always struggled to put women in charge of its fortunes. In one of dad's letters written many months after the end of the war in 1945 dad wrote to his MP to tell her about many like him in the 8th Army who had not had home leave since 1942. He received a supportive reply. Dad never trusted Straw who he saw as a career politician who changed his political position as the political wind changed, with the sole pursuit of personal power. He also liked but was suspicious of Margaret Thatcher. He liked that she was knew what she wanted, was a plain speaker and was not afraid to follow her principles. But he disliked many of her policies.

The Royal Family V Politicians

Growing up dad was not aware of politics or its machinations. What stands out in his memory is King George V's silver jubilee in 1935 when the town organised grand and memorable celebrations. All the school children were given an item of commemorative pottery to mark the occasion. More impressive parties and commemorations were provided for the King's subjects than for the late Queen's Diamond Jubilee. Everyone took part in the organised events such as fireworks in Corporation Park; no one stayed away from a street or other party. Everyone joined in a national festival of thanksgiving and glorification of the monarch. Another change since the '30s. United Kingdom citizens were more respectful of the royal family in 1935; there was more deference to the monarchy and to the ruling and society's elite. It was taught in schools, churches, and homes—it was expected that king and country would be served; the world was changing slowly despite the shocks to the national system of class hierarchy caused by the Great War. No revolution at home; but the ideas of communism were emerging following the establishment of a Soviet Russia after the Bolshevik revolution.

The British constitution relies on a constitutional monarchy as one of its constituent parts. Dad sees the Crown as representing him as British citizen to the rest of the world. He is not an abolitionist or republican. He believes the royal family stands for quality and tradition. He saw his Queen as having high standards in her behaviour and conduct. That respect though has dimmed in recent times with the behaviour of the Monarch's children, in particular the adultery of the heir to the throne who will on taking the Crown become head of the Church of England which has as one of its principles, the confidence that the Ten Commandments as handed down by God to Moses is the word of God. "Thou shalt not commit adultery" being one of them. Dad cannot understand how the future head of the Church of England can be respected and accepted as such because of his infidelity to his wife, Princess Diana. Likewise, he is perplexed and somewhat hurt by Prince Andrew's friendship with a paedophile and the inability to acknowledge what the evidence says that he was a friend of Ghislaine Maxwell and Jeffrey Epstein.

The Queen had the respect of so many peoples and nations. Dad was unhappy when the Royal Yacht Britannia was scrapped because he saw it as representing British values of quality and prestige in the countries it visited. It exuded British character of stability when it pulled into a foreign port. He felt it spoke of quiet power combined with gracious friendship. Dad's main reason for retaining a constitutional monarchy is answered by this question he asked—"Anyhow, who could you have as a president?" He is clearly not in favour of a politician becoming head of state; a celebrity would be ghastly—although the young Royals and their partners, in particular are sometimes exploited or engage in self-promotion that in turns feeds a gossip industry selling magazines, newspapers, providing twitter feed and endless stories on countless web pages. People who have to work hard and have few holidays are amazed by statements from Harry and Meghan that they needed a six-week holiday after their South African tour. Most people would love to travel first class and then be shown around a country being provided with the best food and drink, staying in the nicest accommodation. Hypocrisy nags at the fair minded.

Queen Elizabeth II by her dignified reserve never allowed herself to become a celebrity. Shut up and put up has worked well for her, but newspapers did not have to compete against other news media in the '30s. There was no television, no internet. If you went to the cinema to watch a movie then, there might be a news reel. The radio had news broadcasts, but not every house had a radio. Newspapers exercised a huge influence as to how world, national and local events were communicated to the populace. Newspaper owners had even greater power, than they do now. They could give a picture of life or a news story that may not be totally accurate. Newspaper owners dictated and controlled the publication of news preventing the truth about the activities of the young Royals then—George and Edward reaching public ears. There were two million unemployed and massive destitution and poverty. Hundreds starved to death, yet these princes continued to live the high life and in the case of Edward push for similar politics that had infiltrated Germany. A Nazi sympathiser by no means alone in his views which were sometimes shared by the aristocratic society in which he moved. Edward was protected by the newspaper owners, not only his political views were kept off the pages, but his partying and womanising. A newspaper baron may decide not to publish a very important event for reasons that were unrelated to the needs of the public to be given news. The public were deliberately kept in the dark. The ruling class protected their own. Dad gave an example of this manipulation of the people's right to have truthful information.

The affair of Edward and Mrs Simpson was well known to the upper classes and the circles in which they lived. The public were ignorant of the affair and its consequences to the future of the monarchy. It was only when the Bishop of Bradford gave a sermon from the pulpit rightly indignant that the future head of the Church of England had committed adultery that the story broke. Until then the aristocratic newspaper owners had kept silent, keeping the public in the dark, protecting their mates. The Bishop's name was "Blunt"—he was Blunt by name, and blunt by nature.

Dad cannot remember vandalism existing before the Second World War. It did exist because in 1861 the Malicious Damage Act had been passed. It became more prevalent in the 1960s. This was one such occurrence remembered from that decade "Once walking down to work through Corporation Park I saw that the flower urns had been toppled over. It was shocking. The park was well looked after by its gardeners and enjoyed by all. No one was ever caught. It was put down to drunks leaving East Lancashire Cricket club across the road from the park. Public property was respected."

Growing up in the post war years the velvet expanses of green lawns in Corporation Park, stretching between paths and promenades were initially immaculate. No one walked on them because it would destroy the grass. There were many places for people to sit on benches at the side of the lawns, along the paths and the Broad Walk, the long open space created in the cotton famine that ran across the top of Corporation Park. But with social liberation came a disrespect for public property. Personal freedom was often interpreted as free choice without consequence to the gardeners who wished to maintain the beauty of the park for all and other users who preferred a vista of green grass rather than litter strewn places, peppered with dog muck.

Many dog owners are responsible and pick up and bin the poo. Another change for the good. Dog owning has become much more prevalent than in the 20th Century. Prosperity has made dog owning possible. For many years people simply could not afford to feed themselves never mind a dog.

School

In 1927 state education was provided from the age of 4 to 14. One sunny morning his dad told him he was taking him for a walk. Dad got ready, putting on his shoes thinking he might be going to feed the ducks in the park. But something much more memorable was his destination. He and his dad walked down to the bottom of Park Street to watch Blackburn Rovers football team parade triumphantly through the town on a bus with the FA cup which they had won by beating Huddersfield Town 3-1 on 21 April 1928. Harry Heelless was the captain. Dad was five years old when Rovers brought back that cup, the age at which he went off to start his school life at St Silas Primary School.

Let's hear the words of dad himself about starting school.

"I was 4 I think when I started school and it was very good at school—quite enjoyable. Was it strict? Yes. I think I got the ruler on the hand, but very rarely. Did I heck do well at primary! No good at maths. I remember the school trips though. They were great."

School trips were a whole town affair. All the children from the town would travel together on a chartered train. The cost of the trip was paid for by weekly subscription. 6d a week was paid towards a total cost of 11s 6d, the weekly payments being recorded on a card. Families had little spare cash and savings, as is often the case today, and the cost of the excursion could be paid in instalments over time from each week's wages.

At 10 year's old, Dad's first school excursion was a day trip to Oxford. It seemed a long way to go for a day. Train travel to Oxford from Blackburn now takes 3 hours and 51 minutes with two changes. A day trip would not be worth the expense and time. Setting off say at 08.00 and arriving at 12.00 to return home for 18.00 would mean only two hours in Oxford. Train travel was quicker in 1933 because it was more direct and efficient. One of dad's work mates after the war was called Arthur Finch. Arthur had started at age 14 working on the railways shovelling the coal into the fires that generated the heat to make the steam that powered the trains. Arthur said that the steam trains were always on time such that the engine driver never needed to use a watch much. Coming out of Bamber Bridge if 2 minutes down—the train driver knew the steam train would make it up by the time it reached Pleasington station. According to Arthur Finch trains were always on time. The best journey Arthur said was down the Eden Valley to Carlisle after crossing the Pennines at Ribblehead where an engine was required at both the front and back of the train. It was down to the fireman to get the train over the viaduct and up the hill by Whernside as quickly as possible. The fireman had to be quick and powerful in shovelling coal into the fire.

Despite having electric trains and modern technology today, fewer people are being moved around the country at slower and less effective speeds. Our train system is a disgrace for a country which should have a first world transportation provision. Steam trains went everywhere before the war because there was a comprehensive line coverage. Much of that was cut after the war. Such a shame as those railway lines could have provided public transport routes such as electric tramways or guided bus routes at a time when petrol and diesel car usage need to be replaced by non-carbon energy sources. Some of the railway lines were saved as off-road cycle and walking routes, but many were not and are now fenced off and overgrown.

Dad's school excursion to Oxford took place in the last year before he left junior school. All the children from the town were entitled to join the trip. It was a community event where children from across the whole town came together for an exciting day out. Oxford was a long way from Blackburn. Most children would have only travelled as far as the Fylde Coast by train—to St Anne's on Sea or Blackpool or Thornton Cleveleys. Or they may have travelled by bus to Clitheroe. In Oxford the school children visited some of the old University Colleges and the Morris motor car factory. Dad remembers that one of the workers when asked whether the owner of the factory William Morris came to work in a big, fancy car such as a Rolls Royce replied with some indignation— "No he doesn't. He drives one of those," pointing to the cheapest and most basic car. William Morris became Lord Nuffield and in 1943 established The Nuffield Foundation. It is a charitable trust funding research and innovation through science and social science with the aim of improving the well-being of society. Lord Nuffield used his fortune to provide a long lasting, meaningful legacy. This is a statement from the Foundation's website showing the benefits to society from one man's decision to give away his money to a worthy cause, rather than spend it on luxury, ostentatious goods which have no real value.

"We want to improve people's lives, and their ability to participate in society, by understanding the social and economic factors that affect their chances in life. The research we fund aims to improve the design and operation of social policy, particularly in Education, Welfare, and Justice."

He gave great value to all, rather than a few.

Another trip took Blackburn school children to London, but this was when dad was in secondary school. They were taken round London to see the sights in open top buses and he particularly remembers the tour of the Tower of London and seeing the Crown Jewels.

Edinburgh was another destination. Dad still remembers the sight of the castle towering up above the railway line, as it does till this day, before the train reaches the end of its journey on pulling into Waverley Station. He recollects his visit to the Scottish War Memorial; an imposing structure which he thought looked unfinished, but it was opened in 1927 some years before the youth of Blackburn invaded Scotland's capital.

A week's holiday might be spent at Arnside or LLanfairfechan—a sign of affluence. Most people could not afford a holiday in the depression of the 20s and 30s. There may be a day trip to Blackpool or Morecambe for some. If the mills and factory wheels were turning, then a wake's week holiday may just have been affordable.

Dad has a great brain. So knowledgeable, always reading, but only a few passed to the Grammar School. It did not bother him as he explained his maths let him down, "You had to be good at school with maths to pass to go to the Grammar School. I went to Blakey Moor. It was a secondary modern school, but very good. Half a dozen passed an entrance exam to a Grammar School. Your parents did not pay to go to Grammar School. If you did not pass it did not matter. A lot of parents would push now to get children to grammar school by extra tuition on the side but not then because it just wasn't done. I got a School Certificate. I left at 14 from Blakey Moor. The ones who went to Grammar School who left at 16 got office jobs in a bank or solicitors. Jim my cousin was top of the class. He ended up as an Inspector of Taxes for the Midlands area. The ones who made most money were the ones who went to Blakey Moor like me, but I didn't make money. They got jobs doing a trade. Alan Lacey in my class, we were friends, he got killed in the Abbeystead Disaster. He was high up, a district manager in the North West Water Authority—a top engineer. He left at 14 went to work as a plumber. Took exams became a water engineer."

George Alan Lacey known as Alan Lacey was conducting a tour of 44 visitors around the Abbeystead pumping station from St Michael's on the Wyre, a village that lay some miles to the west in a flood plain. Abbeystead is a hamlet, inhabited at times by the Duke of Westminster when he comes to his country retreat and shooting lodge. The Duke of Edinburgh, was a frequent visitor over the years shooting thousands of birds off the grouse moors which rise upwards from the village. It is said that this area known as Bowland, was one of the Queen's favourite places. It is a land of unforgiving bogs, heather and rough tangled grasses, wild and bleak in its public face but offering some delightful nooks and crannies when viewed up close which is now possible since open access was enacted.

St Michael's on the Wyre residents had complained that flooding of their homes and land had been caused by the Water Authority pumping water from the River Lune to the River Wyre. The River Wyre's headwaters originated in those grouse moors so frequented by Queen Elizabeth II and her late husband. The river descends from these hills through the Abbeystead valley, flowing onwards until it reaches the flat lands of the Fylde coast exiting between Fleetwood and Knott End on Sea where it joins the end of Morecambe Bay before finally merging with the Irish Sea. St Michaels's on the Wyre residents blamed the flooding on the increase of water flow caused by taking water from the River Lune and dumping it, as they saw it, in their river. The reason the Water Authority took water out of the Lune and pumped it into the Wyre was to stop the River Lune flooding in Lancaster. The solution for one river became a problem for another. The Water Authority thought it ought to explain how and why it was pumping water into the Wyre. It was a public relations exercise. Give a tour of the pumping station, provide some interesting facts and figures, alleviate the anxieties, and demonstrate that the transfer scheme of water from the Lune to the Wyre did not cause flooding. The plan literally backfired with catastrophic results. When the pumps were switched on, they caused a sudden rush of air which propelled a seepage of methane gas that had accumulated from coal deposits 1200 metres underground, a distance just 145 metres short of Ben Nevis Britain's highest mountain. Some of the gas had seeped up through layers of limestone and found its way into an empty pipeline where it lay in wait unable to escape further into open air. It lay silent and undetected.

It was on the evening of 23 May 1984 at 7.20 pm when 44 St Michael's on the Wyre visitors, including children, started a tour of the subterranean pumping house. Alan Lacey oversaw the tour, ready to demonstrate the system of valves and mechanical devices which sucked masses of water from the Lune to the Wyre. He phoned the pumping station on the River Lune to ask for the pumping to start. He waited and the visitors waited, but no water appeared. As no water had come through from the River Lune he made another call some 10 minutes later asking for a more powerful pump to be switched on. Disaster. The power of the water pushing air forwards caused a mass escape of the methane gas which then ignited. There was a huge explosion causing 30 concrete roof beams each of them weighing 2 tons to be thrown upwards through the earth that covered the top of the underground building. Crashing back down into the space below, it seems amazing that only 8 people were killed immediately. Dad's friend Alan was one of them. Tragically many were seriously injured with another 8 subsequently dying, making a total of 16 deaths from the incident. Some had terrible burns, many had life changing injuries. The spark that lit the gas has never been identified.

Methane gas is a very powerful substance. There is a lot of it underground especially in the Arctic and under the Arctic sea. Permafrost keeps that methane gas safely locked away from the atmosphere. The permafrost is melting, and methane is escaping. Permafrost covers the Arctic Ocean's seabed. The Arctic region is subject to phenomenal warming. If the seabed permafrost melts there is the possibility of a massive escape of methane. This could result in the heating of the planet to temperature which would lead to an almost immediate extinction of life including human. Greta Thunberg has called it right. We are living with a potential time bomb.

But back to 1937 when no such worries beset the planet—just the evil of Nazism.

Dad continued to talk about the success of his friends who had not been to a Grammar School:

"Bill a joiner he became in charge of building works for Manchester. He had 300 under him. The ones who went to work as tradesman did well. They had initiative I suppose. Ernie another pal passed for Grammar School he went to work as a compositor in a printers. Ernie left school at age 14. The headmaster went wild. Ernie's father had left his mother and she had 3 children to bring up. Ernie had to go to work to earn money for his mother and brothers and sisters. There were hardly any benefits like now. People had to work. Ernie was very clever. There was the dole if you could not get work. I did not know anyone on the dole as when I was 14 in 1937 it was just before the war and things were picking up because of work in the Fuse factory at Lower Darwen. The government had started to prepare for war. There was a gasmask factory in Blackburn. Work picked up because we were rearming."

So many who failed the equivalent of the later 11 plus introduced in 1944 by the Butler Education Act of 1944 had more successful careers than those who passed a grammar school entrance exam.

He continues:

"Not sure if it is better now or then. It depends what you mean by better. I played out when I was a young lad, mainly football on the spare ground on Cheltenham Street. We did a lot of walking with pals, took a picnic a sandwich and a bottle of pop. We went up on the Yellow Hills with the boys." (Remember that is where his great grandparents lived when they were hand loom weavers—across from the Yellow Hills—so called because of the golden blooms from the gorse bushes). "George Temple was my best friend. He lived on Leamington Road. He lived at the first house past the Baptist church. Ernie Crossley lived round the corner on Cheltenham Street. Ken Holt lived on Burlington Street. We all had a good laugh together."

"It was when I was out walking with the lads in Corporation Park that I bumped into mum. We had grown up. We had enjoyed ourselves when children at Aunty Lucy's parties, but now we were teenagers and we still liked each other. It was a natural progression really."

"I never knew anyone who could not read or write when they left school at 14. I started work at 14 as a butcher's boy and on a Monday, it was my job to walk the beef cattle down from where they had been left in a field after being purchased by my father from the farmer. I was up at around 5am. If there was some slaughtering to do, a contractor would be paid at the Blackburn slaughterhouse in the centre of Blackburn. The cattle were left in a field in summer until we needed them for the shops. Lilian would often ride her bike up to the field when school had finished or during the holidays to check on the cattle. At 5 am on Monday morning I walked up onto the field near Billinge End Road to collect the cattle and I walked them down Preston New Road to the abattoir in Blackburn centre. There was not as much traffic in those days. Couldn't do it now, too busy. If you are droving cattle under the law of the land you have priority on the road—you can stop traffic. It was very early in the morning so there was no traffic around really and the trams had not started to run at that time.

Main job was to keep the cattle quiet and calm—they stay in the lairage where they store cattle. The lairage is a place where the cattle can settle down. The main Blackburn abattoir was located on Sumner Street near the railway sidings and the fire station and the lairage was near there."

"We also went to the auction mart to buy meat. It is where farmers come to sell the cattle. We bought one or two in a week. A stock train came from Clitheroe arriving around 5 am at Blackburn station on a Monday morning. If my dad was in Clitheroe he would go and buy lambs; they could be put on the train and hopefully if they got the early train, we would arrange for 20 lambs to be slaughtered on a Monday afternoon. Then we left the carcasses hung up in the slaughterhouse. These were small slaughterhouses rented off by Blackburn Corporation. All the instruments for slaughter were there—everything was kept nice and clean."

"I met with other butcher friends on a Monday morning at the abattoir, but after I took the cows down to the lairage I had to quickly get to the shop to scrub it down, clean everything, polish brasses, sharpen knives and make everything spotless. I then went home in the afternoon. On Tuesday we made sausages. Bits and Pieces of meat went in mincer and then into the sausage machine to make the sausages. We cut all meat up and put it through the sausage maker. All the beef fat left over from the previous week was boiled up to make dripping. On Tuesday morning at 7 am my dad would take the car and trailer to collect the lambs that had been slaughtered on a Monday. The lambs should have come into Blackburn on Monday by train from where he had bought them in Clitheroe or dad would go and buy lambs on farms such as those around Ribchester and put them in trailer and bring them to the abattoir ready for slaughter. Sometimes dad would transport sheep in the car. Lilian and I would be squashed in the back seat sometimes with a couple of lambs."

"Another of my duties was to deliver orders around the area served by our shops. I took the orders out on my push bike. I pedalled around Billinge Avenue, Buncer Lane—these were wealthy areas at the top of Preston New Road served by the good top shop. The bottom shop was in a poor area. We sold cheaper meat cuts there, but it was still top quality. For instance, English Lamb was sold in the top shop, but never New Zealand lamb which was sold in the bottom shop as it was cheaper, but just as good. New Zealand lamb obviously arrived frozen. Friday was the busiest day when many customers came to the shop. Our pigs came from wholesale butchers and we sold chickens from local farmers. Eggs were also on sale, again supplied by local farmers. I wanted to be a butcher but did not like dealing with customers. Through the week the shops closed at 7pm, but Fridays the shops were open until 8pm. On Saturday we would try and get closed early in the afternoon when I was a lad so that we could get to a football match. Rovers' games would start about 2pm and I wanted to finish in time to arrive for the kick-off. Saturday night was always spent at home where we all sat around the radio listening to the music hall."

"Then when I was older at 16 war started so the life as before stopped. Everything went on rations. Peace had been short lived."

The war to end all wars feels like a myth pedalled to justify the suffering and killing of the First World War. Peace lasted 21 years. In 1939 following the Third Reich's—Germany's invasion of Poland, Great Britain and its considerable empire declared war.

1939

"How we got our meat products into the shops changed once the war came along. We could no longer purchase our own animals for slaughter. We could no longer buy it even after it was slaughtered. The meat was sent to us from the abattoirs and wholesale butchers. There was no choice; we had to take what was sent. At the beginning of rationing there was not much of a difference; there was plenty of food to buy and eat. Then the food supply dropped because of the war in the Atlantic. Food supplies, especially corned beef from the Americas became scarce, as German U Boats sunk cargo ships coming across the Atlantic.

"I was never hungry in the war before I joined up. Nothing was wasted; everything was used. I used to cycle in any spare time; just loved it, but the bikes didn't have the fancy gears and brakes like they do now. It was just one gear which meant for a tiring time when going up hills like Fleet Moss in Yorkshire above Hawes. Cyclists have it easy now, but it made us fit."

Dad was a keen cyclist. Along with reading, playing, and watching cricket and football, it was one of his favourite pastimes. He started riding a bike when he was 12 years old but on his 16[th,] birthday was given what he describes as the first proper bike—a sports bike. A modern model at the time. Dad would cycle for hours on a Sunday thinking nothing of cycling over 100 miles to Windermere or Coniston and back, often on that ride stopping off for a mug of tea at the Gilpin Bridge Hotel at the bottom of the Lyth valley, now just off the A590. He rode out with one or two other riders called Harry Taylor and Harry Robinson. The latter was a married greengrocer who had been wounded in the First World War so was much older than dad.

One day a ride with the older Harry turned into a much longer expedition than planned. They set out in the morning for the Yorkshire Dales travelling through Skipton, on past Kilnsey Crag to Kettlewell where the first major climb of the day faced them after about 42 miles of riding, up the hill called Park Rash, a nearly vertical climb it feels on a bike. The ascent successfully completed they carried on, realising that it would be a long way back home via Coverdale, East Witton, Masham to reach Pateley Bridge. Already having cycled well over 50 miles, another 25 miles including some more big climbs would see them only reach Pateley Bridge, and it was a further 50 miles to cycle home to Blackburn. An epic day of cycling over 125 miles or 201 kilometres with many feet of climbing. If it was a leg in The Tour de France it would have been one of the toughest.

Wondering if carrying their bikes across the moor would reduce their journey they spied what they believed to be a short cut to Pateley Bridge, and this was their undoing. In the distance they saw a reservoir being built with what looked to be a nice, new road running along its shore. Believing it would reduce the journey home, instead of turning around and going back the way they came, they embarked on this ambitious, yet ultimately fool hardy plan. Turning around would have been the more sensible option, but dad ever the adventurer loves veering off the beaten path to forge his own route. His so called "short cuts" usually led to long circuitous diversions where if on foot would require climbing over all sorts of barriers such as walls and fences or fighting a way through a thick forest. Before they reached this illusory track which they believed would speed them onwards to Pateley Bridge, a heather moor had to be first crossed and descended. After the war dad sometimes went riding with "The Rough Stuff". This group would go where no mountain bike would now go. Nothing would prevent them going cross country if that is the route they chose. Mountain Bikers these days believe they are adventurers as they ride along in expensive kit on expensive bikes, but they have it so easy compared to what dad did in his younger years before the war and in his middle-aged years with The Rough Stuff.

Pushing and carrying their bikes, cyclocross style through tussocky grass, marshes and heather, they eventually reached what they thought was an easy road by the reservoir. New it might have been but tarmacked or even graded or gravelled it was not. It was rutted with tracks left by the earth moving vehicles that had built the reservoir constructed to provide water to Bradford. The reservoir was the Scar House reservoir in Nidderdale. Work started in 1921 and was not completed until 1936. Dad's visit to the reservoir was in 1940. Miles and miles they pushed their bikes over rugged ground until they eventually reached Pateley Bridge. This had been no short cut. In Pateley Bridge they stopped for a drink in a pub and when they left it was going dark. At least they were able to start riding their bikes again on the road down to Bolton Abbey to meet the A59 at Bolton Bridge. Their route home should then have been straightforward back through Skipton and home to Blackburn. When they joined the A59 it was after midnight.

Going through Chatburn, near Clitheroe in the dead of the early morning a policeman stopped them as the dynamo powering dad's light had packed in and he had no spare with him. He was riding without any lights but had to get home as it was already Monday and work started at 5.30am. The policeman told them that without lights they would have to dismount and push their bikes the 13 miles back to Blackburn. Dad thought the policeman was over officious as there was no traffic, a blessing as without lights he could have been hit by a vehicle. All street and other lights extinguished by the blackout meant riding along a cross country main road without bike lights was extremely hazardous. Obeying the policeman as good law abiding citizens the bikes were pushed to the top of a hill out of sight of the policeman where they were remounted and the pair rode on in the dark of the night. They eventually arrived back in Blackburn having cycled or pushed their bikes for nearly 150 miles.

Harry's house was the first drop off. As dad rode past Harry's house he shouted back to his cycling pal, "I hope your missus will make you a cup of tea and some eggs and bacon for your breakfast." The "missus" heard dad. She was obviously awake looking out of her bedroom window onto the street, worried sick about her husband who had not arrived home at the expected time for his Sunday tea. No mobile phones and the Robinson's did not have a land line. She must have been out of her mind with worry, but dad thought it highly amusing that her husband had spent the night trying to get home from the Yorkshire Dales, knowing that his wife would be extremely angry and frantic with concern for her husband.

It was 5 am on Monday morning when dad eventually arrived home. Dropping straight asleep as he fell into his bed, 30 minutes later he was woken up by his parents refusing to let their son catch up on his lost hours or recover from his mammoth cycling expedition. The experience did not stop him cycling in the future, but he was less reluctant to venture off on untracked escapades on his bike. Although many times his short cuts when out walking have lengthened into assault courses for him and his family as bogs and rivers are forded, walls, gates and fences climbed or crawled under and fields sprinted across to avoid angry bulls, landowners and cows.

Dad's passion for bike exploration stayed with him throughout the war. Letter writing occupied any free time and some of the letters he sent to mum were kept by her and survive to this day. The letters sent by her to dad are no longer in existence, probably because a soldier on the move has limited amount of space to carry personal possessions. When abroad in Italy dad wrote to mum detailing routes she should go off and try on her own. He wrote the suggestion for what even now with the most advanced bike would be a demanding ride both in terms of the fitness required and the navigation. Dad encouraged mum to go out in the middle of winter in the middle of the war on her bike in a remote part of the country to try out his suggestions. This is what he wrote to her on 24 February 1944. The words in Italics have been added to clarify certain places.

Before going on leave I sent a letter to you by air, in reply to one you sent me. I've been wondering whether you went on any rides I wrote down, here's another. Try going to Whalley over York *(this is not the York in Yorkshire, but a tiny hamlet above the A59 on the old road to Whalley from Blackburn)* some time, it's worth the climb. I'm trying to think of one, there is a smashing spot of rough stuff over the moors from Slaidburn to Wray home through Lancaster *(a rough track)*, it's a bit too far though, tell you what! The Trough (*of Bowland)* this week, it's a six hour ride and easy full day, we used to do it on a half day holiday. Here goes from starting at Whitewell *(it is a 15 miles cycle ride from where mum lived to the Inn at Whitewell and that is where she has to start dad's directions)* have your food there, the hotel makes good tea. Picking up the bikes walk to the road which drops gently down through the wood, just follow the road soon you will come to the first bridge then another, another two miles and you're at Dunsop Bridge. The road to the right is the Slaidburn Newton one, pass it and you are now on the Trough road. There's an R.C. Chapel on your left and soon the first gate across the road, you should manage the hill on your bottom gear, I never do. For the next five miles it's up and down until you come to the hill with the boundary of Lancashire and Yorkshire at the top. It's a real stiff climb *(a typical dad underestimate),* but repays itself on the run down, it's best up there when clouds and mist come over the tops of the hills.

I'm skipping over the Trough road you can't go wrong, you've landed by the side of the Wyre now on your left running through the trees with the moors as a background. Passing the gamekeeper's cottage on your right keep hitting the trail, through the gate across the road, you take a gentle rise through the trees look out for a road on your left which drops towards the river passing the farm on its right, you can't mistake it being the first road

on your left. At the bottom there's a ford not worth riding through, I tried it when the river was a bit too deep. Water gets in the bottom bracket and you're riding home listening to cracking and crunching then. Cross the footbridge and keep going, over the hill, you've a nice ride across the moors now to the next water splash at the bottom of a steep hill, keep on this road you're going home, Bleasdale way via Longridge. O.K. You're heading away from ford number two, keep to the road. I'm a bit hazy here stick to it you will find yourself among green fields once again bearing to the first crossroads.

You turn left by the house on the corner as you get the road over Bleasdale you're okay you won't go far wrong anyway. It's grand on Bleasdale on a clear day you can see for miles. After turning left you pass a pub, tea here as well, have it here you're heading for a moorland road again another nice climb or walk, they're well worth it. You can't go wrong, we are on Bleasedale's highest point now. You drop down, cross a small bridge up again and then a good straight run down to another junction. This is it that's your way to the right. If you feel ready for another river crossing then open the gate in front, the two dashes mark it (*dad included a little diagram showing the gate to river crossing*).

Carry on down the rough track to the river and up the opposite bank you will soon hit a good road, turn right, first left and through winding lanes to Longridge, up through the town over the level crossing turn left at the top of the hill, there's a library on the corner, first right down the hill, left again on the main road another pub on your left, fork right, hold it there and you're in Ribchester.

Before Brock bottoms if you don't want to go over the river turn right at the T junction, then left again, this is always a puzzle. I'm rather vague on it. I believe it's right, you'll soon be able to put yourself right. I wouldn't go round the Trough until you feel like it, it's not a hard run but it's really pleasant the way I've told you doesn't include many main roads, only Blackburn Whalley Ribchester, if you do go Peggy you'll feel it's well worthwhile. *(A 60 mile route with many hills—some very challenging, navigationally difficult as dad could not remember himself all the turnings— not sure if mum ever took up his suggestion. She did though record some of her cycle outings in her 1945 diary, the only one surviving. On Whitsuntide Monday the 21ˢᵗ May 1945 which was a Bank Holiday she rode with her friend*

Kathleen around Whalley and Clitheroe. Roads would obviously be much quieter then, but still a 25 mile round journey from her home.)

Dad always believes anything is possible and unless he literally cannot do something will carry on regardless of pain, problems and protestations from anyone with him. He seems fearless or almost immune to fear, worry and chaos.

Not having experienced aerial bombardment having lived in a time and place of peace, the thought alone of something dropping down from the sky to kill you, I find terrifying. I asked dad about how he felt about the risk of being bombed when still living and working in Blackburn or when out and about on his bike. A usual characteristic relaxed and casual reaction.

"I remember the first air raid, it was nothing. In October 1940 the Germans tried to bomb the fuse factory at Lower Darwen, but missed by a mile or more. Again in 1940 I once saw a plane come over Preston New Road. Then I heard an explosion. It was an enemy plane that had dropped a bomb on Ainsworth Street in the very centre of the town. It killed a couple of people and few others were injured. The war was right on our doorsteps, not on battlefields thousands of miles away. Everyone was involved and in danger, but we did not really think like that—just got on with our lives."

The Germans dropped bombs on the cotton mill in Chatburn where dad was stopped by the policeman for riding his bike without lights in the middle of the night. Fortunately it was after this encounter with the law. Chatburn is such a small place, no more than a village the other side of Clitheroe. It was an opportunistic terror raid with no military strategic importance. The pilot was a sneak raider who had come over on his own in daylight avoiding detection by flying under the radar. The pilot chose to drop a bomb on a mill in Chatburn on 30 October 1940. Dad again cycling into the Yorkshire Dales from home saw the damage that had been done by the bomb. "On my usual weekend cycle out I went past the scene of the explosion. Everything was shattered. A man from the mill had watched the plane bank round the factory chimney flying very low. A fellow on the main road with a petrol tanker got out to look at the plane. He was killed, even though his petrol tanker was not blown up. If he had stayed in his cab he would have remained untouched, but he got out of the tanker and was unlucky. Tiles were blown off rooves and windows were smashed. A house was demolished, hit by a bomb and two residents were also killed."

This is a report from the local newspaper at the time the "Clitheroe Advertiser and Times".

BOMBS ON NORTH-WEST VILLAGE
TWO PEOPLE KILLED AND OTHERS INJURED
DAYLIGHT RAID

"Two bombs were dropped on a North-west village on Wednesday afternoon, killing two people, gravely injuring two more and a number of others received minor injuries. The two killed were—Mrs Mary Elizabeth Wilson, widow, and Lawrence Westwood, the driver of a petrol wagon which was being driven through the village whilst the raid was taking place.

"The gravely injured residents are Miss Alice Robinson (53) whose house was demolished, and Elijah Halstead (62) who received injuries about the head and eyes when his cottage was damaged. Both are in hospital.

"Among others detained in hospital on Wednesday night were: Mrs Graham Wood, Miss Taylor, Mrs Walton, Walter Forrest and Jean Wignall, while others who were allowed to go home after receiving treatment were: Mrs W Hartley, Mrs E Monk, Mrs Arthur, Mrs Harwood, Robert W Graham and Emma Leigh.

"Probably a further dozen villagers who received minor injuries were treated by first-aid parties on the spot."

This is of Alice Robinson's house which took a direct hit from the bomb and was demolished; the German pilot missing the target. A full description of the bombing features on the Chatburn Village website, excellently researched and described. Here is the link—

http://www.chatburnvillage.org.uk/Bombing_story.html

Dad's account is how he remembers it, seeing the devastation after the bombing, riding through on his bicycle, a 17-year-old.

Dad shared more memories "During 1941 Manchester and Liverpool were heavily bombed. The light from the fires could be seen in Blackburn. I often heard planes go over. They were probably going over to bomb the ship yards of Barrow in Furness or Belfast. You could see the searchlights trying to pick the planes out from the vast night sky.

"The day war broke out was a Sunday. I was not upset. I was relieved. We all knew after Munich that it was only a matter of time. Neville Chamberlain wanted to keep giving in so there would be peace. There had been ongoing signs of the war to come in the years before 1939. Mussolini had invaded Abyssinia and the Spanish civil war had been an opportunity for the Nazis to try out their airplanes and bombs on Guernica. That was terrible. We knew what we were in for when war broke out on 3rd September 1939.

"It's surprising the gossip I heard in the butcher's shop, and I don't mean local tittle tattle. I cannot remember the name of this fellow but he used to come into the top shop. His family were tripe dressers in Blackburn and they lived up on Preston New Road."

Sir Neville Meyrick Henderson GCMG was a British diplomat and Ambassador of the United Kingdom to Nazi Germany from 1937 to 1939. The tripe dresser's son became chief interpreter to Neville Henderson in Berlin, quite a prestigious line of work from someone who was born the son of a tripe dresser.

"This interpreter had been at school with my dad—they were old school pals. I remember my dad saying to him in the shop as he came in to buy some meat 'You have made a right mess of it this time. What have you being doing over there in Germany—there's going to be another war, isn't that right?"

This fellow replied to my dad, 'Whatever you say do not blame our negotiations in Berlin. It is not our fault. We have been warning the Foreign Office for years what's been going on in Germany. Been telling the Government that they are rearming. They did not take the slightest bit of notice.'

His warnings went on, 'I tell you something else—we are going to lose this war.'

My dad says, 'Nahh. Don't say that.'

He replied, 'We are going to lose it. The Germans have much better equipment than we have and more of it.'

Dad overhearing this conversation at the tender and impressionable age of 16 did not feel fear or anxious, more fascinated and excited by someone who had been in Berlin listening to the conversations of the British Prime Minister and the Fuhrer himself.

Sanguine and realistic as always looking back on what he heard in his parent's butchers shop all those years ago dad realised there could have been a different outcome.

"Well, he was nearly right, wasn't he? We could have surrendered or been beaten. Dunkirk was a big defeat—that was a let off as we managed to rescue a lot of the troops. It was a good thing Russia came in and took a lot of pressure off us and then the Yanks came in. Almighty Germany you can see his point. I always remember dad saying to me when war broke out 'You'll be in the army. It won't be over in a few months, it will be a few years. You are 16 and you are a boy and you want to be in it but don't worry as you will be in it.' When you are 16 it seems a long time off until you are old enough to join up."

It is hard to understand how a political movement that led to the destruction of millions of people, including many Germans had come to power in the first place. Hitler was elected to power by the German people because they had starved during the workless years of the 1920s after the First World War. They positively welcomed him bringing them work and turning some of their lives around. But the lives of millions were not turned around for the better, they were turned to ashes. The lives of so many were destroyed—the unwelcome minorities, disabled people, socialists, gypsies, Slavs, Jews, homosexuals, lesbians—the list goes on and on and on—so, so many were annihilated. Millions of innocent civilians—the residents of villages, towns and cities who got in the way of the advancing armies and were not classed as racially pure by the Nazis.

Many millions of fighters died. There were soldiers, like dad, who could not wait to start what dad thought of as being a big adventure. Others conscripted and reluctant; others who had been brainwashed, their minds turned to a destructive, hating, evil force by Hitler's white supremacist ideology or the Emperor of Japan's support for ultra-nationalism and militarism.

383,770 British service personnel and 67,200 British civilians perished during the war. This is out of a population of forty seven and a half million. Compare this to the numbers that have died because of the coronavirus. The population is much greater now, 66.65 million in 2019, but even taking into account a larger population the death toll from the pandemic is a national grief, and a personal one for all those who have died and those who mourn their passing.

Around 4.3 million German soldiers and between 1.5 and 3 million German civilians perished out of a population of 69 million. The German government exterminated a significant proportion of their own civilian population. The Nazi regime killed those with the wrong skin colour, political beliefs, gender identity, sexual preference, religious conviction, and race or for not fitting it to their warped idea of human perfection. Millions of Germans therefore survived the war to build the peace, or face further tyranny under the communist government that took power after the war in the east of Germany.

The statistics of survival were not as favourable if you lived in the Soviet Union. A country of nearly 189 million it had more bodies to throw against Germany. Stalin ordered millions of his subjects into battle. They were though fighting for their lives. Being conquered by Hitler would mean certain slavery or death. Under Stalin there was a better chance of not facing a firing squad or being sent to a prison camp. It was by sheer force of numbers alone, a sacrifice by the Soviet fighting man and woman and the civilian population that led to the defeat of the German army on the Eastern Front. Around 27 million Soviet peoples lost their lives—8 million were military deaths and 19 million civilian. An enormous death toll. And even whilst this slaughter of his country's women and men was happening, Stalin continued with his own persecution—3 million dying in the Gulag prison camps of Siberia.

The world lost around 70 to 85 million from its population. It truly was a world war.

The European Convention of Human Rights was created to stop the holocaust and other atrocities happening ever again in Europe after the Second World War. Sadly human rights laws can never stop individuals or governments intent on destroying people who do not comply with their beliefs and politics. Governments can repeal such laws or ignore them—genocide in the former Yugoslavia is just one example when Bosnians were killed by Serbs from 1992—1995.

Learn the lessons of history. If it happened once, it can happen again and again. A careful vigilance must be kept by each and every one because be it death by war or death by pandemic or death through climate change consequences the risk is ever present and everything must be done to reduce it.

The European Convention of Human Rights was enacted into British domestic law by the Human Rights Act 1988. A government can change the law. Any country who is a signatory to any Convention can decide to stop being bound by its rules. It can tear it up.

The United Kingdom had some ancient laws that protect the human rights of its citizens. Habeus Corpus is one of them and the judicial review powers of the Courts. Laws can be used to persecute and destroy people such as the apartheid laws in South Africa, the racist laws in certain southern states of the USA, and laws that sent people to their death in Nazi concentration camps. Laws can only be changed by governments, so it is up to us to make sure that the governments we elect protect us all and our human rights to live at peace with our loved ones and neighbours.

The Holocaust horror was well under way when the war started; little seems to have been done about it by British and other diplomats working in Berlin. But what could be done to change this Teutonic killing machine, more deathly than anything imagined.

Dad had to wait three years before he was of an age to join the British Army. But one of his letters to mum revealed a secret that he had never disclosed since. He applied seven times to join the merchant navy once war was declared. Fortunately for him he was always refused, probably because he was too young. The death rate for merchant seamen during World War Two was higher proportionately than in any of the armed forces including the RAF which suffered heavy losses from its cadre.

Whilst her son was secretly trying to run away to sea his ever resourceful mother was making preparations on the home front. At the outbreak of the war she made sure that the family would be as prepared as possible for the shortages she knew would be coming from her past experience of living through the First World War. Lizzie got the front room furnished and had a fitted carpet laid down. She made sure that all four of them had new suits of clothes and coats, because such items would become scarce as the war effort concentrated on supplying the forces. Uniforms, blankets, kit bags needed manufacturing in their millions. There would eventually be less for civilians. She stocked up on essentials. She hoarded sugar and flour, hiding them away. She would have put away a lot more if her husband had let her. Dad never got to wear his new suit, coat and shoes before he became a member of the British army. Initially aired and moth proofed in a wardrobe to await his home coming, the expected shortages soon meant there was no cloth to make clothes so his sister Lilian cut up his new suit and coat to make herself new skirts, dresses and jackets. Nothing went to waste.

Having lived through times of shortage helps people value what they may miss. It nudges them to value and care for what they have in case it runs out and disappears from the shelves or market place web pages. Margarine was never on the Hindle' table after the war and the end of rationing, never used on bread or toast, only butter, it having been in short supply. Its golden buttery taste could once again be enjoyed. Butter is such a simple product, now like so much taken for granted. Choices have multiplied—so all dietary needs and preferences are catered for. Organic, free traded, vegan, low salt, low fat, locally produced, gluten free are just some of the options we may need to buy. The variety of foods on offer now coming from all global cuisines is truly astonishing. But what would happen if we returned to war time conditions?

Fortunate to have parents who needed a vehicle for their business Dad learnt to drive in 1940 in the family's Austin 10 on his 17th birthday. He was taught by his father. When the Second World War started driving was permitted on a provisional licence. He never actually took his driving test until after the war yet had driven ten ton lorries through North Africa, Sicily, right up the whole boot of Italy until finishing his war amongst the beautiful mountains and lakes of Austria.

Sometime about April 1942 he received a letter requiring him to report for a medical at St Peter's Street Blackburn as he had been called up for service and his suitability had to be assessed. At the medical centre he queued up with the other conscripts before being examined by a number of doctors each with a specialism. He was given a Grade 2 for his heart—his medical records which he had sight of some years later gave the reason as "possible tachycardia". He had been for a medical to join the RAF the week before and had been found fully fit. Between the two medical examinations he had caught flu and this may have affected his heart rhythm, as when demobbed he was passed fully fit. But that temporary ill health from the flu may have given him more chances of surviving the war as he was enlisted as a driver. He was not drafted into the infantry.

This is what dad said about joining the British Army.

"I was called up when I was 19. I did volunteer the week before for the RAF as if you think about it, all lads want to go and fly an aeroplane and that was my ambition too. But my eyes were not good enough so I waited till I got called up to the army. When I got the letter I was pleased because well we were daft weren't we to be pleased? It was an adventure. Nobody thought much of getting killed. Before the war started we were aware of Germany but there was no television. I did not really think about Germany before the war; it was miles away—foreign parts. There was lots of propaganda coming out of Germany and we were sceptical of what they said. We knew Jews were being persecuted but it is somewhere else so it is not real. Like Syria today when there was gas attacks. Powers that be were often pro-Nazi. All the toffs they were fascists. Churchill was aware of the danger. Toffs and the fascists were frightened of communists.

It is understandable. They travelled and probably had friends in Russia who had not survived Stalin's purges. Aristocrats knew what would happen to them if the communists took over. I knew this because of my friend Percy who met the Russians in Europe at the end of the war. He was in a tank corps in the war. Tanks corps were cavalry regiments, mechanisation had replaced horses. Percy served in The Royal Scots Greys, a regiment attracting aristocratic officers because of its traditions and links with the Crown. When they met the Russians as normal the ordinary lads had a great time getting on with the Ruski soldier, but the British officers were going mad wanting to have a go at the Russians, revenge for Stalin's murdering purges that had killed millions."

Because Stalin was an ally of the British it was only after the war ended and the cold war emerged that his crimes against his people started to be slowly identified and quantified. But the horror he wreaked has never attracted the same level of opprobrium as the Holocaust or later large scale massacres in Africa or Asia. Stalin raged a campaign of genocide against his own people. That he sent 3 million of his subjects to near certain death in the Gulag during the war is a dreadful statistic in itself but a relatively small number when compared to the total numbers he had killed, terrorised, starved and persecuted. Some estimates say at least 20 million.

The life of a Russian and of all the other races, peoples and countries that were submerged into the Union of Soviet Socialist Republics was worthless to and expendable to the autocrat, demonic Stalin. His fighting forces were totally expendable. Attack was the only option; a relentless continuous onslaught of men and weaponry, the German guns eventually could not cope and ceased working. A continuous wave of bodies unstoppable by fire power. The West owes so much to these brave USSR soldiers who died for our freedom when they themselves were not free. Without their sacrificial demolition of the German army on the Eastern front we may not have won the war. The 75th anniversary of the ending of the war in Europe was commemorated and celebrated by the removal of the May Day Bank Holiday, usually held on the first Monday in May to the Friday, 8th May 2020. In the midst of the coronavirus lockdown many regaled their isolation homes with the fluttering of Union Jacks, the Stars and Stripes, the French Tricolour, the European Union flag, but the Hammer and Sickle on a red background—the USSR flag or its successor—the current flag of the Russian state was absent. Many coherent and valid reasons for this absence— possibly not wanting to be seen as associated with a Putin led dictatorial government. VE anniversary day was a commemoration of war years, not now. All those who died that we are now free should be remembered.

It was not just the aristocrats that were killed, no section of society was left untouched by Stalin's terror which had raged with a demonic intensity during the 1930s when he had done away with comrades, members of the communist party, Christians, Moslems, anyone whom his spies named. To say it was an awful time for the Jewish and other peoples not deemed to be sufficiently genetically acceptable to the Nazis, and all those who lived in the USSR (as no one was safe from Stalin) is an understatement. Better words than these express the horror for these people who suffered under these two dictatorial systems of fascism and communism. Many more millions died in the years after the war in China under the communist rule of Mao Zedong—another dictator, another murderer.

Percy was one of dad's good friends. Percy had fought in a tank after the D Day landings in France. He ended up in Germany where the two fronts the Western and the Eastern came together and that is where he made his acquaintance with Russian soldiers. His Captain was no other than the 8th Earl Spencer of Althorp. The Earl was one of the lads according to Percy. Percy said he would leave his letters on top of the radio for Percy to take back to headquarters. The Viscount Spencer would say, "Percy, would you mind posting them for me?" And when Percy picked up the letters they would be addressed to the then Queen (who became the Queen Mother) and to her daughter Princess Elizabeth who became Queen on 06 February 1952, on the death of her father. In the regiment there was obviously some discussion as to whether he was lined up to marry Princess Elizabeth. The men thought he would make a good match for the heir in line to the throne, because of his sound judgement and leadership of his men. Of course Queen Elizabeth must have had many young men trying to become her husband, but she had only eyes for one man right through the war. That was of course another serving officer Philip who won her hand in marriage. Earl Spencer as we all may know, was the father of the late Princess Diana. Dad's explanation of his early life in the army continued.

"I did not decide that I would drive a lorry in the army. I was put in the Royal Army Service Corps. There was no selection process. I did not fill in an application form. The Army did not know that I could already drive. They would have taught me to drive as those who could not, were given lessons. I left Blackburn on 21 May 1942 catching the train from the station to my eventual destination in Chesterfield. As it does now the line runs south to Manchester from Blackburn where I changed trains. The station in Manchester I changed at is where the conference centre is now at the back of the Midland Hotel. The journey then went through Sheffield, but I cannot remember whether the train was direct from Manchester to Chesterfield or if I had to change trains.

"To begin with there was a lot of square bashing and then learning to drive the wagons. Even though I could drive a car I needed to learn how to manage a big vehicle. I was taught there for a month, then I went to Clay Cross near Alfreton to learn about vehicle maintenance and map reading. Stuff I needed to know to perform as a driver in the Service Corps."

On 21 May 1942, John Hindle left his home in Blackburn with a suitcase packed with his worldly possessions to report for initial training at Chesterfield. Like so many young men and women as he hugged his parents feeling the excitement of an unknown future, he had no idea of the experiences and adventures that war would bring him. Some would be terrible and heart breaking; others heart-warming and amusing. His first barracks was a requisitioned school on Chesterfield's outskirts. Chesterfield is famous for its leaning church steeple that dominates this former mining town. On arrival the new recruits visited the quartermaster's stores to be kitted out with their army gear and equipment. The first item was a large kit bag into which was placed two battle dress outfits, two pairs of boots, socks, a blanket, mess tins to cook and eat from, and a rifle, but obviously no ammunition at this stage. Other vital items such as a gas mask were slung into the kit bag and a series of belts which held the uniform and the other bits and pieces together. He struggled at first to work out how the uniform fit together with the webbing, but soon mastered it with practice.

He also received a single mattress cover to be filled with straw to make a mattress. The problem was that there was not much straw so he ended up sleeping on the floor with only the cover between him and the ground. There was no hot water; showers were cold.

The day started at 5 am with a wash, shave and then a breakfast of tea, porridge, bread and marmalade from the canteen. This was the way he started his new daily routine. He had been enlisted into the Service Corps, but his initial four week training was identical to that of all soldiers including the infantry. He was taught how to march and drill and salute; constant parading up and down the former school playground. He learnt how to strip down a rifle, put it together again and fire it. He had bayonet practice sticking the blade into straw bags.

He said he was not bullied and was never aware of any bullying. He spent a month being trained as an infantry soldier at the former school at Chesterfield before moving on to his allotted job of driving a lorry. Already a driver he still needed to learn how to handle a huge truck. This he did at Alfreton returning in the evening to sleep in his Chesterfield billet, on the hard floor of the old school.

He then got posted to a company at Glen Corse barracks near Pennicuik just outside of Edinburgh where he described his life as "just messing around". He was there about a month and enjoyed himself driving three ton wagons. He had no responsibility and was able to carry out his duties with ease. Next was assault training, he described it as playing at being soldiers, enjoying himself as he climbed over obstacles, crawled through drain pipes, ran around in the local countryside. By now he was living in a tent. The food was good and plenty with stew, a staple. He was never hungry. There was not much social life outside the base and little free time off. The new recruits would amuse themselves in whatever time they had off playing football or cricket.

The platoon was then posted to Lockerbie to carry out manoeuvres. He joined some other men from the Service Corps who had developed a side line. Whilst there they would offer to help out the locals for a small charge if anyone wanted furniture moving or were "flitting". They had a little business going where they would move furniture for the locals. It was war time and difficult for civilians to find a removal van. One day the trucks which were open to the elements apart from tarpaulin covers, were out on the road with some Lockerbie resident's furniture in the back when the Commanding Officer came along in his staff car from the opposite direction. He stopped his car and asked the lads how they were getting on. "Fine", dad said. It was a good thing that he did not look in back of the lorry as he was transporting a load of possessions, a settee, sideboard and beds for a grateful Scot. Dad wondered whether the CO did have a good look in the lorry as he drove past and saw the furniture, but knowing that his men were helping out the locals decided to turn a blind eye. Everyone really was in it together.

After finishing the training in Lockerbie the company moved back to Edinburgh and life got even better for him. He was and is always one for enjoying female company.

Dad kept laughing and chuckling to himself as he remembered his time back in Edinburgh. The main reason was the plentiful supply of youngish women who arrived every fortnight. Every fortnight two thousand Auxiliary Territorial

Service female recruits came into his base. During this time he was given a detached duty for two weeks in the centre of Edinburgh. He was stationed right in the middle of Edinburgh at the junction of Leith Street and Princess Street, next to the North British Hotel, now The Balmoral. He was trained mainly by members of the Home Guard. The very popular television programme "Dad's Army" is based on the exploits of the Home Guard in a fictional town on the south coast of England. The members of "Dad's Army" are portrayed as bumbling or pompous or useless, but the story lines always have them triumphantly succeeding against whatever is thrown at them. Dad has massive respect for the members of the Home Guard who trained him in Edinburgh because they were veterans of the First World War. They were survivors who were skilful, wily and experienced fighters. He learnt about sniping, ambush, camouflage—techniques of guerrilla war fare really. Dad described them as "proper soldiers." Learning from these hardened and skilful soldiers gave him an advantage in the years of fighting he was yet to face. He looked up to these experienced soldiers who were tough, having already experienced bloody trench warfare.

He came out of Waverley Station, turned left and that was his billet. Right in the middle of this great city he enjoyed wandering around exploring Edinburgh. Dancing in the open air in Princes Street Gardens was another pleasure. He could not remember whether there were any air raids to disrupt his waltz, fox trot and quick step.

On 7 December 1941 Japan attacked the USA by bombing its war ships in their naval base at Pearl Harbour in Honolulu, Hawaii. No warning of the attack was given so the Americans suffered many casualties and the loss of many ships and equipment. War was soon declared between the USA and Japan, Italy and Germany and on 26 January 1942 USA forces arrived in the United Kingdom, their boots first touching down on Northern Irish soil in Belfast. During the war a total of 300,000 American troops were stationed in Northern Ireland. They were given a hand book called "Pocket Book to Northern Ireland" of how to behave, familiarise themselves with Irish ways and identify and understand the differences between American and Northern Irish culture. Advice ranged from how to relate to Irish women. The guidance for the GI was "You will find the Irish very friendly. Do not assume you are the most wonderful guy in the world if an Irish girl smiles and talks with you. It means only Irish friendliness. When out socially there are two topics of conversation about which you must not comment: politics and religion." Nothing much has changed—these are two topics to definitely avoid when in Northern Ireland. The Americans gathered some of their ships in Belfast Lough before the D Day landings in 1944, but dad also saw some of their fleet anchored in the Firth of Forth when he was stationed in Edinburgh.

The USA fleet docked just down the road from where he stayed near Leith Street and Walk. Leith is the sea side town for Edinburgh named after the road that runs down from Edinburgh to the sea. Dad enjoyed his time in Edinburgh and always speaks of it with fondness. Scotland has always been his favourite holiday destination, particularly its mountainous west coast and islands.

After his month in Edinburgh he was sent to another Company in Sevenoaks in Kent. He described the change of moving from a happy relaxing place where he was accepted and welcomed by Scottish folk to Sevenoaks in Kent. His feeling of ease stopped with the move south. He was in the Kent commuter belt and the locals had no time for British soldiers. "They were miserable and snobbish folk who did not want us in their town," according to him.

Dad's words: "The Civvies looked after us in Scotland. Not so down south. We were billeted in a big residential house just outside Sevenoaks. Our Captain was Cyril Raphael Rex-Hassan, who before the war worked for Simpsons of Piccadilly, a department clothing store established in the 1930s." Dad described him as being just like Captain Peacock in the sitcom "Are you being served?" which was set in a department store called "Grace Brothers." Possibly Captain Peacock's character was based on Captain Hassan because one of the writers and producers of the TV show had worked in Simpsons of Piccadilly. It is not known whether Captain Rex-Hassan had returned to work in the store selling menswear after leaving the army, but if he had, no doubt the future character had been born out of this former soldier persona as witnessed by dad.

Their Captain' grandiose pretentions caused much hilarity amongst his troops as Rex-Hassan's projects often ended up disastrously for him. Here are just four recollections;

"Captain Rex-Hassan's girlfriend happened to live in Sevenoaks where we were billeted. He had us on parade on the town's roads. He marched us to the road where his girlfriend lived drilling us there, up and down the street outside his girlfriend's house. A nice detached house. He was showing off. He was balling and shouting at us, obviously trying to impress his girlfriend by demonstrating his authority and control over his men. He was making such a racket telling us what to do. All of a sudden this young woman came out of one of the houses, went up to her boyfriend and pleaded 'Cyril darling, stop shouting at those men.' She stamped her foot, turned around and went back in the house, slamming the door behind her. Well we all had a good laugh to ourselves.

"In Sevenoaks I was driving a 15 hundredweight wagon which we parked in a nearby wood. One day Captain Hassan decided that the wagon must be camouflaged and hidden deep in the wood. He took it upon himself to do this, but when the next day came and he went to find it, the wagon could not be located. Walking round in circles, thrashing the undergrowth he had forgotten its location. The camouflage had certainly done its job. He had to ask us all to search for it. Again the poor man was the laughing stock of the company.

"Captain Rex-Hassan lived with us, sleeping up in the attic. One of lads could play the trumpet. Every morning the captain had him play reveille to get us up. Stan Donaldson was our cook at Sevenoaks and he made us a brew of tea bringing it round to our bed rooms. We lived like lords having a cup of tea. We always had our tea before the trumpet started up. Stan never gave a cup of tea to the Captain. When he found out he did not get a cup of tea from Stan he accused the cook of stealing tea. The cook was a clever guy—he was a lawyer in Civvy Street and knew his stuff. He looked up the Army rules and regulations. Because the Captain had accused Stan of stealing tea when he had not done, Stan himself reported the false allegation to his commanding officer. That meant the allegation would have to be investigated fully and Stan knew a false allegation by the Captain had been made against him and he could prove it was false. Stan the cook was sent to see the Commanding Officer who was a sound man who took no nonsense from jumped up types. Stan marched in and got a telling off from the Major for making tea for the ranks, but not their officer. The Major dismissed him and told him to stand and wait in the lobby. This was so he could hear the Major then go on and discipline the Captain. Captain Hassan was then called in and the Major tore a strip off him saying he had wrongly accused the cook of stealing. The Major told the Captain. 'You are supposed to be an officer and gentleman, I find you are neither—get out.'

"One day we had to go up to London in convoy. The Captain had planned that the convoy should drive past his old workplace Simpson's in Piccadilly so that he could show off to the staff, his former work colleagues. The sergeant was in control of the convoy, up front leading it. The Captain was right behind him in his own vehicle—a jeep I think. We were all behind him in our vehicles, trucks and the like. The sergeant on the motorbike arriving first at Piccadilly told the policeman who was directing traffic around Piccadilly Circus that he had to stop all the traffic to let the convoy through. The policeman refused. Rex-Hassan continued driving his vehicle past the policeman who was talking to the sergeant. The rest of the convoy stopped and waited for the sergeant to finish his conversation with the policeman. Rex-Hassan carried on driving down Piccadilly leaving his convoy behind him. He drove down Piccadilly alone passing Simpsons where all the staff were at the windows waiting to see this former employee pass by at the head of a long convoy of military vehicles. Rex-Hassan never had his drive past moment of glory. It never happened. We had to wait until the policeman let us through a few at a time around the Circus and onto Piccadilly. He provided such amusement for us."

The times of carefree life sharing jokes and games of football with his army pals, helping out locals with their removal worries, dancing under the stars were running out. Endless marching and parading done, HGV training completed, weapon handling and firing passed, he was a fully ready soldier primed to go into action. The world of war would soon become a terrifying reality testing his fortitude and resilience.

This is the first of dad's letters written to mum. It tells of his last visit home before leaving the world of being a new trainee recruit to become a fighting soldier.

Home Address
John Hindle
79 Leamington Road Blackburn Lancs. Service address Sevenoaks
Date: November 25th 1942

Dear Peggy,
I thought that perhaps it was time that I dropped you a line, I'm still the same as usual but there's a lot more to look forward to than before. You will probably guess by the look of things it won't be long before I'm seeing Harry, was he called Harry? I've clean forgotten. I'm looking forward to it all, it's the looking back on it that I'm worried very slightly about.
I hope everything is O.K. with you as they are with me. Last Sunday morning a corporal and I had a nice hike home from Preston. They gave me a 48 hours leave with warrant on Sat. so I came home. The train arrived in

Preston at 4 AM Sunday morning. The B'burn train was 6 hours later so I walked it home. I'd been on guard Fri. Night after having a route march in full marching order. Saturday I was working and in the afternoon just as I was going to change my boots, the D.R. came round with the offer of an immediate leave. I dashed off, got my pass and came home. It was well worth it. I had a look round London before catching my train, and then I spent a grand day in civvies at home. I came back Monday, I thoroughly enjoyed it all, it was a grand break. It was perhaps the last leave from many moons so I made the best of it, I'm sorry that it wasn't possible for me to see you. I was more out Pleasington way than the park—side.

Your Ronnie will be coming to the end of his training before long, won't he? Tell him to look out for me when he gets posted. We not sure where we are going by the news films, the kitbag numbers though seem on some news films tally with ours, but you never know. When I get to the end of the trip I will let you know what it's like. I'm looking forward to it, when you see the films it makes you want to be driving the lorry all the way to Berlin, maybe I'm too optimistic.

It's time I signed off Peggy. If you reply please send it to my home address. I've always been glad to have known you Peggy and be a friend of yours, as you probably know I've been out with somebody else since the last leave but one, but whether I go out with ones or hundreds, I still hope to be your friend.

All the best

Yours Jack

PS sorry for the dirty paper, written at work as usual

From this letter dad clearly did not view mum as his girlfriend at the beginning of his war. They were friends, having known each other for years since childhood from those New Year parties. Dad refers to a girlfriend, someone who he had been out with in the last paragraph of the letter. Characteristic behaviour from him. He always has enjoyed female company and continues to do so. Dad was part of a friendship group which included some of his mates and some of mum's girlfriends. They would all go out on a Thursday night either for a bike ride in the summer or on darker nights to a dance.

Absence makes the heart grow fonder. Their separation as friends warmed their relationship over the next three years. It grew deeper and more profound by their many exchange of letters. The war changed him and mum as it did everyone.

Convoy

The time had come to leave Great Britain to fight the enemy. Dad, as with many others who had been called up was headed to North Africa to fight General Rommel's army. A new major took over dad's company who also failed to gain his troops' respect on the battlefields of North Africa and Italy. Major Butcher was his name and he came from a Birmingham family firm of printers.

North Africa had been invaded by the Allies in November 1942. Dad was deployed there as part of the 8th Army in December of that year. Travelling overnight by train from Sevenoaks to Liverpool where their transport ship was docked was the first part of a long and subsequently dangerous journey. Marching from Liverpool Lime Street station down to the docks Red Caps, the military police, patrolled street corners to stop any deserters. This was when the fun of the training and playing at soldiers stopped and reality set in. As they marched past a street running down to the docks one of the lads said he lived up the street. He kept on marching like the rest of them. "This is what we had spent the last 6 months preparing for; there was no turning back now," dad recalled. Here is his account of what he described as his most terrifying experience of the war.

"We were told very little about where we were going or how we were getting there. There were a few ships lined up in the docks to carry troops. We were supporting the North Africa invasion. I knew nothing. We were told nothing. Our ship was called the Empire Pride. We set sail from the quay side at Liverpool docks on 10 December 1942. We had no idea where we were going. It was war time, naturally secrecy clouded everything including our eventual destination. Since the war began in 1939 the government had made it clear to us all that careless talk costs lives, so we had been told next to nothing.

"More crucially we had no idea of the weather forecast. To be honest it was the last thing on our minds to find out whether it would rain, snow or the wind would blow hard in the coming days. Little did we know the weather would be a much more important factor in our survival whilst on board our troop carrier, than the destination. I remember all these big ships in the River Mersey anchored one after the other next to the dockside. Some were big liners, their steel flanks towering high above us. Before the war broke out they had been built to transport people around our then British Empire or across the Atlantic Ocean to the USA or Canada. Air travel was affordable by only a privileged few.

"The Duchess of Atholl was one such ship in our convoy. Before the war its usual voyage was across the Atlantic transporting people and their treasured possessions between the UK and Canada. I had remembered seeing its launch reported on news reels at the cinema.

"We marched through the gates to the dock until our company was halted alongside a ship called the Empire Pride. This was to be my home for the next week or more. As we walked up the gangplank I wondered when my feet would once again be standing on the earth of my birth. I was leaving England, the only home I had known."

Here is dad's letter written when he had boarded the troop ship. The elation was not to last.

Driver John Hindle 10704283, A Platoon, 276 General Transport Company. Royal Army Service Corp.
C/O APO 4330
Date: November 1942 (as written when on the troopship).

Dear Peggy,
    Whoopee!
    We're off! Do not ask me where or what I am on or intend doing, because I haven't to. The next week or two I will be following your Ronnie's profession, I am dead scared of following the fishes even so I feel kind of elated. It's a little cramped in the new billet. These places aren't hotels, you settle down to things as you always do in the Army.

    My one regret is not being able to be home last leave, it's a mess having to leave Old England without first going home, but it's the way of the army so why worry? I would like to have seen you Peggy, going away like this makes you feel as you do when leaving school. Going into the unknown always makes you feel different, it makes things more interesting. When I reach my new destination I will send you an unvarnished account of how things are. This is a lot better than living in training, no more blancoing, parading, square bashing, and all the other small but foolish things which gets a soldier browned off. Where I am now would perhaps make you feel a

bit more mad at old Hitler. If ever you want to see the living example of sardines in a tin this is it. We have plenty of laughs you can bet there will be more tonight when we try to get in bed it will be a scream. Army life is full of laughs, I thoroughly enjoy it when the boys get together. As long as it is run without the Daft red tape et cetera we have our own word for it, I do not mind. A little bit of a rough or even a lot of it never gets us down, because you can always have a laugh over something.

The O. C. is going to give us a lecture so I will have to say au revoir! (I hope) for the present, hoping to see you as pretty as ever in about three years' time, please give my kind regards to Marion and a good and Merry Christmas to you all at home. Mine will be merry not half! Hope you keep well Peggy and I hope Ronnie knocks along safe and sound, this war it's a serious business. Perhaps I have said it before and I will say it again, it has been grand knowing you Peggy and I intend taking you out and having a real good night with you, or would a day be better? A reunion with the boys and, the girls would just be okay for celebrations after. Maybe I sound optimistic but it is always best to look on the bright side of things, but whatever happens it has been worthwhile. Albert Brown's photo was in last week's Blackburn Times, he is going in for piloting in Rhodesia.

I will have to say goodbye for the present, I hope!

All the best of everything

Your old friend Jack.

Dad mentions Ronnie in his letter. This is mum's brother who joined the Royal Navy. My Uncle Ron developed an abscess on his spinal column which required an operation and many months in a hospital in a frame without moving to heal his damaged back. Marion was mum's friend. As later letters show their friendship grew into a special relationship during dad's absence from the UK with dad eventually revealing his long standing attraction to his future wife first recognised by him when they used to go dancing or cycling as a group of mates before he joined the army. He signs off "Your old friend, Jack." No endearments or expressions of personal affection. They were to come later.

Dad carried on chatting to me about the troop ship he boarded at Liverpool where he lived in cramped conditions below deck as he described in his letter to mum.

"Records show that the Empire Pride was part of a convoy that left the River Clyde in Scotland on 12 December 1942; but the records do not show that many troops boarded ships in Liverpool like I did, a place I know quite well as I am from Lancashire and Liverpool was part of Lancashire then. Liverpool has since left the proud red rose county of Lancashire and has become part of Merseyside. There were many ships in the convoy including HMS Argus which was an aging aircraft carrier. It was part of the convoy so it could provide air cover from attacking enemy planes. There were 9 escort ships in total accompanying the convoy. These were Royal Navy ships intended to protect the convoy from torpedoes fired by U Boats and enemy air power. The convoy also included 9 ships carrying between them thousands of troops. There were a couple of ships carrying just stores. I found this out afterwards. As I say none of us knew nothing. We just did what we were told."

"We set off up the Mersey estuary going north past Blackpool. I could see mountains in the distant gloom of a winter's day. We were passing the Lake District' mountains, a place I knew well from my long cycling trips up there. On 12 December more ships waiting in the River Clyde joined us. One of those ships was the Strathallan. Little did we know then that she would come to a tragic end during the final stages of our voyage.

"The Strathallan was a beautiful vessel, built by Vickers Armstrong in their Barrow in Furness ship yard, another place I know well as family friends of my parents lived there, butchers like my father and me. It was a liner built for the Peninsular and Oriental Steam Navigation Company, now known as P & O, who operate cruise ships. I see their adverts on the television. I have never wanted to go on a cruise; perhaps because of my experience in the convoy.

"The Strathallan was launched at Barrow on 23 September 1937 and had her maiden voyage on 18 March 1938 sailing from London to Brisbane in Australia so my daughter tells me. Such care free sailing days were necessarily doomed by the impending stirrings of war and she was requisitioned by the Royal Navy to support the Anglo-American invasion of North Africa in 1942. This invasion was called Operation Torch. A lot is made of the Normandy landings but we 8th Army had already been fighting for nearly two years by the time the Allies invaded France having had to land in a foreign continent, very far from home with long supply lines. It is easier to visit the beaches and battle fields of Normandy than those of Northern Africa, as they are just over the English Channel. But the 8th Army was the second UK force to invade Europe, when we went into Italy. The first was the British Expeditionary Force, famous for its Dunkirk evacuation.

"We continued our sail up the west coast of Scotland with their glorious mountains in the distance which we could just make out when we were allowed up on deck for exercise. The days were short in that final month of the year and we were kept well below deck in very cramped conditions. I had a hammock to sleep in; others put their bed out on the floor.

"I have a good sense of direction and know the geography of the British Isles. I knew we were far up the north coastline of Scotland around the Western Isles or Outer Hebrides as they are often called. Their silence of where we were going continued even though we could not have told anyone else other than someone else on the ship. There were no mobile phones then and none of us had a wireless.

"I tried to work out where we might be headed as we were sailing so far north—could it be to Russia? I didn't fancy that and thought that the passage through the Barents' sea to Murmansk would be too cold and full of icebergs for my liking. We all knew what had happened to the Titanic 30 years before. We were living through the last month of the year but the coming of Christmas

146

seemed a fantasy. The sea would be bitterly cold. If our ship went down and we ended up in the Barents's sea then death would be swift as a vicious cold creeping through the body would switch off the ability to move. Even if held up by a life jacket; hypothermia would get me. Death was a certainty.

"Then I stopped bothering about anything because I was sick as a dog as we must have sailed west into the Atlantic. As soon as we turned away from the relatively sheltered waters of the west of Scotland and into the big and fathomless waters of the Atlantic I started to be sea sick. The weather turned wild as we headed out into the stormy Atlantic. The waves were exceptionally high, driven by hurricane force winds. I have been told since that there was flooding in the Isle of Portland as low pressure fell to 940 millibars.

"The bad weather had a benefit for all of us as it kept the U-Boats away from our convoy and for those unaffected by the tossing and turning of the ship, they had double rations of eggs and bacon as so many of us could not face any food and certainly not a fry up.

"We must have travelled way out into the Atlantic before circling round to travel back east to reach the apparent calm of the straights of Gibraltar. This was a terrific storm. It was said to be the worst one for 50 years, but it kept us safe from enemy attack as the waves were so high, it was difficult for submarines and other vessels to spot us. We were down one minute and then up the next. It took me three days to get over the seasickness. Once over it and used to the heaving movement of the ship it was great. I enjoyed the sailing. We were allowed up on the deck at times to get some fresh, sea air. I liked looking out over the large expanse of wild water, the ship forcing its way through the rough, tempestuous waves. One of our company damaged his fingers in a door blown shut by the ferocious wind.

"I remember one of the destroyers accompanying us came alongside one evening just as it was going dusk. Through their loud hailer they shouted to the crew to put out a light that was shining on our starboard side. A blackout at sea and our Empire Pride had broken it. Other ships in the convoy were not always in view; we were pretty spread out. I was 19 years old, on an adventure with lots of other lads my age. It was exciting.

"Then we sailed past Gibraltar. The Rock was an obvious landmark. There was no mistaking the Rock. I also remember there was a line in the water where the Mediterranean Sea meets the Atlantic Ocean. Pleased to be going somewhere warm I started to really relax thinking the long journey from Liverpool was nearly over. We left Gibraltar in day light sailing past the southern coast of Spain. It is now full of villas, apartments and hotels, the chaotic result of often wild unplanned development, a large proportion of it said to be driven by corruption particularly in Marbella. The prolonged building boom which fizzled out in the crash of 2008 would not have been so long lived if it had not been for us Northern Europeans seeking a sunny holiday or retirement home. Or when what is now termed the Costa del Sol first started to be developed and there was no extradition treaty with Spain, it was an escape route from justice—a country where suspected offenders could live without prosecution from criminal offences in their own country. I always refused to go to Spain whilst Franco was alive. He was a fascist and I had seen what they were capable of doing in the war. Mum and I did only bought the holiday apartment in Spain after Franco died. We went in winter to escape the British cold and damp. But that was in future—the tower blocks of Torremolinos were still to be built. Looking over to the Spanish coastline, there were obvious settlements, one of which was quite noticeable. We could make out buildings huddled along the shoreline; now I know it was Malaga, behind which snow topped mountains in the distance could be made out—the Sierra Nevada—now home on its Granada side to that skiing place which we visited with you when we had the apartment. I felt happy and relaxed looking out over the calm blue waters of the Mediterranean to a country which in years to come would provide me, like so many of my country men and women who survived the war, with many happy times. But then it all went wrong.

The next night all hell let loose as the convoy was attacked by German and Italian planes and submarines. At first we had to stay out on the boat deck in case the ship was hit by a torpedo but when the aircraft attacked from above we were sent below to the mess deck. I became apprehensive. I don't think I was ever as frightened as I was then. But it was all just part of life.

"Looking back over my life including my years of war service this was the most awful time of all times. I wondered what would happen if a torpedo hit the ship whilst I was sitting there next to the bulkhead. I thought the ship might sink and I would be trapped beneath the decks unable to get out. The thought of death by drowning when I could do little to save myself was a horrible image and thought. But there was nothing I could do but obey the orders to go down below. It was so terribly noisy with explosions, firing of shells, the relentless scream of fighter aircraft and the omnipresent throb of the ships engines feeling too close to call. I wanted to be up on deck where I felt I might have a better chance if the

Empire Pride started to sink. I was young. I was fit from all my cycling and square bashing since joining the army. I would find myself a life saver and take my chance in the sea rather than be trapped below and suffer a watery death, trapped below with no escape. But there was no chance to get back on deck. I kicked myself I had never learnt to swim. There were no swimming lessons like there are today. I had to stay with my pals below deck where we tried to make jokes and believe we would come out the other end. These days, my children said it would be 'thinking positively'. But we did not have such words then in every day speech. Being positive was last on our minds. We just fretted listening and waiting.

"Many of the ships in the convoy were attacked. Someone said we were hit with a torpedo that turned out to be a dud. Others said that two torpedoes were fired at us but because the Empire Pride had took evasive action, the torpedoes had passed either side of the ship. When I go to Ulverston I always go and look at a glass work model of the Strathallan in a store opposite Booth's supermarket. It is a beautiful work of art. I often look at it and think that I was lucky. Our boat did not get hit. But the Strathallan did. I always felt it was shocking that a beautiful ocean liner built through the sweat and toil of working men was sunk so far away from where it was created. Sentimental I know, and maybe it stopped me thinking about how I was lucky, not to have been on that ship, but on the Empire Pride.

"The Strathallan was hit by a torpedo. The worse bit was that the convoy had nearly reached its destination. One of the chaps I worked with after the war had been in the same convoy and was on the Strathallan being transported like me to Algiers in North Africa. Him and his pal were having a good nosey about the Strathallan during the voyage and had explored the boat from down below. Motivated by a realisation that there were a number of water tight doors down below where they were billeted which may keep them trapped and unable to escape should the unthinkable, but possible happen ,which it did, this duo had planned their own evacuation. Such foresight paid off. In their explorations of the ships inners in the cause of self-preservation they had discovered a ladder. Climbing this ladder they had found it led up to a funnel and eventually to a way out onto the open deck. These days there would be health and safety prohibitions against their wanderings around the bowels of the ship, but in those days and certainly during the voyage from Liverpool we could please ourselves where we went and what we did for a lot of the time.

"When the torpedo struck the Strathallan they were able to escape from being trapped below using that same ladder. They arrived up on deck to find that the ship was nearly deserted. The ship had not yet sunk. My work pal actually was one of the last to be evacuated off the ship. He told me he did not even get his feet wet. He had survived and like me would survive the war and come back to build a life in Blackburn. Like many of us he was just one more who had been so near to death, but had dodged its clutches. We carried on and came home to build lives after the war; many did not. They had sacrificed their lives for their King and country. Looking around now at our country I sometimes wonder why. Is this what they fought for?"

Dad was emphatic that it was the most frightening experience of his life when the convoy was attacked so near to its final destination and safe harbour. There would be many more scary moments and events as his war continued for three more years after arriving in North Africa. Life after the war had many life threatening episodes. He is definitely the man with more lives than a cat—he has cheated death more than 9 times. Possibly it is due to his lifelong Christian faith and trust in a loving God. He never believes his time is up and always knows there is more life to be lived.

Africa

Dad continued his description of life after leaving his temporary home on the Empire Pride.

"We landed in Algiers on 20 December 1942. It looked lovely from the sea. I read somewhere that Algiers was one of the best sights from the sea. But when we get on shore the smells from Africa were unusual and unpleasant at times. We were billeted first in a local football ground. We made our camp in the stands. It was winter and cold. I was uncomfortable as I had to sleep on concrete. There was though a reminder from home in our compo rations which were handed out to us. We were given enough meals to last a number of days and one of those meals was Tattersall's sausages in a tin. They were made in Blackburn. It was where mum worked as an accounts clerk. One of the Tattersall family was a successful submarine commander whose submarine sunk a lot of Italian ships in the Mediterranean saving British lives as there were less enemy shipping to hunt down British ships carrying troops and equipment to North Africa. He was a hero to us who had to enter the relatively confined waters of the Mediterranean Sea. When back in Civvy Street after the war serving customers in the family shop in King William Street, nobody would have known what he did in the war. Only those who were there knew how he saved so many lives. There is so much made about the D Day landings, that it seems as though the rest of us who fought the enemy have been forgotten, maybe because the invasion of France across the Normandy beaches was close to home just across the channel. But the 8th Army invaded many countries—Egypt, Tunisia, Algeria, and Sicily then the Italian mainland and finally Austria."

Here's the first letter dad wrote after arriving in Algeria. It is missing a page or more at the end so finishes abruptly. He doesn't say much about the convoy being attacked other than saying he doesn't like being below deck. He would not want to have passed on such a frightening experience to those at home; it would have caused more worry.

December 1942 Algeria
10704283 Driver John Hindle, A Platoon 276 General Transport Company.
R.A.S.C. c/o A.P.O. 4330
December 30th

Dear Peggy,

I have nothing to do this afternoon so I have decided to write a few letters. It means I can make the time go quicker to teatime, I'm a poor do at spending time in bed. We cannot go in the local town because a couple of our lads came in at 10:30 pm instead of 8.30 which means we have to stay in this sports stadium which is our temporary home or rather shelter. We have lovely mattresses of concrete, last night I managed to keep warm for the first time. I am billeted along with the rest of the boys in the stadium, my place is next to the top step. It is the first and I hope it's the last time when we shall use a grandstand for a bedroom. We have a good view of the local A.A. fire when there is an air raid. It is just like it's on the pictures when the guns open up, we had a grand firework display on Christmas night. It almost made me feel homesick, we had one bomb which shook our beds, the plane dived and something swished past, my heart nearly choked me. That is about the only news out of the ordinary as you might say. Coming over we had to get out of our hammocks and go on deck, but we landed safe and sound thanks to the Navy, your Ronnie will be okay. I am never so sure of that as I am now. You feel a lot better on land when a warning goes than on a boat below decks. The water sounded too close for me as it slapped against the sides, it's all right being at sea as a sailor when you have a job to do, but as a soldier it's not much use. It's hard not to imagine things when the guns etc. are going off upstairs and you hear that water, always reminding you how wet it is. Now that we have landed it's hard to believe you are out of England once in the streets you see a big difference. High percentage dress like tramps out here and carry other things besides their selves on legs, that is one reason why you are not allowed to ride on the trams. The whites are not any better than the Arabs who live in the district which stinks like Blackburn's fish market with all the rotten vegetables thrown in. It is out of bounds to us. I wouldn't fancy walking through the narrow alleys in the daytime never mind night. We are not allowed in for safety's sake. 8:30 pm it's the time to clock in if you go out. The N. African district is a long way from being like our own country but it is very interesting watching these people live and going into cafes and trying out the cuisenerrie, sorry I cannot spell. The best places are out of bounds for rankers but 7/6 a week doesn't go far in any country. Christmas Eve we went in a small cafe and had a nicely cooked dinner, we had wine to finish it off, the cost 1/6d each. You couldn't say "Merry Christmas" with any real meaning this time so we wished all at home in the England one, I hope you had a good time. We had a good time but by any stretch of imagination it could not be called English. We have plenty of fun and it is better serving here than in England up to now, you do not get browned off as you do back home, no need to bother about leave and then we are here to do the job we are in the Army for, it's hard to say how you feel but it's better than, over there. We will have a much worse time before all is done with but we will perhaps get more satisfaction from our work. The boys who have come back say it's pretty bad farther up, when I go please do not expect any letters, we will be too busy getting things done. They tell me transport is having it rough, the roads are deep in sludge and run over difficult country mountains etc. and Jerry will not help things, I will write in due course though. The other day we had Tattersall's sausages for breakfast. I pulled your leg enough saying I would never eat them, but I had to do or else go hungry, they tasted good too. Maybe you will be fed up with seeing the coppery coloured tins, we have had them every day for the last six days, other brands as well of course. When I spied those black letters Sausages Wm. Tatt. & Sons. they were packed 7/42 I almost started to feel homesick, for the first time or else it was the thought of have having to eat them, after I had run your sausages down. The stuff from whatever they are made with didn't interest me, they tasted well though. We have army stew for dinner every day, it is good though, there is not any bread only biscuits, if we don't get worse food, we will be O.K. I have no complaints. Christmas dinner was also stew and everything we eat and drink comes out of a tin. I feel tin plated almost.

Have you been to any dances lately? It must be quiet at home all the lads will have gone up, I wonder what it's going to be like when they come back, there is going to be a lot of competition in my opinion. If the 4 of us get together again things will be lively we all intend having a celebration. How are things going on at night school? I could just do with your help when I

struggle to patch one or two odds and ends up, I can darn O.K. But patching or other fastening a barbed wire tear in my pants almost made

And that where it ends, the last page or pages missing.

Dad continued to recall fighting in North Africa.

"We stayed in the football stadium until the wagons were unloaded from the ships and I could then use my lorry as my sleeping quarters. I lived in my lorry, but especially once the autumn rains and winter came I slept under it as it was dry. The tarpaulin covers that went over the top of the lorry would let in water so sleeping under the lorry kept me out of the rain. It also gave some protection from enemy fire. It was only later when in Italy I had the luxury of sleeping in a proper tent. My home was my lorry. I remember when in Algiers the Germans bombed the docks producing a terrific fire work display. We watched it from our football stadium terraces. The planes came over wave after wave. There were no air raid shelters, but fortunately the Germans were not after the football ground."

In one of our long conversations Dad said that he always felt sorry for Germans and their General Rommel was the best military leader in the war. This was an expression of dad's lifelong humanity and innate ability never to take offence, always forgiving and finding the good in everybody and everything, apart from when his youngest daughter announced she was pregnant at the age of 17—then there were fireworks.

Dad knew the back story. Many Germans were fighting a war which they probably did not want still being scarred from the memories and experiences of the First World War and the widespread destitution and shame following their defeat. Humiliation was not a medicine that goes down well with this proudly efficient and fastidious country that had been broken by the Great War and the punitive peace treaty of Versailles. Understandable that the victorious French and British and other allies wished to ensure Germany never posed a threat in the future and anxious to be recompensed for their losses, even though nothing can make amends for death and destruction and damage. Hindsight is such a remarkable and useless exercise. To look back with knowledge and say with the lessons learnt, it would have all been done differently so that Germany would not have been penalised for losing the First World War and it would not have suffered from the crushing poverty brought about by the humiliating terms of the Treaty of Versailles. By 1923 through hyperinflation a loaf of bread cost 200,000,000,000 German marks. Money had lost its value. Even though there was some short lived recovery the 1929 Wall Street Crash resulted in widespread economic depression with falling wages and mass unemployment. Identical effects from the Crash had been experienced throughout the Western world. The Germans became disillusioned with the Weimar Republic government. They wanted their problems solved—many had had enough of extreme poverty and the suffering caused.

Hitler had come to power surreptitiously but yet obviously. In the December 1924 election, only 15 years before the start of the 2nd World War, Hitler's Nazi party received 3% of the electorate's vote. In May 1928 the Nazi party won 12 seats in the election taking even a smaller share of the vote. Eleven years later they were able to declare war, demolishing the British and French resistance as they powered their way to the English Channel. So how did Hitler gain such absolute power in a decade? There are many reasons but remembering how quickly this dictator took power and then wreaked havoc and destruction should make us all think. Knowledge of the past is vital for the making of a wise future. Protect democracy at all costs; demand integrity and honesty from politicians; don't let power corrupt decent and ethical standards of political conduct.

Dad soon settled in North Africa, happy to be outside camping in his truck. Sleeping in a tent would be a luxury, compared to the isolation sometimes felt when all alone sleeping under or on the flat bed of his lorry. In the winter, heat from the desert the sun warmed up his lorry during the day, but once the sun set over the horizon the temperatures dropped, as they do in the desert, to freezing.

Dad was not too keen on the French colonists.

"I remember having an argument with a French colonialist. He called himself La Chef—he said he was a sergeant. I argued with him because he said he was La Chef and I knew from school it was Le as it was masculine. We moved out of Algiers and up in to the country side, to the hills where the war was and it was alright. The 8th army was coming from Cairo, from the east. We had to block the Germans. The Germans had wanted to get Egypt and the Suez Canal—we had to block off the Suez Canal to them and the 8th Army did that. It was very difficult country to work in. It was not possible to drive with the lights on, but you soon get used to driving without lights when moving around in the dark. A light on the differential was on the vehicle in front of you on the back of a truck driving ahead which meant I could sometimes follow it. There was a line of wagons. I carried everything from ammunitions to men. Paratroopers did not like being transported by a wagon as they felt it was a big target. They did not always get into the right position in coming down from the sky. At times I had to take them up to their front line positions in the dark. They would quickly jump off the tailboard glad to be free of the confines of my wagon. I never not get lost in the desert. The ground was just rough to drive over. The landscape varied, sometimes it was desert and other times it was cultivated land. What astounded me when driving through Tunisia is that I would be in the middle of the country side and come across a big Roman arch standing there all on its own. Our Major explained they were the remains of the Roman buildings and their stones had not been used for other purposes by the Arabs who came after the Romans. There were still many Roman ruins around.

"I had learnt to drive a Bedford truck back home which were better in muddy conditions if driven very slow, than the 3 ton Chevrolet four wheel drive I was given in Algiers. Built in Canada it was a great vehicle and I soon learnt how to deal with any minor mechanical problem, changing the wheels and oil—had good tools to do it. Anything more the workshop platoon would come and mend it. Petrol came first in tins, then 4 gallon Gerry cans. The Germans designed them—that's why they are called Gerry cans. We used petrol for all sorts of things. Everyone had a tin can which they used as their stove to boil water or heat up the food like soup or meat and veg which came to us in cans. I had a can and all the drivers had one—you would see them hung on the tow hook.

"You would put petrol in an empty can, set the petrol alight, and then put another can on top of this stove as your pan or kettle. We weren't given any stoves or cooking equipment. We all knew how to make the most of what we had. We used petrol for lots of things. Occasionally and it was rare we would get tins of beer. It was very weak. We put the beer in the sand and then poured petrol over the tin. It would cause evaporation which cooled the tin and the beer inside it.

"We did our own washing and kept ourselves clean as best we could. By the time we had got to Italy, the Royal Engineers had set up mobile laundries and showers. There were all sorts of mobile provisions by then, such as bakeries. When in Italy after a shower we could change all our clothes for clean clothes. But uniform was free and easy; there was no dress code—we could wear what we wanted really from what we had in our kit bags, although we bought the local scarves to wear around our necks and cover our noses and mouths when there was a sandstorm. We looked a bit rag, tag and bobtail. The infantry had suede boots which were better in the desert conditions. We never had to dress up to parade which were very occasional in any event and did not have to report every day. There were no drills. It was very free and easy. I would much rather be in the field of a war than mess around in barracks in England where you have to parade, drill and dress up all the time. As long as you did your job property everything was ok; I might have to salute an officer now and then, but it was all informal.

"One day I gave a lift to a Roman Catholic padre after Tunis had fallen. He was an Irish priest. A bonny girl, not a local Arab as the women were kept indoors mostly, but of French settler descent, jumped onto the running board that ran along the bottom of my driver's door. She gave me a kiss. She was kissing all us liberators. The Priest said to my astonishment—'Drag her in my boy.' I being a lad looked at him, was very shocked—he was dead serious; he wanted to join in the hugs and kisses that the girls wanted to share at their delight in being free from the Germans."

Dad naturally did not stop his vehicle but can still remember as a 19 year young lad, his shock at the priest's apparently serious and potentially concerning banter. Dad explained the day after their liberation these white French settlers would not have anything to do with their liberators possibly because they were frightened as to what may happen next. War was still on their doorstep. Who knew what may happen if the Germans counterattacked and retook the land just occupied by the Allies? The French colonialists decided to keep their options open.

Perhaps the priest away from the claustrophobic and unnatural rules of celibacy imposed by the Roman Catholic Church found himself freed both spiritually and sexually. I think it was the words used by the Priest "Drag her in" suggesting that she be taken by force that shocked and upset dad. Dad has always respected women and defended their right to self-determination. If a man could be a feminist, then he was one of the first ones.

Dad acknowledges he was lucky in not being in the infantry or part of a front line fighting force. He was though shot at regularly in North Africa particularly when the Germans had air superiority. At first it would just be one plane—a Messerschmitt that would chase down his wagon as he was driving along the routes to and from the front. If he heard or saw a plane he would dive out of his cab and run as far away from the vehicle as he could and throw himself on the ground. There was little cover and nowhere to hide as the terrain was desert with few trees or buildings. At first the single Luftwaffe plane was only interested in attacking and destroying the lorry, not dad. That changed when the Germans started to attack using three planes side by side. The central plane would fire at the vehicle, the other planes would chase down the drivers who had left their lorry attempting to escape being blown up if the fuel tank was hit by a bullet. Dad wondered if the change to hunting down the driver came about because of a change in the experience of the pilots. He thought they may have been on the Russian front where the hostilities were totally brutal and merciless. Moving to the hot sun of Africa did not warm the hearts of these pilots as they sought to kill their enemy who was fleeing over the stony rubble of the North African countryside.

Dad remembered another occasion which he witnessed where an Auster plane was chased down from the sky by a German fighter plane. The Auster aircraft was designed as a small reconnaissance plane to fly over land to obtain an aerial view of the ground collecting information as to whether guns had hit their target. This information helped in assessing military strategy, assisted forward planning and helped the artillery to improve the sighting of their weapons. Dad said that when he saw the Auster plane in the sky with the German fighter plane on its tail, it had been plotting where British shells had landed as it flew above him. Eight such aircraft had landed in Algiers on 12 November 1942 as the first contingent. The Auster had a maximum speed of 90 horse power. The Messerschmitt had a horsepower of 610. No way could the Auster pilot out run or out manoeuvre the German plane that was on his tail. The plane had a single propeller at the front. Out of the sky a German fighter plane appeared and started to hunt down the Auster. The little plane dropped down in ever decreasing circles. The German fighter plane did not fire on the Auster. It just kept moving away and then coming around above the Auster. Eventually the British plane landed and the pilot got out and ran away. It was only then that the German pilot fired on the Auster destroying it. The German pilot then came round again and waved to the pilot in greeting before flying off. Such humanity was shown by that German pilot in using his power to kill the enemy object but not the enemy person.

Dad had great respect for the German army in North Africa especially their General Rommel as he thought they fought fairly and respected each other as soldiers warring on behalf of their nation. Many years after the war dad became friends with a German soldier who had fought in North Africa. Both men were retired and enjoyed their holiday homes in La Manga, Spain. They agreed the fight in the deserts which lay directly across the Mediterranean Sea which their apartments looked out over, had been a fair one. Sometimes the drivers received warning of an attack from signals allowing avoidance tactics, but there was a particular stretch of highway which the drivers called Messerschmitt Alley because there was always an attack guaranteed on that part of their journey.

In Afghanistan, Iraq, Syria, countries where the American air force has bombed and attacked in recent times, there have been occasions when innocent lives have been tragically lost because the bomb was dropped on the wrong target. Human error? In the days of computer directed drones and other advanced technology it is disgraceful and alarming that such mistakes have been made. Maybe the pilot and gunner are sometimes reckless. They certainly were in dad's day. Not only was he attacked by the German Air Force; he was shot at by the USA Air Force. Obviously a mistake, but one that could have cost his life.

The explanation for such errors was provided by dad's close friend Harry Durham who was a navigator in a Lancaster Bomber during the war. Making many take offs from the airfield he was stationed in Lincolnshire using only rulers, pencils and his mathematical brain he plotted routes for the aircraft to bomb the cities, factories and installations of the Third Reich. Harry had flown with the Yanks (as dad called them) teaching them aerial navigation. After the war, when dad and Harry were discussing dad being shot at not once, but on two different occasions by the Yankee air force Harry defended our American cousins by saying, "You can't blame the Yanks—they are not up to it. They are used to flying over a huge country and have difficulties assessing scale." It appears that they had not learnt accurate navigation when flying their aircraft given their inability to find the right target at times.

Total concentration ensured accurate navigation and there was no better at plotting his aircraft's course to avoid enemy attack than Harry Durham. He changed course every 6 minutes calculating their exact position by detailed mathematical formulas depending on altitude, speed and other factors. For the length of the whole flight the navigator's calculations were made sitting at a desk behind the pilot. Every 6 minutes the compass bearing to be followed by the Lancaster aeroplane was announced by its navigator to the pilot. Sky orienteers plotted the route from England to targets all over Europe, but particularly Germany. Harry's skill of zig zagging the route, rather than flying in a straight line kept him and his crew members alive despite many bombing missions. If he was more than one minute out from his scheduled time in arriving at the Lancaster's destination he considered it a personal failure.

Having a cup of tea in a Malham tea shop one day, the topic came up with the owner of the café of Harry's war service and that he had been air crew. Apparently the lady believed that German aircraft had been flying over Malham tarn, and onwards over the cove saying she often heard their aircraft overhead. Harry did not wish to spoil the lady's belief that the then sleepy Yorkshire Dales village of Malham had regularly been the target of German aircraft, even though no bombs had dropped on the village of Malham. He chuckled saying that his Lancaster had had many training runs over the area practising low flying over the water of Malham Tarn as did the Dam Buster pilots and crews.

Between 1939 and 1945 125,000 airmen and women served in Bomber Command. The losses were horrific. 55,500 were killed, more than 8000 wounded. Awful odds—nearly a 50% chance of dying or injury. Possibly because the airplanes that Harry oriented returned home to his airfield base in Lincolnshire his flights were considered to be a safe bet by the BBC for one of their most trusted reporters to join. On one bombing mission to Berlin the famous BBC broadcaster Richard Dimbleby joined Harry's plane to report on the raid. The risk of dying did not leave journalists untouched. Two of the three that flew on raids never returned. Dimbleby did, possibly through Harry's clever navigation.

Harry was lucky. He survived many crash landings, his aeroplane just making it onto the runway. It put him off flying. He never flew again. Harry and his wife Amy never holidayed abroad. He would ask dad when mum and dad were off to Spain from Manchester Airport—"Don't you think it's dangerous flying?" This from the man who had a 50—50 chance of dying in the war. Maybe he thought his luck had run out. He survived when so many had not—he was not going to tempt that cruel beast of fate.

Dad said that it was quite common that bombs were dropped where they should not have been. Dad was not at Monte Cassino. The 8th Army advanced headquarters overseeing that campaign to secure the way to Rome were housed in caravans. A bomb was dropped right in the middle of the encampment.

Dad's stories of his war in Africa fascinate. This next one relates to some of the first battles fought by the USA forces in the war, where they had to be rescued by the British 1st Army. Dad also did some rescuing to help an American soldier get back to his base.

The Kasserine Pass runs from North to South between the Atlas mountain range. Jebel Chambi at 1,544 metres is Tunisia's highest mountain and lies to the south west of the Kasserine Pass which is a 2.3 kilometre gap. The pass was defended by American forces. On the 19 February 1943 the German Army under the leadership of General Rommel attacked. Dad was working to the north of pass. He was stopped by numerous American soldiers on their way to the Kasserine Pass battlefields asking for directions.

"These innocent greenhorn Yanks kept passing through in their jeeps and tanks and say things like—'Hey where is the shooting gallery bud?'—these lads were off to the Kasserine and likely to be killed" dad said.

In these remarkable days of instant news, providing a device such as a smart phone, tablet or lap top is at hand to connect to an available and functioning Wi fi or satellite connection, nothing, unless censored, cannot be known if out there on the World Wide Web. Mobile phones did not exist for many years. The only method of instantaneous communication was the radio and that was used for conveying and receiving messages in and around the battle field. No information was given to the troops unless the Army chiefs agreed. Keeping troops motivated and ensuring their morale was buoyed up meant that the news given to the troops was carefully controlled. So unless directly witnessed or experienced no report of a disaster affecting the Allies was heard about at the time, until some days later when newspapers from Great Britain arrived in North Africa, following the long sea journey to North Africa. So Dad did not know about the routing of the American forces at Kasserine. He heard about it later.

Dad thought the Americans were overoptimistic and not as determined as the British. It was probably because the USA was far removed from the war. They had only recently entered it and had not experienced the Blitz, Dunkirk and all the other traumas inflicted by the Nazis on the British people. The Turks refused to fight with the American army saying that they were unreliable. The Turks would only fight with the British because of their reputation as an effective fighting force. Dad described how he was cross to read in the British newspapers that the USA army had retreated from the Kasserine Pass in 1943 because they were described in the papers as "inexperienced". Dad had not been in North Africa long and this was new terrain to the 1st army. He had no more experience than an American soldier. The British newspapers did not give the 1st and 8th Armies the same degree of sympathy showed to their American allies. The USA army suffered a bitter defeat in trying to defend this two mile wide valley.

Rommel was fighting the Allies on two fronts, squeezed in the middle in the eastern part of Tunisia. He nearly succeeding in defeating the combined forces of the Allies.

The American troops suffered disastrous casualties so the papers were obviously reassuring their readers that their country's new allies were not incompetent in this defeat by giving a reason that they were inexperienced. The truth was that the American forces lacked tactical and military competence particularly in its leadership. Dad helped out a jeep driver who was low on fuel who had to retreat from the battle front after the American advance had failed. Massive losses had been sustained. The man he met was an African/American soldier and stopped dad to see if he had any "gas".

"Do you have any gas bud?" he asked after dad had pulled up to chat to him. Dad gave him a can asking him what he needed it for and where he was heading.

He replied, "I'm retreating."

Dad asked him where he was retreating to.

"Souk Ahras—I don't like it up there. We are all gettin' shot at back there," was his reply as both drove off their separate ways.

This American soldier had made the sensible choice to retreat and fight another day when he probably hoped the USA battle plan was better thought through and carried out. Souk Ahras was 40 miles away so dad given him enough fuel to get back to his base and safety.

Dad noticed the extra freedoms that the American soldiers enjoyed such as being able to take photographs which the British troops were prohibited from doing. It was said to be in case he was captured and the photographs were developed by the Germans. Dad though did have a camera, and the rebel that he is, took some photos, but these were not of the battlefield. They were of his pals or of his lorry inscribed with the name "Peggy".

After two days of advance by the German and Italian troops, the US forces had lost 16,000 men and were left with one third of their original tanks, two thirds having been destroyed. Dad said it was the British 6th Armoured Division that saved the day for the Allies when in the evening of 21 February 1943 their Commander sent his last 6 tanks into battle against the Germans. Dad's words summed up his feelings at this British victory as follows:

"Our 1st Army lads came over the hills; they were blooming marvellous— just rolled over the hills the Americans had been trying to take for ages. They just did it."

The Battle of Kasserine Pass was in February 1943. The armies were still fighting hard and there was no peace as this letter tells. Dad got into trouble when he knocked a light off another lorry. He was speeding along a road, just like the blokes do on "Top Gear" when racing around, although for dad it was a matter of life and death, not for idiotic fun and entertainment.

10704283 Dvr. John Hindle A Platt. 276 C.T.C. R.A.S.C. B.N.A.F. Mar 29th 1943

Dear Peggy,

Many thanks for your letter which I received yesterday, it was good to hear from you and to know you're having a good time. But here we've been driving night and day, the Major has got us a day off today and we needed it, all of us were just about worn out, but it's well worth it, to know the boys farther up are getting their shells etc., you do get the satisfaction of doing a job. Driving out here is rather different than going around Blackburn. At night it's without lights over pretty high hills on bad roads but it's well worth it, sorry for the repeats, I never like giving descriptions of what we do because thoughts are always of home, I'm not homesick but it's the main thing and all of us are thankful the war is being fought away from England. Honest Peggy there is no glory in it as many think it's just one big ghastly waste. No wonder the last war soldiers don't talk about it. I see very little of it in comparison to those who live amongst it, but when you think of the use which could be made of the money and then in making things far better back home it's pretty awful, if I'd my way anybody who tried to do a bit of warmongering after, as Jerry did, they will soon be put down. It's a distasteful job and the sooner we wade into it and get it over the better, I never worry about things, but the only way is the hard way and if we invade Europe you will see some fireworks back home or rather my pals will but there it is. I'm not going to try and be a blinkin' general and say what should be done, I've no complaints about being out here but I just felt that way, if we once start, you back home will have to put up with a lot, that's enough about the war, I prefer to be on the bright side even though things overshadow it at times.

I am sorry to hear that the parcel which I sent hasn't arrived. A lot of mail didn't arrive home, they received one from me at home, sent a bit

before yours Peggy. If it doesn't arrive I will try and send another if ever I'm back where it can be bought. There's nothing for miles around where I am at the moment, but things are sure to change.

According to the last letter from Ernie he isn't courting Barbara Stirrup. Dash it all, it seems bad telling tales out of school but I thought you'd have known he seemed to be fairly spliced with one from his old training centre, he has even invited her to come to B'burn. The poor lad he's scared of breaking it to his mother. I told him to take the bull by the horns and tell her, sparks might fly but it's the best way, if he's set on getting spliced sometime in the future why hang back? Don't you think it's right? When Ernie tells me he's going to be faithful it's like hearing a startling bit of news, I'm the same way but have not got like that, I've never chucked any girl but I must confess , I've never really stuck to one, begging your pardon Peggy, but I must give it to you, you're the best girlfriend I've had and there's been a few on and off, I value your friendship and you've always been jolly decent, I don't often say things like this but when away you don't half realise who were the best. When you mention dancing it brings to mind the night when you pulled me around the floor at the Butchers' dance, I can't see how you could enjoy yourself trying to teach me dancing, I was very thankful for it though, keep it up and have a good time. We want to see the ball rolling when we come home as all others intend doing. It would be a suck if people let things like that die down, some have the opinion they should do the same as us and go without pleasures because there's a war on, I say have a good time while there's a chance, do your work well and enjoy yourself, after it, I did. We will go potholing as you say and I'll take you up in the Craven district, forcefully if need be and show you the difference between a cave and a pothole, I'm hoping to do Alum Pot after, it's a good game finding your way through them, it has a certain amount of pleasurable adventure in it, there hasn't been any time for hiking out here, I've seen enough of this country, it must be better than being in the desert though, always count the smallness of your losses, or rather it's the smallness of your wants which count. It's like being bombed as you may put it. You can always say thank goodness I'm not sitting on a load of petrol, even if it's a bit of high explosive you are hiding behind in the wagon. If there is a poor dinner to eat always be thankful you aren't going without, if you're going without you can always be thankful for the emergency ration. I don't think we will need to go without food, I've always a spare tin of M & V in my lorry.

I hope your social was a big success sorry. I couldn't come lieutenant, queer to spell isn't it. Let me know when you're having another, and I will put in for a 48 hours pass and 3 weeks travelling time. But then I may only annoy the Major. I've done that pretty badly lately, but I'm still waiting for orderly room parade—defaulter, quick march etc. and then halt! The old boy will read out my charge. Driver JH on March 28 at 2 PM or rather 14:00 hours whilst proceeding along road so-and-so commonly known as Messerschmitt alley overtook a vehicle at excessive speed, sorry security, and knocked a sidelight off the other lorry, badly dented a mudguard. The charge is pretty formidable. I've no excuse, and I deserve punishment it's the foolish speed work which got me, if it had been worse there wouldn't have been any lorry or drivers left, you can bet I will be grounded or rather be going out as a spare driver, which is better for a lot of things. I feel that I've let the side down doing a foolish thing like that, I'd a load on which had to be delivered and it nearly went west and me with it, you can bet I will drive the proper way next time. The trouble was, I was making home and I put a bit of speed on after doing 20 hours driving. It isn't the same, you've a ragged patience and a splitting headache and you feel like going hell for leather to get it done with, it's done now so I can just await the results, it's the first accident I've had driving so even though it was a slight one I hope it's the last.

I'm glad to hear Marion is going on all right, and Gwen seems to be liking her job, I know that I wouldn't and it's good to hear your work is going down well. I received your airgraph via ordinary mail, pity you are mad keen about joining up. If you have to go, there's plenty of fun in it, but it's always better at home. For heaven's sake don't join up to wear a uniform, you will be all right. A bit of common sense goes a long way, if you're lucky enough to have it, as I haven't. You're sure to be all right though, if you volunteer you deserve … well never mind. I've put my name down to join things so I can't talk.

I will sign off now and write some more letters this afternoon. I'll be glad when I haven't to write them, I will start counting the pages, it's a good job I got 2 writing pads from home, there won't be any time to use them up though. It's time I , hoping this letter finds you well and as happy as always and all at home as well, things out here are the same as usual, plenty of work, little sleep, all that can be expected. The last I heard of the boys was they are doing fine, and there's high hopes for the foursome getting together again soon, it's going to be a while yet though. The boys ask after you and Marion so may I please convey their good wishes from the four of us. All the best and a snorting Easter and a good time, during and after the dancing. The moon has a different meaning than it had a year ago to me and thousands more, what a lot there is to look forward to, and that is after only 4 months out here.

Cheerio! For the time being

Your old pal Jack

PS 10 pages what a bore!

Dad refers to mum as a lieutenant. She helped run a Girl Guides troop at home becoming their Captain.

The next letter reveals dad's sense of humour which is often tinged with sarcasm or scepticism. He writes about wishing he could send his cigarette ration to his father who liked his tobacco, so much so that he developed vascular dementia in his early 60s, dying many years before his beloved wife Lizzie. As was the case with the then unknown risks of sun exposure, the dangers of smoking lay dormant ready to be researched and exposed. Fortunately, dad was never interested in cigarettes or the consumption of alcohol. He enjoyed a drink now and then, but has preserved his health and a lot of money by not having an addiction to nicotine or alcohol.

10704283 John Hindle A Platt. 276 Corps Transport Coy R.A.S.C B.N.A.F. Easter Mon (*April 25th 1943*)

Dear Peggy

Sorry I haven't written for a month or two—time is taken up pretty fully so please don't think you're going to be browned off as much with my letter. It will be short. I received your welcome letter Good Fri. Containing the very welcome hankies, thanks a million They were just what was needed. I'd just lost nearly all my kit when they came and was trying to think out how to make a shirt out of them. My kit was in the middle of a field, I found it the day after, I was expecting a few months in the mush, I'm always a jammy sort of getting away with it, I got away with the accident I had, by fixing up the wing. One of our lads made a proper job of wrecking his lorry Good Friday night when it set fire and a fat load of ammo blew up. Taffy the driver was safe, 7.2's swished over our heads. Thanking our lucky stars the trucks were altogether or else a few guns would have strafed. We've seen a few wrecked lorries but his beat old Jerry's handiwork. We pulled his leg a bit unmercifully, congratulating him as well for getting rid of one of those lorries.

You told me in your letter that you'd been dancing again at the old place, mentioning that it was the place you found out that we weren't T.T. not T.B. You're a bit mistaken all of us are T.T. and don't drink. Well I mean to say we have an odd one occasionally. We had a binge in a cafe before coming up here, that's the only time I've been slewed, and it's the last but it's excusable I hope. Ernie is in the same mind, after being drunk at a Christmas party. Ken is strictly a water drinker, George tops the scales above 12 stone now and thrives on it. I don't think you will need to worry about our welfare Peggy, we are dead against it, but in the army you've often to let things go or something else would go. I'm not smoking, my pals benefit by my ration. It's a pity that I can't send them home to dad but he'd rather buy his own.

I also received your letter telling me that you'd received the parcel, glad to know the stuff suits, I brought all my French linguistic experience to bear and told her the colour of your hair and eyes, but I'm not sure on that point, they say you should know the colour of a girls eyes—I said Brown. You must be finding things dull, is there any dancing partners left? If the Yanks are at home, they will be pretty entertaining, it's about all they can do, but I better not get sarcastic.

This afternoon I had a bath down in the little valley filled with lovely flowers, it isn't tiled but it's really luxurious out here. Half a metal barrel cut in half length ways, a length of sacking around the bath about two inches of water in the bottom and voilà! The bath, one of the boys is generally handy for the position of importance, the back scrubber. It's really good bathing under a hot African sun. I will have to try and get my laundry done soon. There's a little patching to be done as well. We shall make good housewives, navies, cooks and bottle washers, and camp experts, guarantee to train you to sleep in any hole until you wonder whether to join the ancient order of Fakirs, but I've no complaints in that direction, it's just how you make it.

You will probably be on the Easter fair rides having a rare old time as I write. It would just be up my alley to spend my credits, if I have any, on the fair but then you don't get much of kick out of it, roundabouts are too controlled, maybe it's exhilarating in one way but not so thrilling is it? Are you doing a lot of Jitterbugging at Blackburn's rhythm club dances? You seem to be going to church as usual, I went to a service yesterday in the open of course. The padre gave us a lecture on Hell, we see a lot of it already. It's a place of big differences out here, you can never think there's a war at times but that's enough of that subject. The padre told us we shall go to Paradise first and then graduate into heaven. I'm going to be a long while graduating even if I scrape into Paradise. He gave us a good sermon and you take a lot more notice out here and a voluntary church parade is very pleasant. Of course we sang Onward Christian Soldiers. Before I left Edinburgh we had hymn singing in the church after a good tea and when they started playing the hymn tune to "When this b…y war is over" I'd to hide my face behind the hymnbook. None of us knew what was coming and it took us by storm, we've had all sorts of laughs, there's always something to laugh at.

I'm stuck for anything else to tell you Peggy and thanks a lot for the handkerchiefs, hoping to be seeing you soon, the boys are doing fine and still in England where I hope they can stay. You were a little out about my birthday I was 20 last Jan 14th. It's time that I signed off. Could you let me know when it's your birthday and I'll send you a stick of Tunis rock? I'm glad to hear Ronald is ready for sailing, it's a tough job, and I never forget those destroyers when we came over. The worst storm for five years and we were on the poop hanging on for grim death and a little destroyer could be seen bashing away through a sea which looked like grey moors, always moving.

Page 8 is missing

Sorry to hear you've been off colour it won't be a long job I hope. Don't worry Peggy by the time this letter reaches you I hope you're feeling as much in the pink as I am. It won't be long before I'm off-colour. We are issued with yellow tablets as a malaria preventative and they say the skin turns yellow, when I come home you will see a grey haired Chinaman, with narrow eyes through scanning with night driving. Also with eating stacks of corned beef I won't be able to pass a haystack without having a sample. Glad to hear Gwen is enjoying life, she should do in a men's ward. I would be in a ladies' ward but then I'm slipping on unsafe ground so I'll sign off now, remember me to Marion and Gwen. See you in Blighty.

Yours from the orange land

Jack

With the 8th Army in the east of Tunisia, and the 1st to its west it was not long before the enemy troops were squeezed into surrendering on 13 May 1943 yielding over 275,000 prisoners of war. It was at Cap Bon, the end of a rocky, windswept, barren peninsula jutting out into the Mediterranean Sea to the east of Tunis that the German and Italian forces surrendered.

Many of dad's letters refer to Blancoing. It was the term used in the rank and file of the army for the whitening of certain pieces of kit—webbing, belts and so forth. Anything that was expected to be white had to be treated with a blanco substance. Dad saw it as a waste of time to be forever making bits of war torn kit perfect for inspection. It wasn't being shot at which got him. It was the insistence of his commanders that he should spend hours cleaning his gear so that it was spotless when the same kit would be soon dirtied once more.

10704283 Dvr. John Hindle A Platt. 276 C.T.C. R.A.S.C. B.N.A.F. May 25th posted 29th

Dear Peggy,

I thought I'd bore you stiff again in all probability writing my letters, I've just written to the boys telling them how browned off I am. We've finished the job to start once more keeping up the tradition of Aldershot, instead of having the sport we thought was coming we get ready for the Blanco convoy, so less said the better Peggy. Only a suffering British squaddie knows what it means, I don't care how soon we get cracking in the final.

The last few weeks has seen the end of it all out here and we are truly thankful and to the greatest army England could ever have, the 8th, it's admired by us all, those lads have roughed it, and we are satisfied as well.

Thousands of enemy prisoners went back a short while ago, you would have seen more than me on the news, some of our lads were filmed I was too late. I've been in Tunis and will be there tomorrow, it's a disappointing place after what we expected but nice to see a little civilisation. The bombing has been accurate, the docks were smashed. Bizerte is in a worse state. The Mediterranean looked tempting, for all its blueness I prefer leaning on a Blackpool rail looking at the grey Irish Sea. Things have never been too bad. Naturally I've had a little tour of the area and got some satisfaction out of it, the feeling of a job done. The lads who live in the line have my sympathy. They cracked the crack Nazi regiments all right, it's sobered me up has this lot. Graves are found aiways around these places and I must give credit where it's due, Jerry buries the dead well, trim black and white crosses making miniature cemeteries. Ours will probably be improved later on, it's generally a rough wooden cross name written in pencil may be a bottle or tin with a paper with the boy's name on. I shall skip other sights. The country is a scrap dump, tanks, guns and lorries litter the fields, planes and bits and pieces are also there. One of our boys spotted an unknown Australian's grave in a Jerry Cemetery without any flowers on it. The Jerry's had quite a show on theirs, so he diligently planted flowers on it, a good act in my opinion. The sky pilot, we have put flowers on the old man's pet falcon's grave, or rather did when the bird died. I will finish that part of the doings out here and tell you how happy we are. We are quite browned off as I told you earlier instead of football and sport, we get the rest with a tightening of discipline. Everybody in the army is scared of his superiors bar the ordinary rankers who have to do what is ordered like sheep.

Tomorrow I will be going to watch a football match in Tunis Anglais v Francais. They're jolly good footballers too are the French, but an English pitch would be too heavy, it's often very funny when the French fall out with the referee. They gesticulate wildly and shout down and nearly fall on each other's necks. You can bet we shall have some fun, when back in Algiers our company and others used to have a great time yelling the old cup tie calls. One of our corporals has a tremendous Roman nose bigger than mine by about twice. The call went out, come on George you'd do better with your nose. They are pretty merciless in their comments, but you take it all in good part. *There is a line of the letter cut out by the censor.* The Arab quarters are out of bounds in these big cities, we like to go hunting for Arab dives to stare at with first repulse and a sensitive nose, but you can get used to anything. Houses lean over on top of you and you feel the mystery of the East. You can just imagine a door opening and being whipped away like you read about in those novels. The Arab wives have a rough time in the country. The well-to-do in the city seemed different altogether and I must admit it we would like to see them without the veils, the women have a fair skin. The French women are not up to much. I've still to see the milk and roses complexion of you back home in Blighty, they put a tremendous amount of grease and powder on spoiling their self, they know how to dress though. There is quite a lot of eye-catching quality about them but they most certainly lacked that something. In Tunis they're Italian. Life is on a lower standard than England they don't hide the low joints as at home, it's a mixture of European and Eastern races.

I will soon be in bed on a farm cart, we sleep out in the fresh air it's better than in a bivvy. We have equipped it well and have a storm lamp, 4 gallon tin of oil, a table and a form. Reason is we moved the Quartermaster's stores, and took a sample, the table can be seen easy enough but we've a nice excuse ready. Sit down meals, now a posh bed, its luxury. I borrowed a sack, well for keeps, and raided a large hay rick and a comfy mattress was produced. I like to camp in luxury. The place swarms with flies, drinking tea even can be a trial, with a marvellous stock of fleas all grades, species and sizes, even flying beetles which whine like Stuckers. Lizards—about in the grass with an occasional snake or adder, marvellous wildlife! Last but not least the ants, blast them, burn them, but they still come, they are well organised.

P.S.S. Just received your letter and enjoying my camping out, ants are the real pest but as you remark about snakes, it's not as bad as all that, scorpions live under stones, they don't cause any trouble. I tried to skin a snake the other day but after cutting round its neck below the head and pulling the skin, the head came off in my hands so I'm waiting to have another go, hang out the skin to dry, cut it long ways in half and there's a belt. Your Ronald will probably be on the blue waters by now. I hope he wasn't seasick, it's really awful. Frank may soon be doing the victory roll who knows? If you have to go up Peggy and land in the ATS it will make the trio. Please thank Gwen for remembering me and I hope she hasn't to do any knife work on me, please don't think that's an insult, I have a horror of that.

(Gwen was a nurse)

You seem to have been away from the social life of Blackburn being laid up in dock as we say, I was glad to hear you was out of it and ready for work again.

Continued back of page 2

So you didn't go on any hikes? I did think you'd have tackled Pendle, I suppose it's still there. The main hill out here was Longstop not a patch on Pendle. I've lived among them such a long while that now I'm on the plains worse luck, my feet feel lighter and I will have to cure the leaning forward as I walk and tying myself to the bed rather the cart, to stop rolling off the cliff, maybe I stretch the point a terrific long way. I prefer living in the hills it's much cooler, a river will be nice to bathe in, the Med is too far off to walk to. Nearer than the sea is to home by 10 miles so. That will be the day when we will be billeted in Venice and able to dive into the street, rowing around the town serenading, some hopes! It will be a great advantage towards the ideal place no roads no lorries, whoopee! I will let you know how it is, who knows? Any soldier who had a grudge against his C.S.M. would only need to push him off the...that's...ain't it? Hope I don't get detention for writing that, got to be careful you know, the international situation you know, excuse the repeats.

Page 3 now

So church bells are ringing. We heard about it but didn't hear them. It must have sounded pleasant and now a women's Home Guard. These husbands will have to be careful now, going on fake parades in one of Blackburn's various clubs and etceteras, or else the Mrs will find out. We in the army wonder what is going to happen next. I suppose we will be having women bossing us around in the army, quite upsetting the married men who realise what the peace in war is. I guess I'm getting a bit sarcastic. The real truth is most married men all nearly worship their wives. Just shows how they realise how much they mean. I'm really sorry for those who have left children as well, it's hard then when they can't see them grow up. One has lost his wife, cleared off with his son and another fellow. Broken engagements run into dozens almost, they worry most about the rings. It's hard for a bloke when he's been saving up to get married for a long while and that comes, it's harder out here for them.

I see there's been a lot of parading for the wings for victory. Just a mess for the poor squaddies in it, they are a pest those parades. It wouldn't be too bad for a little thing like that, it's when a big brass shot comes when you do all the rehearsing. It's becoming dark now so I will finish this.

P.S. Just written a 20 page letter home my record over here 3 days ago I think.

P.S. You will find a small souvenir in this letter a Jerry hat band, if the sensor lets it through.

I will now start on the home news if any. P.T.O paper ration.

I've had regular airmails from home and I'm waiting for the ordinary mail. How's the guiding going on lieutenant? Please be a friend to your ranks and treat them as equals and you're the top-notch officer. I wish you were my lieutenant, I'd make a good Batman, I'm now a dab hand at darning, sewing and laundry work. A brush, soap, water and you will find a rival to Mr Wu. My Persil was such a problem it made me sneeze so awfully. Did you hear about Mrs Driver J. Hindle who smart guy as he was boiled her socks. These wash days are a problem aren't they luv? So leave the leaning over your garden wall wash day gossip. I will now get ready to sign off. Well Peggy I feel that before many years have passed and may one day be seeing you again and dear old snuffy Blackburn and the hot tattie cart. Gosh don't we look forward to that day. Every day we talk and dream of home and hope you are all doing fine. I hope Ronnie gets plenty of leaves home and not the hell of war, he will be an old salt now. He's with the grandest lads on earth. Ask any squaddie over here.

Cheerio and enjoy yourself, your old friend John

The next letter explains how dad came into possession of the hat band mentioned in his second P.S. of his last letter. He had obviously "found" it when exploring the German stores left over after their defeat. Mum had obviously replied asking how he had come across it. Another recurring feature of their letters is that they keep apologising to each other for their "boring" letter. Obviously wanting to receive reassurance that their letter writing was appreciated and not in vain.

T10704283 Dvr. John Hindle A Platt. 276 C.T.C. R.A.S.C. B.N.A.F. Aug 22nd Sun

Dear Peggy,

I received a very welcome letter from you today (July 12th), please don't think they're boring because they are definitely not. It wasn't many days ago since I last wrote. Whenever a letter from home arrived I always like to reply even if I've just written one. Phew! Isn't my writing terrible, thoughts come into my head quicker than the pen can move, sometimes I can't write anything.

Another thing which made me want to write is this, my friend Harry Taylor in Kenya is going to be a missionary. Gosh! Peggy it's one of the finest examples of self-sacrifice I've heard of or seen. I shall put down extracts of his letter maybe it's wrong, but I know Harry. This is what happened. He came to Africa finishing up in Kenya. During leaves he went to stay at a missionary's house, travelling around with them, this is what he says.

"It's really marvellous here." If he was here, I'd raise my hat good and proper. He says after living with the missionaries (John & Sophia) and their hospitality he began to realise it was something more. "Something more to live for than self-glory and money, how to attain this? I didn't know but I went back to camp with a resolution to lead a new life and live up to the standards of John and Sophia." (Later on he goes on leave again after passing time with them his time is near for departure.) They ask me questions then all of a sudden out of the blue Sophia says, "Harry have you made a stand for Christ?" I immediately answered back 'yes' out of"

Pages 3 and 4 are missing. Dad was being sarcastic when he says that it is one of the finest examples of self-sacrifice he has heard or seen. Dad did not much have time for missionaries and he probably saw Harry Taylor's decision to become one as a self-serving, neat escape from going back to the war.

I'm well blessed, everything is fine at home, good friends, myself feeling well and happy, there's a lot to be thankful for, isn't there?

I'd better start answering your letter Peggy, sorry you hadn't received any letter for a while, I see the Afrika Corps hat band arrived. This is how

I got it. Jerry was coming for me in a Tiger Tank. A 100 yards away was a 25 pounder gun, so jumping off a lorry going at 40 mph to get it, I doubled to the gun, tucked it under my arm and shot at the tank, but he came on. He was on top of me! Ah! My jack-knife I pulled out the tin opener, cut open the tank capturing the crew, that's the story of the hat band, well.

The truth is as we was going down to Tunis for a swim we arrived at a place called Tebourba, well in the remains we sniffed a Quartermaster's store where we stopped. We raided it. Jerry had left thousands of those hat bands. Needless to say we brought clothes, half of Krupps away with us. All souvenirs have since been handed in, so you see there's no story attached to it. There is to Tebourba and the 155ths stand there to defeat Jerry, it's great to be British. Makes sense. So you liked my description of the women (European) out here, you don't need to worry Peggy I shan't bring any home white or black. I couldn't tell really many tales because they turn the other way all the time, if they don't that means they are after your chocolate ration. There isn't a man over here who prefers the girls here to our own, but you know how it is, we can't go home. Might as well try counting the flies of Africa, it will be easier than getting leave to Blighty.

I'm promoted from the farm cart to a tent, the lap of luxury, we slept on the cart for coolness. When I read about, "Is your journey really necessary?", it reminded me of the day we left England, one of the last notices we saw, a good hearty laugh went up, with a touch of grimness in it, kind of a grim humour.

Glad to hear you were going on holiday to Blackpool, there's nothing like it. If you didn't catch a train home you'd be able to walk the 30 miles. What's your cycling time? We reckon 1 1/2 hrs but if I'd do it now, rather try to, I'd be stiff and sore. There's nothing like a run into the country to clear away a fed up feeling, it's great. Been over Pendle lately? Out here we play rounders and have a great time, plenty of sport in the game. One platoon plays another, the bat is a pickaxe shaft.

Since I started on this page it is now Thursday. Best if you took notice of the date the sensor puts on the letter.

So Marion has started courting? Please give her my best wishes for her future happiness. Hard luck on you having to split from her, but as you say we've probably to start some time, who's the boy? Maybe it's wrong on my part but if I was going to start courting I'd like to with you. I hope that my abruptness hasn't hurt your feelings Peggy, I've got a load off my chest. Even so it doesn't seem as if I'm playing the game. Just be candid with me, that is only my side but if I was right in my hopes I'd never do anything till after the war. With everything as it is there is always the, if, in it. I don't ask for promises but I'd like to know where I stand and above all be good friends. Maybe you can understand my feelings, it's taken a war to show up what really is true value. Maybe I shall be home sooner than I dare hope, which should help to straighten things out. I had better sign off now hoping you're feeling well and happy after the week at Blackpool, knocking up the mileage on the bike, in short having a rare good time.

Cheerio

Your very sincere friend
Jack

P.S. Part one orders. All brasses will be polished, what a life! My silver is in Davy Jones's locker. Address should be ON INACTIVE SERVICE. 11th Commandment. Thou shalt use thy soap and brush for cleaning webbing, if thou goest before my face, ye and comrades will be exceedingly silvered unto illustrious brightness, in the name of the major, and all who obey his command. Amen.

In this last letter, dad is asking for a commitment from mum to start courting. An old fashion term in the 21st century when dating apps offer instant coupling. Courting was the time of getting to know each other more than as friends as a prelude to commitment. The North African invasion had been a success.

The fighting was over for a time for dad and the 1st and 8th armies now based in Tunis and its surrounding areas. Summer had arrived and these forces were located next to or very near the Mediterranean Sea, a place that would give many hours of rest, relaxation and enjoyment. Dad still had many jobs to do moving around goods and stores. End of hostilities opened up opportunities for catching up on jobs that had been put off, like repairs or maintenance of equipment. But there was plenty of spare time to enjoy themselves and forget the realities of war.

Every day a group of soldiers would get in his wagon and he would drive them down to the beach about 20 miles away where they would swim, enjoying the sun and life by the Mediterranean. This was before the dangers of unprotected sun bathing were widely known. Sun screen creams had first been invented in 1928, but not marketed until a fair skinned chemist who enjoyed sailing wanted to find a solution to his risk of sunburn whist following his favourite past time. L'Oréal is a household name. Its founder was called Eugene Schueller and he told his company's chemists to develop a cream to prevent him getting sun burnt. The chemists came up with an oil in April 1935 which went on to be mass marketed as Ambre Soleil. In 1942 and 1943 no one, not least the British government, knew little of the existence of this product. The long term dangers of sun exposure causing potentially fatal cancers such as melanoma were unknown then. No soldier or sailor was told to cover up against the sun. Sun screen was not provided. Dad knew nothing of the danger he was in for exposing his pale northern skin to the hot African summer sun. He and his pals just wanted to enjoy the blue skies, sea and sun. They had no idea of the permanent damage to their skin that the sun would cause. Many years later dad developed basal cell skin carcinoma on his head and face. He had to have operations to remove the cancers. The personal scars war inflicts are not always visible and can take a long time to surface.

For a couple of months there was sun bathing and sea swimming at Hammamet, today a popular holiday destination for Northern Europeans, whilst the invasion force that was to cross the sea into Europe gathered around the nearest land point in North Africa before the crossing of the Mediterranean to Sicily. The invasion of Europe from Africa called Operation Husky began on 9 July 1943 and continued until 17 August 1943 by which time all enemy forces had fled the island. From May to September 1943 dad's life remained settled and fairly risk free as he had not been part of the invasion force. There was no enemy to attack him as he continued to drive supplies and equipment from the North African battlefields where they were no longer needed to the port where they were ready to be shipped to the future battlefields of Sicily and mainland Italy.

Dad expressed slight irritation that the 8th Army was not given more credit for its long term fighting commitment and engagement. A lot is made of the Normandy landings in 1944 but the 8th Army had already been fighting for a number of years by 1944. The 1st and 8th Armies had invaded across water on three occasions—firstly going in to North Africa, then to Sicily and then mainland Italy. These armies conquered more land, travelled further and engaged the enemy in more fighting than the forces that invaded Normandy on 06 June 1944—The D Day landings.

One veteran of the 8th Army a Lance-Sergeant Harry Pynn of the Tank Rescue Section, 19 Army Fire Brigade wrote a song to express the frustration of his fighting comrades who felt that they had been overlooked in their sacrifices and that after the European "D Day" invasion priority was given to support the forces campaigning eastwards towards Germany and its capital Berlin. The 8th Army had been fighting for years without a break or return home for a vacation. True enough after the surrender in North Africa there was some pleasurable down time by the Mediterranean Sea, but this was short lived for many as the Allied landings on Sicily were soon planned and put into place. 23,000 Allied service men and women died invading the island and many more were to die at Monte Cassino and the landings from the sea at Salerno near Naples.

The song written by the disgruntled Harry Pynn was called "D-Day Dodgers" and was set to the tune of "Lily Marleen", that was a popular song amongst all soldiers on both sides. The tune was well known to all so was used to accompany the sarcastic words written to express their disappointment for being overlooked by those in charge back in the UK.

So if you enjoy singing find the tune to Lily Marleen and sing the "D-Day Dodgers" song, or *you could just read it—*

We're the D-Day Dodgers out in Italy
Always on the vino, always on the spree.
Eighth army scroungers and their tank
We live in Rome—among the Yanks.
We are the D-Day Dodgers, over here in Ital

We landed at Salerno, a holiday with pay,
Jerry brought the band down to cheer us on our way
Showed us the sights and gave us tea,
We all sang songs, the beer was free.
We are the D-Day Dodgers, way out in Italy.

The Volturno and Cassino were taken in our stride.
We didn't have to fight there.
We just went for the ride.
Anzio and Sangro were all forlorn.
We did not do a thing from dusk to dawn.

For we are the D-Day Dodgers, over here in Italy

On our way to Florence we had a lovely time.
We ran a bus to Rimini right through the Gothic Line.
On to Bologna we did go.
Then we went bathing in the Po.
For we are the D-Day Dodgers, over here in Italy.

Once we had a blue light that we were going home
Back to dear old Blighty, never more to roam.
Then somebody said in France you'll fight.
We said never mind, we'll just sit tight,
The windy D-Day Dodgers, out in Sunny Italy

Now Lady Astor, get a load of this.
Don't stand up on a platform and talk a load of piss.
You're the nation's sweetheart, the nation's pride
We think your mouth's too bloody wide.
We are the D-Day Dodgers, in Sunny Italy.

When you look 'round the mountains, through the mud and rain
You'll find the crosses, some which bear no name.
Heartbreak, and toil and suffering gone
The boys beneath them slumber on
They were the D-Day Dodgers, who'll stay in Italy.

So listen all you people, over land and foam
Even though we've parted, our hearts are close to home.
When we return we hope you'll say
"You did your little bit, though far away
All of the D-Day Dodgers, way out there in Italy."

Before leaving the North African theatre of war and finding out what dad did in Sicily, Italy and beyond, two other people who have been very close to dad in the years after the war, in one case many years after, were also in the 8th Army. Not where dad was in Tunisia and Algeria, but in Egypt. One future relative fighting at the battles of El Alamein, the other , a close female friend nursing the injured and dying from that battle and other armed engagements.

David

David Bullen married his sister Lilian in the early 1960s and became his brother-in-law. Like dad he was in the Service Corps driving a wagon up to the front and fought in the crucial battles of El Alamein which prevented the advance of the German and Italian forces whose aim had been to capture Cairo and access to the Suez Canal. David spent the entire war in the army and was one of the first British soldiers to enter the Bergen-Belsen Concentration Camp. The experience of witnessing the horror of thousands of dead, dying or barely alive in the most horrendous conditions stayed with him for life. He never spoke much about this experience, but was left with agonising nightmares for the rest of his life.

Anyone reading this book may wish now to follow this link to gain an understanding of what David saw and why he could never sleep peacefully again, if not already aware of the horrors of a Nazi Concentration Camp— https://www.iwm.org.uk/history/the-liberation-of-bergen-belsen. It is very distressing and even these words are an understatement of the impact of knowing what human beings can do to each other.

Beatrice

Always one to enjoy female company, at the age of 96, dad started a friendship with a lady who lived close by. She was walking to the post box to despatch a letter in the box at the edge of the courtyard in front of the flat in which dad lives. He saw her, was attracted by her blonde hair, her stylish clothes and determined to get to know her better. Lucky Jack as always—he had a cleaner who also cleaned for the attractive lady. His cleaner became dad's Tinder app. The lady accepted dad's invitation to visit him for a cup of tea. Dad in his usual daft way described himself as a toy boy—the real lady's name has been changed to protect her privacy so I am calling her Beatrice and she was 100 year's old when he first met her.

They became close companions, one of the reasons is they have a shared history. She too had been in North Africa in 1942. She had nursed the wounded in field hospitals starting with the battle of El Alamein in October 1942. It was a huge shock to a young nurse to see the bodies of young men devastated by bullets and shrapnel. She had trained as a nurse in Cheltenham, but had no experience,

180

as the majority of the nurses, of the wounds of war. She joined the Queen Alexandra's Imperial Military Nursing Service.

The offensive against the German and Italian forces in North Africa was fought on two fronts. The first front started when after the declaration of war by Mussolini, British forces attacked Italian forces in Libya. Mussolini retaliated by ordering his army to attack Egypt on 8 August 1940. Operation Torch starting in November 1942, which was dad's first posting, began with the Allied invasion of Tunisia opening up another front in the western desert of North Africa. In between the Allied forces were the Axis forces of the Italians and the Germans. Field hospitals were needed in both the east and the west, on either flank. Instead of transporting Queen Alexandra's nurses through the dangerous waters of the Mediterranean to Cairo where convoys were easily attacked from under the sea by U boats and from the air by bombers as had happened to dad, Beatrice along with many other medical staff went by that optimistically named land's end at the bottom of the African continent called the Cape of Good Hope.

Beatrice recalls their troop ship stopping off in Cape Town in Southern Africa. A delightful destination now that apartheid has been abolished. In the 1940s white supremacy reigned, the black African man and woman discriminated against just because of their skin colour. The nurses enjoyed the status of honoured guests, their food paid for in restaurants, invited to parties and shown a good time by their white skinned hosts who lived in the villas and bungalows under the buttresses of Table Mountain. After enjoying the hospitality in Cape Town the troop ship left the Atlantic Ocean, heading round into the warmer waters of the Indian Ocean.

Their route followed the eastern sea board of the African continent up around the Gulf of Aden and into the Red Sea. Sailing through the Red Sea their ship collided with another ship—a cargo ship. The cargo ship sunk and their ship rescued its crew. Even though their ship was not damaged, their kit bags holding all their belongings were damaged, through the fault of one of the seamen who went down into the hold to have a cigarette. It was forbidden because a smouldering cigarette could lead to a fire. This is what nearly happened. When the seaman heard the crash, feeling the tremendous collision he threw his cigarette away in a panic, not making sure that it was extinguished. It lay alight in the hold amongst the kit bags. Fire did not break out immediately, but some of the kit bags and their contents started to smoulder. A silent smoke eventually seeped up through the decks alerting the crew to the danger. Water was immediately applied to all the kit bags which by then had been badly smoke damaged and scorched by the heat from the incipient fire. Also sodden with the contents of the fire hoses, they were ruined and had to be dispensed with—into the Red Sea. A dumping that would be inconceivable now by the British Navy, as the pollution of the oceans is a global and environmental scandal and disaster. But such problems were not foremost in the midst of a world war in 1942. The contents of the kit bags were probably mostly biodegradable, plastic production being minimal until the 1950s. The ship was undamaged and sailed on to the port of disembarkation. The last but one leg of their journey was in sight as they landed in Egypt. A transport to Cairo for induction in a hospital before the reaching their journey's end—a field hospital behind the battle front lines.

On arrival in their Cairo hospital it was made quite clear by a stony faced and autocratic matron that their previous weeks of cruising around Africa were over and that life would be different and demanding. The Matron was only giving a message of reality, making the nurses aware of the work, living demands and conditions they had to cope with. They just had to get on with it.

Most people back home in the UK were also getting on with it. There was no room for making a complaint or grievance. The threat facing the country was immense. A life and death situation required every man, woman and child to dig deep for those human characteristics of resilience, self-reliance and resourcefulness. These are characteristics we all have; we must have had to survive and flourish as a race since the first women and men roamed the plains of Africa in search of meat and fruits. These days those characteristics are often still needed but have fallen into disuse. The nurses had only the clothes which they wore—their possessions lying at the bottom of the Red Sea. They were given a sheet and given a place to sleep, the floor of a room in the hospital which had its fair share of insects and creepy crawlies running around.

It was a huge change for these women whose lives prior to training as nurses was one of middle-class comfort, safety and ease. Much more fundamental challenges were to confront Beatrice once the wounded started to arrive at the field hospital. So many torn and mutilated bodies, not experienced by her as a nurse in civilian life. Some of her nurse colleagues may have nursed Blitz casualties and were therefore prepared for the sight of so much blood, pain and human suffering, but for a young nurse fresh from the orderly and peaceful hospitals of middle England it was a testing experience. The memories stay with her forever and are not forgotten, not because she does not want to forget them, but because they were so powerful. Such memories of the direct and intimate witness of man's cruelty to each other can never disappear. Often mixed up with Post-Traumatic Stress Disorder, memory is a normal process of remembering an event even though the event was distressing and upsetting. Memories should not be sanitised or medicalised unless the medical condition of PTSD is diagnosed by a psychiatrist. We all have bad memories; it is part of the human condition that life causes pain, suffering and ultimately death. How we are able to deal with such experiences depends on our three R resources. Some have few resources because of poverty, upbringing, childhood abuse, domestic violence, prejudice, ill-health, disease, homelessness, worklessness, disability, discrimination and so many other causes of inequality and unfairness in the lottery of life.

Beatrice is a survivor indeed. Happiness came after the sorrow of nursing the wounded from the battlefields of El Alamein. She met her first husband who was serving like her in Egypt marrying under the bright Mediterranean sun. A successful life still being lived to the full at 104 but marked by many sorrows including the loss of a child and many other loved ones. Dad and Beatrice became great friends. He teased her that if he had met her during the war, as she was an officer, he would have had to call her ma'am and she would have been above his love ambitions. Now they are equal. Well not quite equal as Beatrice has the sharpest mind and wit despite her advanced years and has much better mobility than dad, walking outdoors on her own nearly every morning.

Italy

On 10 July 1943 the Allies invaded Sicily. General Dwight D. Eisenhower was in charge of all the Allied forces, an American who went on to be President of the USA for most of the 1950s. His second in command was Sir Harold Alexander. The force was again comprised of American, British and Canadian armies, and divided in to two invasion forces. One was the 8th British Army and 1st Canadian Infantry Division. The other was commanded by General Paton and consisted of the American 7th Army. Dad arrived landing in Catania in September, taken by the Allies on 05 August. Italy had surrendered on the 18 September.

Mount Etna spewed out white smoke as dad sailed in to the port of Catania. It was if it was acknowledging the Italian and German surrender of Sicily, The superior power of the American, British and Canadian forces together with other countries that formed the then Empire and groups such as the Free French had pushed the enemy out of the island. The German Army managed to escape by evacuating the island through the Straits of Messina by 17 August. Some say it was because of rivalry between the British and the American commanders in chief who were squabbling amongst themselves as to who should pursue the Germans. German efficiency was probably the reason; once they knew Sicily could not be defended they made the short exit across to the Italian mainland.

A cunning deception plot was hatched in London to convince the enemy that Sicily was not the allied invasion target after the allied success in North Africa. Ian Fleming, the creator of James Bond 007, had come up with the idea of placing fake top secret papers on a dead body with the expectation that the enemy would be conned into accepting the papers to be genuine. The papers would point the Germans to a planned invasion of Greece, not Sicily. The first pre-requisite for the success of this risky plan was the need for a dead body which would be accepted by the Germans as the dead body of a high ranking officer entrusted to convey top secret papers.

It had to be a body which was untraceable and for which a new identity could be created. Tragically a suicide victim who lived on the streets—a homeless, jobless, alcoholic and probably mentally ill—provided the body. Glyndwr

Michael had took rat poison in a derelict warehouse in King's Cross, London as the new year of 1943 began.

He lost his birth identity and was reincarnated as Major William Martin, having been given parents, an education, an army career and a girlfriend. Documents and other items were placed in his pockets to trick the Germans into believing this was a real Major from the British Army who had drowned and been washed ashore onto the south west Atlantic coast of Spain. The Germans found a briefcase chained to his wrist containing a letter marked "Personal and Most Secret." The Germans were apparently deceived into believing the letter to be authentic. More inquiring minds may have asked the question as to who would keep a briefcase chained to their wrist on what must have been a sea voyage. It would make it impossible to carry out many activities such as eating, washing, using the toilet and sleeping. If he knew he was to be shipwrecked then surely he would have destroyed the letter before going in to the sea or lifeboat. It seemed a farfetched plot. Called Operation Mincemeat it worked and must have saved lives as the Germans and Italians were not prepared for the invasion of Sicily. The story has been made into two films the first called The Man Who Never Was and in 2021 the name of military project itself—"Operation Mincemeat".

Dad remembers it still being very hot when he arrived in Sicily, too hot for him in the Southern Mediterranean summer. As in North Africa his job was to keep the infantry supplied with ammunition, guns, equipment and everything the soldier needs to fight the battles of war. Dad is always puzzled when he sees news films of guns being shot into the air. Such scenes of men firing their weapons to the skies were common in events shown in the news reels of conflicts that have ravaged the Middle East in recent times. It puzzled him as to him it was a waste of bullets. Ammunition must be easier to come by for the modern day insurrectionist or "freedom fighter" than when dad had to drive his lorry up to the front to deliver supplies was his conclusion of this ammunition profligacy.

Sicily also offered a respite from living in his lorry. He became one of five campers, all drivers like him who shared a tent. Dad was so happy living under canvas, one of his favourite habitats, a passion that would last all his life. Living closely with four other soldiers, one of whom was Australian, dad would read out the entertaining letters he received from his sister Lilian. One day after reading out a particularly funny one from Lilian his four tenting neighbours asked if they too could write a letters to Lilian. Here are the letters. Written in pencil they would be too indistinct to read if photocopied onto the page. All written in October 1943, Lilian was a popular woman even amongst the married men who wrote letters. There was nothing underhand about this correspondence exchange. As can be seen from the letters they were written because any contact with home lifted spirits and brought them closer to their own loved ones so far away. Each of them had a driver number and each letter is headed with the number. Six letters in all as dad sent one too.

(No 1) DRIVER

Dear Lilian,

Excuse the liberty of taking the chance of writing this short note, but having read your letter, which by the way was very interesting I can tell you it has certainly passed a few lonely hours away, of course you will realise the army comprises various types of men, but all the same they all appreciate a kindly thought from the folks at home, the freshness of your letter was a welcome break from the sordidness of this sorry business, it is very good of you and your friends, the way you are trying to help them to make them happy in their particular job. I can see that you are making a pretty good job anyhow so keep on with the good work, having sampled some of the ways you at home are trying to make the boys happy I note what it means to them. I hope that all is well with you and all at home as I can safely tell you that Jack is okay and in good company, So I will leave you, wishing you good luck. Yours—W Thomas Stockport

No 2 Driver

Dear Lilian,

I have just read your letter out to some of the boys in our tent, and I meant to say it was very enjoyable, as you say it will pass many a lonely hour and it certainly did, as a matter of fact we had a good old laugh at some of the things you had to talk about, especially the dollop you made on the carpet hope you do not mind me saying this but we had a good old laugh at it anyway, Well Lilian I cannot say a lot more for now as we are limited to one page each, so keep up the good work and let us have a few more letters, we like them very much, so cheerio for now, hope to hear from you soon. All the best of luck,

From Rowley of London

Dear Lilian,

Here is a short note from me no need to guess I bet. My pals who live in the same tent as me and next door read that letter you sent me a while back.

They've certainly liked reading a letter from you, we had a laugh over the spill. We had a good brew up tonight using the tea mother sent, quite a Lord's life.

Bill is married and has two young boys. Rowley has just got a baby daughter, who he has not seen yet, rotten luck is it not? Charlie has twins two girls and a couple of lads one as old as yourself.

Bill Swindells is about 25 single and one of our wags, always a laugh when all the boys are together. They are all good blokes Lilian, maybe we shall meet them sometime after the war, it will be a surprise to get a letter from them I bet.

Here is hoping everything is going on all right at home having plenty of fun and a good time at Slaidburn Y.H. Peggy asked me to go to Tatts dance in November here's hoping.

Cheerio All my Love John

Slaidburn Youth Hostel was a favourite destination from Blackburn and some weekends during the war Lilian and dad's girlfriend and future wife Peggy would cycle there and stay over. Tatts is short for Tattersalls where Peggy worked. Dad was definitely dreaming if he thought he would be home by November to go to her office ball. Faced with an unknown future it's not surprising he imagined waltzing round a ballroom with the love of his life in his arms.

Dad added the following postscript to his letter:

P.S. I am sorry missing Jasper out, he is an old back woodsman in Australia. English though, smokes an awful pipe, old man of the tent, two grandchildren at home like their Pa.

No. 3 Driver

Dear Lilian,

Having read your most welcomed letter, I can say it was greatly appreciated by the boys. The life out here is as you say, very lonely at times. We do manage to make a wee bit of entertainment ourselves. I am glad to hear that you are putting in a bit of good work for the boys at home. Jack himself is in very good health and good company, hoping it is not long before he is back with you again. He sleeps next to me but you would laugh at the bed he has made it takes up all the tent. So keep up the good work, and let us hope that soon we will be united to our families once again, as I am a married man myself with four children and I know what it feels like to be away from them. But we must keep smiling and hope for the best. So cheerio and good luck to you all.

Charlie from Woolwich

No. 4 (DRIVER and BATH KING)

Dear Lilian,
    Having heard your letter to your brother read in the tent I have joined with the others in writing notes to you. We all rather enjoyed your account of your little daily doings and I guessed it is that we all enjoy most about letters from home, just as it is that part of our own lives we are missing most here. We do fairly well for cinemas and Ensa shows but they do not, and cannot, take the place of home contacts. I hope you enjoyed your holiday and did not catch it for too much for the mess on the carpet. My own daughter is pretty good at getting out of scrapes. Well here's good wishes for the future from,

Yours Sincerely O.R. Jasper Canterbury

The grandfather from Canterbury, Australia not Canterbury, Kent did find the time to write Lilian a letter. Ensa—ENSA stands for Entertainments National Service Association. This was the organisation established to provide entertainment for British armed forces personnel during World War II.

My Dear Lil,

Just a short note from a Derbyshire lad who was one of the boys lucky to hear your letter read out to me, I can see you are quite busy trying to entertain the lads at home, and other things besides. Anyway just be on the lookout after (Geo) your office boy in case he gets up to his games, tell him (grins) out here are four men not boys, but if the boys come across a few tin soldiers we will forward same on, so until then he will just have to go on stamp licking hoping the (little boy) will not mind. Well I have nothing more to say, only we are all going to wait for a reply,
Wishing you all the best in the read years,

W Swindells (Fairfield)

The poignancy flowing from these letters is overwhelming reading them now. The constant fear of never returning home to hug children and grandchildren, wondering every day what may happen. Day and after day, week and after week, year after year battling the enemy. Lilian's letter had cheered them all up. Obviously when on holiday she had made a mess by dropping something on the carpet. The something cannot be deciphered from dad's hand written letter. As often when life gets tough, as has been found during the pandemic, it is the simple things which can give pleasure. Dad brewing up for the lads with the tea his mother sent, joking about the Australian grandfather bath giver—Jasper. Dad thinks the bath was "borrowed" from the large house whose grounds provided their campsite. They boiled water up on their stoves enjoying bathing al fresco. Dad does not know what happened to his fellow campers. Many different comrades in arms passed through his war years. Let's hope they all made it back home. The camping life was not to last. There was yet another sea journey.

Dad then moved with the 8th army by sea from Sicily to Taranto sailing in ships around the toe of Italy. Here is his account of his journey in a letter sent to mum and first impressions of the mainland Italy.

T10704283 John Hindle A Platt. 276 Corps Transport Coy
R.A.S.C C.M.F. Nov 2nd

Dear Peggy,

I'm in Italy now as you can see by the address, for a lot of things it's a king to Africa, more civilised and plenty of green to look at. The roads are putrid, other than the main ones, you can't expect anything else when there's a fight on. That's enough of that side, probably be sampling more than enough before long.

As usual I'm camping out and it's too good to last. I've a decent bed, <u>5</u> blankets, 3 rubber cushions, an air pillow, never been so well off, but it won't last. Always the case, next thing will be probably the usual round of things, so I'm making the best of it, not 'arf.

The trip over was smashing, I was never seasick, you've got to be careful what is written, but how would you like to swim in water, bluer than this ink and so clear you can see the bottom scores of feet deep, we'd a great time, one thing I've learned to swim, <u>not</u> to my satisfaction but I may be able to improve sometime, there hasn't been any chance of learning to dive, the Med is a grand place for all that, probably be a long while before we have any spare time. I'm straightened up, all the washing done, round our tent now are strung shirts, towels, vest, holed socks, all drying. Mr Wu isn't in the picture, just him missing. No wonder all housewives detest that, they talk about Beveridge schemes and all those wonderful new ideas but mine would be for first and foremost, electric washers for everybody. You'd have laughed the other day I went to a nearby fast running stream to wash a dirty towel and a pair of socks, needless to say I turned my back on the socks which were anchored by two heavy stones. Turned round and they'd disappeared into a pool, ever tried hunting for a pair of socks (grey) in milky coloured water? After hunting around I found one, but the other, no all the fish in that neighbourhood will be poisoned. Pebbles are certainly hard on bare feet. I bet I looked daft hobbling on one foot then on the other, in my shirt and underpants in a cold stream, there's always something happening.

It was a change to see a brook, this place does look more like home, it all boils down to the same thing wherever you are in the army. We're heading the right way home this time things seem to be going on all right, last news the Russians were 750 miles from Berlin and we are advancing out here, may seem strange to you but I'm willing to bet that you have more knowledge and see more of this place than ever I do. Funny how I used to see the newsreels and then when you're there it's different altogether, you see all the lot bar that which would upset you. Papers come from home and there it is described how on a certain night things were moving. You know something is up as now, it's to be something big though.

When you read about people cheering English troops over here, that is fact, we'd a real reception, thousands lined the roads, and cheered. Italians should never be in a war it just doesn't mix, the soldiers are like they've just stepped out of an opera, especially the officers. They stared goggle eyed at us producing tins and watching the grub appear, all out of a tin. The children are really starving, poor kids I don't think many of us ate all our food. It's hard on children, it's a lot worse here than in England, you live like kings if you only realised it.

It won't be long before it's Christmas seeing as we are now in November, time flies, I hope this one passes better than the last, it will be the first year passed abroad soon, it's been quite interesting. At the time you grouse a lot but you can always have a laugh over it afterwards. Now as I'm abroad I'd like to see it through in the Army, but I don't want to go home for another trip out again.

Two airmails arrived from home yesterday telling me the boys had been on leave. Together I bet they had a good time, I'm impatiently waiting to hear how they went on, and who Ernie's latest is, it's a good laugh reading about what happened.

I am sure you're going to have a good time this Christmas, I'm sorry that I can't send a card it's hard to say in writing. I hope you spend a real Merry Christmas and a grand New Year. In fact all the very best! With all sincerity.

All Yours John

Another mention of dad's friend Ernie who definitely likes female company. This letter is also the second time he has mentioned "Mr Wu" in connection with his laundry activities. The reference comes from the lyrics of the song "Mr Wu's a window cleaner now."

Mr Wu no longer has a laundry. Sad to say the business was flop.

He shouted 'what a hope' as he chewed a bar of soap

And then put up the shutters of the shop.

Said Mr Wu, "What shall I do?" and Mr Wu's a window cleaner now.

The laundry, it didn't pay.

Now there's no clean collars down Limehouse Way.

When he goes out working, interest he arouses

Polishing the windows with worn-out ladies blouses.

He wears a pair of Cami nicks to save his Sunday trousers

Cos Mr Wu's a window cleaner now.

Now little Chinese wifie each day is getting madder,

Tearing her silk stockings, her husband makes her sadder.

All day long he wants to keep on running up the ladder

'Cos Mr Wu's a window cleaner now.

He had his eyesight tested, a most important matter.

Through a bathroom window, a lady he peeps at her

His eyesight's getting better but his nose is getting flatter

'Cos Mr Wu's a window cleaner now.

Said Mr Wu "What Shall I do?" And Mr Wu's a window cleaner now.

The laundry it didn't pay. Now there's no clean collars down Limehouse Way.

Customers he's washed for now are in bad humours.

They feel quite neglected and I've heard the rumours

Lots of girls on winter nights go out without their garters.

'Cos Mr Wu's a window cleaner now.

The movement of the 8th Army up the Italian east coast through the region of Puglia and the towns of Brindisi and Bari was quickly achieved. Puglia is still a poor region of Italy as is Sicily but the poverty and inevitable hunger was extreme in 1943. The children were starving. Wherever they pulled up along the road famished children would appear around his wagon. It was so upsetting to see their wasted bodies that dad and the other drivers and service men, after cooking a meal gave their food to these children. They could not bear to see them so hungry.

In late November 1943 they reached San Severo an old town in Apulia where they sought shelter in a house overnight. A wood partition divided the room in which they bedded down. Knocking could be heard all night from the other side of this dividing wall. In the morning dad realised that it was the family's mule making the noise and disturbing their sleep. The family and its animals slept under the same roof.

Much of the driving of army transport took place at night, obviously without lights. One night pulling up for a break and to get some sleep dad reversed into a wall. Park assist devices were not invented and if they had have been, would probably be an audible signal to any enemy in the vicinity. It was only in the morning that dad realised that he had knocked down a wall when reversing. The lorry was undamaged. The wall had disintegrated. It had uncovered the vertically stacked stone tombs containing the corpses of dead people. The decaying bodies turning or turned to skeletons in their stone graves were revealed. When dad looked out in the morning light, the sight of the decaying dead in their stone resting places one on top of the other, understandably gave him more than a bit of a shock.

He had many scrapes and close calls with disaster. There was an occasion when in Italy he was making a delivery of ammunition to a gun battery. He asked a "Red Cap" from the Indian army who was directing traffic to show him which route to take. The Red Caps are so called because they wear scarlet head gear, but their formal title is the Royal Military Police. The Red Cap did not speak much English and certainly dad did not speak the Red Cap's birth tongue so it is quite understandable that there was a misunderstanding in the direction pointed out by the Indian Military policeman. The road he took turned out to be wrong. Driving down this lane he passed infantry moving forward spread out ready to attack the retreating Germans. He was driving straight into the front line, any further he would be seeing the enemy guns. Being such a large target he has never made a swifter three point turn to get out of the firing line of the German artillery.

This is the last letter written in 1943. A development is that he signs himself off with the word "Love" and he includes kisses at the end. It was way back in his letter of 22 August 1943 that he asked for an exclusive relationship with his future wife. Mum had some reservations, always the sensible, considered and careful one of the partnership she recognised that dad's impulsive and sometimes reckless nature may have resulted in a premature declaration when the outcome of the war was still uncertain and they were thousands of miles apart. She suggested he seek advice from his best friend Ernie, not sure whether that was a wise recommendation or not. Ernie is the one who dropped his girlfriend at home for someone he met when away living in barracks. Possibly mum thought that he would offer impartial advice taking into account dad's personality, wants and needs, being familiar with them as a best friend. Knowing that dad has plenty of girlfriends in the past, mum was being cautious and wanting to take it slowly. Also she must have acknowledged to herself that being a beautiful woman in many ways, she may meet someone other than dad with whom she would enter a committed relationship. Careful not to hurt anyone and especially not dad who had been a long-time friend, she suggested that she ask his best friend the one and only Ernie, for advice on whether dad should pledge himself to mum. Mum obviously thought that Ernie, who seemed to have a commitment phobia in his youth was the man who might test dad's resolve to stay with one woman.

T10704283 John Hindle A Platt. 276 Corps Transport Coy R.A.S.C. C.M.F. Dec 4th

Dear Peggy,

A letter arrived from you last night telling me you were going under for an operation. Here's all my best wishes for a quick recovery, hoping you've forgotten all about it when this letter arrives. I'm always stuck for words when I want the most, but you know what my feelings are, hoping the next letter arrives telling me you're in the pink.

I can just imagine your feelings when the letter arrived telling you to report for the op. It's always the waiting which is the worst, wondering what's in store. I find soon as you set off everything is okay because you're too busy to think about it. As a squaddie, pardon slang, I've always found it so.

I'm glad to hear Ernie and Ken met you, ten to one they are different girls than the previous ones who they tell me they've been with. It's good to hear that they are having a good time in Blighty. If another front opens they're likely to have it sticky for a while, I've told 'em what to do, forewarned is forearmed. Anybody who is in the first round will have my sympathy, I hope it ends quick. All is in the job, thank the Lord we've plenty of fighters, we hadn't for a while in Africa! I'm starting on shop talk, let's forget the war, only it brings things to mind when the boys are home and you naturally look at it as if it may be their last leave for a while. You're right about me asking Ernie for advice but didn't wait for a reply, couldn't be called advice, only when you're abroad everything is different and you see things clearer, only it makes it difficult. I was nervous of insulting you. I was wondering whether it was playing the game. When I sent the letter on to you I thought it was pretty blunt, but I can't for the life of me go around a thing before going straight to it. When you're likely to have an introduction to Jerry it makes you want to have a settled mind one way or the other, and to know it isn't causing anything to be misunderstood at home. As you know promises are very unfair and you are right Peggy, I feel the same. You can be sure I'm hoping to make a promise and both ways always be good friends. Everything will turn someday back in civvies once again, and everything good, what is worth having, we will be able to make our minds up, with a clear mind and a more certain future.

I was glad to hear Gwen is looking well, it's a job I wouldn't fancy that. It seems an age since we used to see you on a Thursday night, all others are in service now, wanting to get out of it, instead of in. Although for a lot of things I wouldn't like to have missed it, certainly makes you realise what you do miss, and it's those Thursday nights. Trips over the moors and dales, and mountains, and home. Yet I very rarely felt homesick. You settle down quickly and think nothing more of it, you can accustom yourself to anything bar feeling tired and hungry, it's hard to say how it affects you. Maybe you're put in khaki and it changes you, there's something somehow. After four years of war we are still kicking, it still certainly included a lot of surprises, and old England hasn't been laid waste as we expected when the war was declared. When it finishes there will be some fun, we'll miss that if we are abroad. When Tunis fell we went into it but there wasn't any mad sprees, but a dead quietness and a large sigh of relief and then plenty of parades, webbing scrubbing, and the unending training, then you sigh for the old times and laugh over it and things happen. One day you're off again and begin comparing Italy to Africa, this time we're in the final and heading for England. Every mile north is one nearer, mud and rains are the biggest enemy, capping it all the same, so there you have it. The war may not last long, but you never can tell, it's quite a do.

When you told me that there was no blackout up in your Church it seemed rather slack, all right for the vicar though. The last time I'd been to a Church service was on Sept. 3rd last, a full-blown parade as well. I like a

Church service but not a compulsory one, the largest piece of hypocrisy going. The order comes on parade after your boots are shone black and your webbing the dead opposite. There's an open order to march, the sun is stewing you, fly strolls down your nose. I'm afraid it doesn't make you feel like praying, but, when the padre starts off it is soon forgotten, then it starts once again after parade till you're dismissed, of course it's for discipline, but it always rankles one. There's the funny side as always with the sergeant major's threats of another parade if you don't come to attention up to standard, and a spate of un-godly words, he's probably only letting off steam in his way, it cuts both ways. Now a voluntary church parade is vastly different, it's sincere, you may go after a trying time when everything went wrong, and believe me you feel as if there's nothing else to cheese you off, it certainly helps immensely.

I'd like to have joined you at the 21st birthday party, a pre-war tea phew! Is she by any chance well in with an R.A.S. tea? Just that's John Bob as we say, it must have been a gay old party. I have a cousin who is following me a fortnight after me over here, he's a way back from where I am , but we'd like to have a do on bully and biscuit if nothing else. We're hoping to celebrate it on our 22nd birthday, you can't abroad though. We had an unofficial party one night in the guardroom, the lad was 21 and in the mush for 6 months. By a miracle there was a bit of beer going so all the guards gave him theirs. He had a decent night. Job was getting him up from sleep. He was sleeping peacefully when the orderly officer came round. The only man in Africa to get drunk off English beer. I bet he will remember his 21st birthday night, the morning after especially.

I've an idea of the sort of film Random Harvest was, we see the reviews and photos in the mags from home.

Glad to hear Ronnie was getting… By the sound of things he's up in the Shetland gales et cetera. I don't envy him, must be rough, all have their drawbacks. The Med is smashing to sail on, swimming off the side of a ship is a grand experience, you're glad to be abroad when it's like that, really marvellous. I see that it is really blue, at Gibraltar you can see the difference, and a change in the weather. On the whole the past year has been full of changes and full of variety. You envy blokes in England in one sense but it's better for soldiering out here, there's nothing to be reminding you what you're missing and time flies. You're travelling all the time and feeling that you're doing a job if it's only our millionth part of the show. In England it's all the repetition, and doing a guard on a Sat night is a tragedy, very rare this browns you off as it did. In Scotland I'd a smashing time, they are grand people. Hence a snobbish place comes from a superiority complex down there in Kent. I've been writing this letter on and off. Oh! For a pushbike. Works going down well Peggy and though we grouse we are happy doing it. Last thing you must think is we're a mournful lot because it's the dead opposite, there's always something to laugh at.

If you've any photos to spare could you send me one on Peggy please, if it isn't asking too much, it's a treasured thing abroad, here's hoping. I'm sorry if I've bored you. It's getting dark now. So cheerio! This hopes you're feeling fit and happy.

See you Soon, Thursday night—? 19—?

Love Jack xxxxxxxx

Letter writing frequency increased in 1944. This is the first one he wrote in that year expressing his usual hyperactive style, but with steroids.

T10704283 Dvr. John Hindle D Platt. 2076 Corps Transport Coy R.A.S.C. C.M.F. Jan 18th

Dear Peggy,

I have just received your very welcome letter Jan 6th, thank you very much for your kind wishes, it's very peaceful over here, so that part has been granted.

Thank you very much for the Christmas gift, it will be put to good use. I chuckled on seeing the Christmas card, I wish we were going Carol singing again. It rather startled Ken's mother that night, me and you on St Silas's Road.

I'd a jolly good Christmas as well, but nothing on the next one I hope, Ronnie must have felt he was in heaven, grand luck was that. Let's hope his next ship brings him the same good luck.

So you've bought a new iron (bike), send your old one to my address, I'd make good use of it. Tandem riding is good fun especially taking it over a nice rough road like I did, in the Lakes, Hard Knot pass in the morning with a climb up Scafell, dinner below the summit, tea in Eskdale, and a night spent on a farmhouse floor. Wartime rations eggs and bacon for breakfast, you can have a rare time. It's a date Peggy. Lilian goes Youth Hostelling occasionally, a pity you've nobody to ride with. As for Blackpool it's a poor ride, nose to the wheel knocking off your past time. Dad rides any iron nowadays, after all the insults he poured on the cyclists, it was often deserved though. It will take me many moons to get in form again. I like to mix it, carry the boots and a rucksack and walk. Go to Malham, and climb the chimney; it's simplicity itself, the more I think of it the more comes in my mind. The Trough is an easy run for an afternoon, the Longridge byways are difficult to explain. I shall have to send a letter and give you a few of my specials, in fact all come in that category. Harry and myself say that rough stuff is best, across the moors on the old tracks. Slaidburn over the fells to Wray is a classic, especially in a storm.

If ever you feel like a run ask Lillian, stay at Slaidburn Y. H. An afternoon's easy run, dancing and plenty of fun night, just the job.

The last news I had from Harry was that he was going to Jerusalem, the Lebanon is out of bounds, so his climbing leave misfired. In Kenya he went on a safari, he likes to get around the out of the way places. I wouldn't like to trust myself among the Arabs but in his case the Africans, maybe we shall manage a joint expedition up the Burma Road. As far as sleeping in the native huts that put the cap on it.

So you have been learning Frank how to dance, do you fall out? At home when Victor Sylvester came on the wireless, back went the table, Dad and Mum retreated. It wasn't often the piano was knocked over by me, maybe we would finish up with the pupil telling the instructor to learn how to dance. Needless to say she writes and tells me my next session is on how to do the fancy steps, you know what that will mean Peggy after your sufferings.

You hope that the description of your supper didn't make my mouth water, what about this, we have white bread, what a vision that must be to you. Sorry to hear the Christmas party at Tattersalls ended too soon, my old job washing up, mother never trusted me with, those white cups and etc. Shelley, isn't it? These air letters finish too quick.

Marion is on the road to, I nearly said the usual thing, she's surprised me, what did I say phew! I often wondered. I shall have to close now, and as you said, away to bed, so goodnight! See you Thursday!

Love John xxxxxx

T10704283 Dvr. John Hindle D Platt. 2076 Corps Transport Coy
R.A.S.C. C.M.F. Feb 24th

Dear Peggy,

Many thanks for your very welcome AG *(AG stands for aerogram—it was similar to an airmail letter but had two pages only to it)* Feb 7 which arrived 4 days ago. I think I had better look through it again and see what's what, I've a terrible memory for letters.

You're certainly being kept busy with Scouts, don't think I've been drinking, I mean Guides. I hope the show went down alright. I'd liked to have seen you doing your stuff, maybe I'd have put you off it. You know clapping at the wrong time and all that. Last week I was on the stage in the opera house at the nearby town of? It was an E.N.S.A. show and a bloke was on the stage cracking a whip. He asked for volunteers, so the three of us who were there went up, gosh it was dazzling. This cowboy, a London one was flicking a piece of paper out of your hand with this stock whip, that was all right but when he had the volunteers doing it, well that went a bit too far, but everything passed off alright. We have plenty of fun. I'm afraid you're liable to let things go when you're having a break from the old job. It's grand here having a rest. I'm waiting to go on a 6 day leave shortly to a rest camp, stay in bed as long as you like, food brought to you, billiards, football, clubrooms, armchairs! And a theatre and shows in the camp. No kidding I'm having an easy time now, it won't last though of course I have a soft job being a batman *(an army batman is a personal servant to a commissioned officer)*. I didn't like it at first, but it turned out to be a good job. Running around with my gaffer in a jeep every now and again. You'd enjoy it Peggy, real good fun, see a big lorry and it's a case of deciding whether to go around or under. It's the driving of a 15 horse power dodgem, toddle along at 55 m.p.h. not bad going. I hope you don't mind but after intending for the last 12 months and forgetting to tell you, I've named my truck after you. Thank goodness I hadn't to write Margaret, it took me a whole afternoon to write Peggy, and has that truck travelled? Alamein to Wapland, next order will be all names to be painted out. The Army's terrific, if that webbing isn't buckled on and a forage cap one inch over the right eye. It doesn't matter what's happening, you're liable for a telling off. Wear a comfy woolly Comforter, by Gad Sir! The war will be lost. It's all in the game though so why panic? Ever had a dehydrated dinner? They're dehydrated mad at the moment, I'm thinking of being processed myself, then I'll use a registered envelope I have to come home.

Three AG's arrived at the same time as yours. Note sorry to others. One from Lilian telling me she'd seen you at the Police Ball, yours saying you'd seen her and the manager of our other shop saying he'd seen Lilian. I believe she is hooked up to a cadet officer. If she takes him home and I'm there I'll pull her leg, if he isn't too big he'll be woofed out of it. She tells me about all her infatuations. I split my sides laughing at her letters, they're a description of the suffering girl's side of dates. At the moment she is dance mad. It's grand to hear you're all having a good time. Some letters I received, say it doesn't seem right that we should be having a good time, and you poor boys out there. Daft I call it, tragedy wouldn't be in it to come home to dear old England and find it lifeless. As for the war well why be perturbed as my old Dad says about news from Italy, old Tedeschi are wading in at Anzio. Thank the Lord I'm not there, oh! I've probably overstepped the censorship rules & regs.

I am about the part of your AG which says about the cycling attractions of Italy, it's not much cop. I had a ride up the road on a Wop (guappo) bike, my legs soon ached, that's what the Army abroad does for you, keeps you out of trim. A petrol engine will do me for the time being, what do you think of Wop land? I expect you see a lot on the pictures. Mother writes have you been to… yet, seeing it on the pictures they think all the gang is there. Tunis was a big disappointment to many who expected the flowers and the run of the town after seeing the first mad day on the newsreels.

We'd a bit of hard luck then. Never mind we'll be having some good fortune one of these days, even if it's to be a day pass into Tokyo. I absolutely dread having to go to Burma way. Let's hope it doesn't last long. The blinking war pushes itself into everything, another two or three years should see us settling down to work again. I hope to be blazing new trails on the old bike as well then, coming?

What do you say about it Peggy? When I think of the country such a lot of places come into my mind that it's a job sorting out which to take. Maybe you are the same, down by the Ribble on a hot summer's afternoon, what a king to the Italian rivers, muddy and barren with a host of olive trees by the banks. Not woods and pleasant bends, a mournful-looking cow is nowhere to be seen on the horizon over here. Italy is a beautiful country I won't dispute the fact, but it's lacking. A beautiful building in the city hides a smelly slum. Maybe there is a war on but all the same you can see what it lacks, a bit of, no a tremendous lot of the stuff a Britisher has got and that's guts. Those who toadied to Mussolini deserve a nice strong rope as a muffler. Ice cream selling is a thing they're good at, and that's about all. It's a cheap country, people who rave about a cruise and Italy only see the places they're meant to. I'm sure they've never been in the small villages and towns which are not far removed from the Arab villages, blow Italy we will have a trip to Germany instead, unless the RAF have sunk it.

It's nearly time for bed now, I'm in a former summer villa at the moment, tea in bed in the morning, straight up! The duty cook brings a brew round for the favoured few at reveille at 6.30 a.m. I arise at 7 a.m. amid grunts and groans. I'm having a good time considering the calm before a storm, it never lasts, when you receive this letter things may be different. I only hope Ronnie is doing all right, I doubt whether he will be having tea in bed, I hope he isn't browned off, you haven't to let it get you down. It's Thursday night, rather a change from those years ago—so I will sign off and warm the spring and feather bed up, hoping for sweet dreams.

Good night & God bless

Yours Love Jack
Xxxxxxx

Southern Italy as now was and is impoverished compared to Northern Italy and to most places in the United Kingdom. Dad noticed the slums. There are degrees of poverty. Blackburn had its slums, like most urban conurbations in 1930s Britain. Probably not as bad as some British places, particularly the industrial cities such as Glasgow and Liverpool. He contrasts the "guts" of the

British with those who followed fascism in Italy. Many Italians did not many giving their lives in the Spanish Civil War in the Garibaldi's—one of the many International Brigades that fought for the democratically elected Republican government against the despot—Franco. But Franco could not have won without the support of his fascist friends Hitler and Mussolini who sent soldiers and pilots to help him out. So dad and all those who fought against fascism in Italy were carrying on where the International Brigades left off. The struggle did not end with their defeat in Spain.

Prison

By now you may have realised that dad had no time for meaningless rules and regulations. Always spontaneous especially when offered an adventure, he decided to visit his cousin who was fighting in the vicinity. He broke a prohibition of disclosing his location when he wrote a letter to his cousin to make arrangements to meet up. He described being in prison—"the mush" in his letter. This is the letter in which he gave mum suggestions for the mega bike ride over the Trough of Bowland. He had nothing else to do in his prison cell—a room at the top of a castle—than fantasise about cycling over his beloved hills.

T10704283 Dvr. John Hindle D Platt. 2076 Corps Transport Coy R.A.S.C. C.M.F. April 9th Sun

Dear Peggy,

It's Easter Sunday as I write this letter, and I bet you'd never guess where I'm writing it, yes and in the mush, or bluntly, prison. "If I had the wings of a dove." I'm in for writing a letter to my cousin over here, he'd seen our lorries passed his door, told me, so I wrote back and told him where I thought he was, naming places, so I've had it. I wanted to meet up with him.

You would have laughed yesterday I came back after spending 7 days of perfect freedom in a rest camp, waiting for me was the R.P. Corporal who put me under close arrest. Later on after taking away my money, photos, razor etc. they don't want me to commit suicide, rules & regs. Well after all that, I am put on open arrest, I'm now waiting for a court martial, we shall see. It's the first time I've come up to that, orderly room is common, but a court martial, I do hope I'm not sent down for a few years.

We'll have to wait and see. I never write home about these things, they'd only worry. Trouble is I had been posted to H.Q. smashing food, but believe me I don't like it. There's nothing like getting out on the road, maybe if I use my loaf they'll post me to another platoon, san-fairian as the French say. It won't make any difference when I'm in a civvy suit. I can't help but laugh, honest I do. They've put me in a room on top of the house, a lovely view. You've even to climb a winding staircase, the turreted castle. In open arrest I don't need an escort, parole as you might say is what I'm on.

That's my latest news, so if I don't write for a while, don't blame me, I'll be digging. That's a good thing about being abroad you don't miss a night out through this.

I'd grand leave Peggy with some Navy boys, four of us and seven sailors, oldest of our lot was twenty two, we stayed in the camp all the time, canteens, cinema, theatre, clubrooms, sports, everything you needed, even waited on for food. It was lovely. We had a game of football against an army team. I played on the Navy side, we lost, score? 12—1 for the Army. They were quite a good team, we were quite a poor one by the scoring. Oh! It was terrific, we trooped on in navy blue and white, cocky as you please, kick-off we watch the ball sail in our net. Never mind it was good fun, for the spectators. Our only goal was brilliant, the opposing goalie stood at one side to let it in. I'd better change the subject from what "I did" that's three pages already.

You will probably be at B'pool now seeing as its Easter Sunday, here's hoping you aren't having the same weather, it's raining hard at the moment, when the sun shines it's really great. I can just imagine you stepping onto the floor at the "Tower", I'm stepping off it onto my bed soon, if I'm not careful this letter will be full of questions you know. Is the Tower still there etc, etc. As soon as you think of someone at a place you're seeing it in your mind. I'll be on the Tower floor some year soon and maybe my mind will slip back over the years to a little white washed room top of a house in Italy, tears will come in my eyes, those were the days, some hopes! That's the worst of a war, it upsets things, but then being locked up or politely confined to a place across the drink is saving you the torture of having me stepping on your toes. If you did go dancing I can only hope you'd have partners as heavy as feathers. There's nothing like hearing of someone at home having a good time, certainly brightens things up over here, doesn't mean to say I'm not. It's been all right up to now, but there's one thing missing, a Thursday night date, that is the objective just plain and simple—home. It's everything, and it does you good to be away. You know I've not one single thing to complain about. I don't include having to parade and etc. I mean the big things. Good health, friends, parents, I'm fortunate, aren't I entirely?

The part of the letter giving instructions about the bike ride was at this point in the letter, but has been taken out because it has already been read, that's if you are reading the book from the front to the back.

I think I'd better sign off hadn't I? Ten pages phew! Must have bored you stiff. It's passed the evening on for me, so I will get in bed. Hoping your Easter went off with a swing, <u>do</u> have a good time. Let's hope we are all making things move soon, cheerio!

Your very sincere friend
Love Jack
xxxxxx

The letter expresses dad's personality so accurately. Hardly anything ever gets him down and that is the secret of his long and happy life. He just makes the most of any situation he is in and always finds something to laugh and smile about.

Moving North

The initial advance up the eastern side of Italy's lower boot was relatively straightforward in military terms with capture of the Adriatic port of Bari and the movement over the flatter lands around Foggia. Progress was steady until the combination of rivers and mountains impeded the advance, natural obstacles used by the Germans to develop their defensive lines. After crossing the River Sangro which claimed many lives and injuries, the push continued by various sections of the 8th Army. It really was a multinational force comprised of Nepalese Gurkhas, a Jewish Brigade from Palestine, Irishmen, South Africans and soldiers from the now Commonwealth countries of Australia, Canada, India and New Zealand. The advance slowed mainly because of extended supply lines, winter weather causing the rivers to flood and the land turned to mud. The 8th pressed on, under Montgomery, determined to keep the front moving forward. The next river to be crossed was the Moro.

Working closely with the Canadians, he enjoyed their informality and absence of snobbery, rank and elitism which characterised some parts of the British Army. For a time he was attached to the Princess Patricia's Canadian Light Infantry, called "Princess Pats" for short. He remembers going to take orders from a Canadian Captain of Princess Pats whom he saluted and addressed as "Sir". "Don't call me Sir, call me Harry" was the reply. A lot of the men he fought with from Canada hailed from British Columbia, working as lumberjacks back home. Wanting dad to emigrate to Canada after the war they told him about their life cutting down trees. His Canadian buddies spoke of a good life of parties and socialising when the snow lay too deep to bring down timber in the winter, and the long days in the summer when they stayed out in the forests. It obviously attracted him, being a lover of the outdoors, but he never went.

So many rivers run down from the Apennine hills cutting across the rugged land to the east. The River Moro is not a wide river but it is at the bottom of a deep valley requiring a bridge to cross the ravine. The Royal Engineers worked through the night in rivers with icy water up to their waists to build vital bridges with as much secrecy and silence as possible. Once the bridge was built dad drove over the river in support of the Princess Pats who had made a successful advance to take a strategic village just before the next main goal which was Ortona. The going had been tough. Just before the start of the assault across the Moro and on to the village a rallying call had been made by the commanding officer to his troops reassuring them they were better equipped having armoured cars whereas the Germans had horse and carts. Because of the waterlogged conditions the Germans' transport performed better, horses being able to cope with the mud whereas the heavy armoured cars became stuck and going was slow.

Ortona was a small port considered to be an important target by British General Montgomery. Capturing its harbour would allow ships carrying vital supplies to dock and offload their cargo so reducing the reliance on long lines of transport travelling up from Bari. Heavily fortified by the Germans who had dug in ready for the assault, it took 8 days to capture and a quarter of all of Canadian soldiers who perished during World War II died at this battle and in the fighting to capture Ortona. Mouse holing was used to move from house to house. This is a tactic where a hole is blown in the inside walls of buildings, so saving the attacker from being out in the street where he was an easy moving target for a sniper in a building overlooking that street. The hole allowed the attacker an element of surprise—after blowing open the hole, the attacker threw in grenades before entering the adjacent building with a machine gun blasting out. Eight long days of fighting room to room, building to building clearing street by street. War is gruesome.

Capturing Ortona meant that the Gustav defensive line constructed by the Germans had been smashed on it east side. The Gustav line stretched from just north of the outlet of the Garigliano River into the Mediterranean Sea, about 100 miles south of Rome through the Apennine Mountains to the mouth of the Sangro River on the Adriatic coast in the east. The campaign did not have such positive results in the west where the seemingly endless battles to take Monte Cassino brought the advance to a halt.

Winter weather of rain, snow and ice held the rest of the 8th Army located to the east of the mountain range. Relentless mud demoralised dad at times when the wheels of his lorry became stuck. Dad was always brilliant at driving in any conditions in any place, techniques and skills learnt through his army driving experiences. With a growing family a Ford van was purchased which he fit out for basic camping. Later he moved up market to VW camper vans. He would relive his youthful days of driving over Italian and Austrian mountain passes by always seeking a tricky road in the UK. The steeper the gradient the better, especially if it had some difficult hairpins—so Hard Knott and Wrynose were his favourites in the Lake District, with Honister and Kirkstone coming somewhat behind. A love of traversing up the steep sides of mountains could have come from an experience of a child when he went in a wagonette over Kirkstone Pass. Kirkstone pass is the route between the lakes of Windermere and Ullswater. A horse drawn wagon fitted with seats it was a form of public transport to link the two lakes. A steep gradient made it impossible for cart horses pulling a wagon laden with goggled eyed tourists. The only way for the wagon to reach the top of the pass was for the passengers to get off and walk; and sometimes they even had to push the wagon. Kirkstone Pass steep enough for horses and cyclists alike is not too much of a challenge for the motorist, Hard Knott being a relentless 1 in 3 gradient, in old money, afflicted with some tortuous bends is always a challenge, especially on non-motorised two wheels which dad used to ride over on his bike.

Dad particularly enjoyed the Bealach na Ba, in English the Pass of the Cattle in Strathcarron, Wester Ross. Driving over one summer to camp at the end of the road destination of Applecross it nearly caused a family move to the west coast of Scotland. At that time there was only one way in and one way out over the pass. This was before the coastal road to Shieldag and Torridon was built. Peggy his wife refused to go back over the Bealach na Ba saying dad would have to sell up everything in Lancashire and move up to Applecross. She quickly changed her mind as a huge storm ripped through and destroyed the tent where we children were sleeping that night. The next day the return journey was made over the pass, with mum hiding under a blanket the whole way. It is not a frightening drive at all—just a narrow road with passing places—like many Highland routes, requiring care, patience and a competent driver as dad always was.

Dad shared comradery with all the nations who fought alongside him. The Australians provided amusement and relief giving much banter. He loved their easy going fearless, tough, straight talking characters. He heard about an Australian officer who wanted to take his two non-commissioned mates into the officer's mess, but was refused because they were not officers. He solved the problem by giving each of them a pip to wear on their uniform temporarily upgrading them so that they could be allowed into the officer's mess. It offered much better dining and alcohol than experienced by the rank and file soldiers.

"Kiwis"—New Zealand soldiers, South Africans, Indians—came to fight and serve King and the Empire. So much gratitude to these men who came from such faraway places. Dad hated the way that American black soldiers were treated. They were segregated from white American soldiers. He and his pals judged people on whether or not they had the same values as them—ready to give a hand, muck in and help, whether they were decent and friendly—not by rank or skin colour. African American men had their own fighting units, separate from the whites. South African black men suffered even greater discrimination. They were prohibited from fighting by their racist government, but allowed to contribute to the war effort by being members of work parties who would carry out tasks such as erecting buildings or shelters, construction of bridges, any work that did not involve fighting. It is hard to find words to describe such dreadful, discriminatory treatment just because of skin colour. These were horrid times and continued to be so in America and South Africa for people who are not white. Even with the abolition of segregation and apartheid people of colour continue to face discrimination and hatred especially in certain states of America. Other countries, including the United Kingdom, still have people and institutions tainted and infected by racism. Improvements there have been in the last 75 years in UK from legislation, policy and cultural changes, but racist behaviour and attitudes continue and there is still much work to be done. The destructive legacy of colonialism and treating people differently just because of who they are, what they look like or where they come from continues.

Dad thought that entering the Common Market in 1973 was a kick in the teeth to the countries he had fought with in the war. He expected the import of products from these countries, such as New Zealand lamb and dairy produce to decline because of the need to comply with the rules made in Brussels. Eventually like most people he accepted and became used to the change.

Dad was no great hero. He was like millions who just did what they had to do to defeat an ideology based on a belief that there was a super race—a Master race that was top of the hierarchy of all other races. This Master race should rule the world, all other races being subservient to this Nazi ideology. These warped beliefs continue to this day. They offend against the best words ever said—"That we should love our neighbours as we love ourselves and do unto others as we would have them do unto us." These words found in the New Testament are now reflected in universal Human Rights law. Such sources of law originate from Jewish law such as the Ten Commandments—Thou shall not kill; Thou shall not steal, or from the Qur'an, the Holy Book of Islam which amongst other commands requires a follower of the faith to give a set proportion of income to charity, to obviously help the less fortunate and those in need. Other religions such as Sikhism believe in equality, justice and serving your fellow human being. All these men who came to fight from different religious, ethnic, cultural backgrounds had the one aim to defeat the abomination that people were not equal, but could be tortured and murdered or enslaved just because they did not have certain physical features that deemed them to be a member of the Master or Aryan race.

We who live now are so grateful for the sacrifice of so many people from the former colonies. The Sangro River cemetery is the second largest Allied forces cemetery in Italy. 2617 soldiers are buried there. But more than that died. Around 500 Indians were cremated in accordance with their Hindu faith so have no grave to mark their sacrifice.

One of the saddest times of dad's service was when two of his platoon were killed in Italy by a shell—one was a really well liked sergeant and the younger brother of dad's mate Ted Butler who held the rank of corporal. There were many traumatic tragedies, death and destruction that he had to live through and personally process, but the telling of this event always causes him some pain in remembering. One of his close pals who he had started off with in North Africa, a driver like him was Ted Butler. Dad has an album of the photographs he took with his prohibited camera. One of them shows a beaming man with a stand of thick, dark, hair on top, Ted Butler. Ted had a brother—their sergeant, also in the same Service Corps. One day some shells dropped just in front of where dad was driving. Ted Butler was behind him in his wagon. Ted Butler's brother lay still by the side of the road, with no visible injuries, other than a trickle of blood at the corner of his mouth. Dad said to Ted—"You drive on. I will see to him." Dad feared his brother was dead. He wanted to save one of his best mates the dreadful experience of this realisation. Dad knew looking at him that there was no hope. It had been an instantaneous death, the shock wave blast from the shell had gone straight through Ted's brother's brain turning it to an internal bloody mess.

During 1944 the 8th Army pushed on up the east coast of Italy eventually reaching Cesena, 25 miles inland from Rimini until the last campaign started. The Irish Brigade was in dad's division at that point in the war and were very enjoyable company. The celebration of St Patrick's Day on 17 March 1945 was uproarious. There was a football match, between the Irish and the rest and the RAF flew low over the football ground in salute demonstrating their flying skills in the process. Dad described the celebrations as "A right wild time. We all had a good booze up drinking lots of Italian wine." The Irish Brigade included in their ranks Free State Irish who volunteered to fight Hitler, in contrast to others in their own country who supported the German war machine. These brave Irish men travelled through Liverpool from Ireland to England. Wearing their British uniform on leave when home in Ireland made them targets for any Irish nationalist who hated the British, so they were careful to put on their civilian clothes before catching the boat home across the Irish Sea. It was still known in the clannish, tight knit communities that characterised much of Ireland in the 1940s that they had fought against Hitler. Some heaped praise on these soldiers, others shunned them.

Whilst enjoying the break in Cesena, news came through that his regiment would be moved to Cairo for a full refit. Moving out of the theatre of fighting even though it would require a sail across the Mediterranean with the risk of attack from submarines, dad's love of exploration and visiting new places quelled his fear of being hit by a torpedo when stuck in the lower depths of a ship. Any hopes or fears he had were in vain. It never happened. Dad never knew why, but found out the reason many years later from a local landowner, fellow parishioner, and neighbour. Brigadier Charles Edward Tryon-Wilson was also in the 8th Army in Italy; at the time he was just Brigadier Tryon. He was in 8th army in Italy, but was on the western side of the Apennine peninsular where he fought at Monte Cassino and was awarded the Distinguished Service Order for his gallantry. Dad did not know him then, only making his acquaintance years later when he and mum retired to the South Lakes. In conversation with the Brigadier sharing their experiences of the 8th Army campaigns dad found out that the proposed plan to go to Cairo for a refit was a smoke screen. He would never have cast his eyes on the pyramids. The real destination was the Russian front. Churchill wanted a British contingent to fight with the Russians. The 8th Army were experienced fighters, but fortunately for dad Turkey would not give permission for Brits to go through the Bosporus and Dardanelles to access the Black Sea most probably to land in the area where Dimitri Karsazky who you will read about later, was born and raised, or possibly on the shores of Romania or Bulgaria. Certainly the weather would have been much colder and the conditions harsher than in Italy, so Turkey saved dad from a bitterly freezing cold winter and possibly much else on the Russian Front.

Only a rule breaker of what in his judgement he perceived as a nonsense regulation, dad must have agreed with most of Army dicta as he was only charged with one offence in his entire army career which landed him in "The Mosh". Possibly other breaches went undetected, concealing his potential misdemeanours, but there was another instance when he was found out and given a much tamer punishment than being locked up in an Italian tower. Ever the writer of long letters he wrote to his Uncle Jim, the Blackburn librarian, saying that his commanding officer, a Major Butcher was never seen on the front line leading his troops, always staying way behind his men waving to them from his staff car as they marched forward. All correspondence was scrutinised because such details, it was said, could be intercepted by the enemy and used against the allied forces. His letter criticising his cowardly major was read; the letter had also described some Roman ruins in Italy that dad had seen. Major Butcher found him in breach of the regulation that careless writing about ancient ruins could costs lives and dad was given a punishment which sounded quite tame. He had to report to the Sergeant at 5.00 pm in the evening where he was given a job such as peeling a large amount of potatoes. This was no trouble for a man who was used to hard work. Developing a speedy spud peeling technique came in very useful for the rest of his life as he nearly always prepped the vegetables for the family evening meal on his return from work.

General Alexander was in charge of the North African and Italian campaigns that dad fought in, becoming the top man in charge of all military operations in the Mediterranean region. This commander was well liked because he looked after his troops. One example was his order that best buildings be taken over for NAAFI. The Navy, Army and Air Force Institutes is an organisation established by the government to organise and operate opportunities for recreation, respite and relaxation for British service men and women. A sanctuary from the war for the junior ranks, Dad experienced the NAAFI as a supportive club. They were staffed by the WRVS ("the Women's Royal Voluntary Service") who were made up of mature women who would give a soldier a cup of tea and a chance to talk. Dad never came into contact with female staff working in secretarial, administrative or support roles other than the Women's Royal Voluntary Service.

Now it would be called a "Talking therapy", when it was the most natural way for a soldier to offload his worries and fears, and feel the care and concern of a mother type figure. One of the reasons that the UK has the highest reliance on anti-depressant medication could be that community ties and support systems have reduced. The family unit has become fragmented with so many societal changes since the 1940s and 1950s when most, certainly working class families, lived in the same neighbourhood, very often in the same or adjacent streets. All of dad's family lived in a small area, less than a quarter of a mile across.

There are a lot of myths believed to be truths. People believe what they are told in the media. For instance I would expect that most people would believe that Vera Lynn's singing the White Cliffs of Dover was heard by every soldier, sailor and airman from Torquay to Timbuctoo. Not true. There were no record players at the front; there were no radios. Only tanks had radios. So dad never heard those rich, tones of Vera trilling out her message of reassurance that he would meet those he had left back in Blighty again. For a long time the 8th Army even in its rest and recuperation stations did not have record players or radios. But then Mrs Mountbatten (General Mountbatten's wife) arranged for the provision of such equipment so weary soldiers could have the pleasure of listening to the radio and music on the gramophone, as it was then called.

There was little patience with and respect for higher ranks who did not appreciate the difficulties of the prolonged and interminable campaign fought by the 8th Army. One such instance dad described was a mechanic from dad's platoon who operated a mobile workshop. He was working under a wagon in the thick Italian mud when what dad described as a "twit of a major" asked what the mechanic was doing. The mechanic replied with choice language; he was that fed up with struggling to keep the vehicles in working order, dealing with awful conditions. "What the f... do you think I am doing?" was the reply.

The Major, wisely, just walked on, realising he had asked a stupid question. It was obvious what his sapper was doing—a better and more supportive question would have been to find out if he could do anything to help.

Dad enjoyed the sun of an Italian summer and some sightseeing as this next letter to mum shows, before the final push towards victory.

T10704283 Dvr. John Hindle D Platt. 2076 Corps Transport Coy
R.A.S.C. C.M.F. July 13th – 14th

Dear Peggy,

Thanks a lot for your very welcome airmail sent on the 8th, I believe, hard luck your holiday will just be ending now. Your letter just arrived at the right time. Yes I was feeling really cheesed off, I think this war has browned all of us off. Anyhow I've woke up from dreams of years and more before we crash into Blighty. I give myself no less than six months, it will soon pass. If I was home now the brass hats would be sending the unfortunates into the Norman shooting gallery. I'm thankful I'm not unfortunate. Gosh I'm sorry to have told all that with opinions.

I'd better look through your air letter , I'm sorry I didn't write more often, but I didn't know, whether I was on my head or my tail, I'm just about on a normal basis now, sleeping well, it's a lazy life. I was glad to hear Lilian's boy was a good sort. I hope I haven't hurt her, a letter puts words in a different meaning. I must have taken the leg pull too far, I will have to put her mind at rest. You know how it is, teasing her. I feel real guilty, poor kid. She sends me photos out and I can certainly see a difference as you say, she is quite a young lady. Your letters aren't censored, I think it is only military mail which is blue pencilled. The names of places passed alright, I wouldn't have minded a trip through Hellifield to Malham especially. I've done a little hiking in the evenings around here. It is certainly lovely in places over in Italy, but beautiful scenery means so much more work for an army, all the same it is well worth the effort to get out and do a spot of climbing or else a few miles across country. Three of us generally go out together, a former Liverpool stevedore and a headmaster from Stoke way, it's surprising what a mixture we are.

I only hope you are having the same kind of weather as we are enjoying in Italy, it's been sunny and hot for weeks all the time. I've only worn a singlet and shorts, bar the evenings when slacks and shirts have to be worn. Maybe you'd find us playing cricket, I can't get within a yard of the stumps at bowling, and I'm terrible.

I don't think I told you I've seen Naples and Pompei, a little grey wisp of smoke was coming out of the crater of Vesuvius. Censorship restrictions don't apply in that line so I won't get whipped in for a month or two. Naples isn't a patch on our Naples of the North, Llandudno. I doubt if there is another place in the world with as much vice to the square mile as that city. There's plenty of shops selling luxuries at crazy prices. I wouldn't give the wops a cent of English money if I could help it, we would need to be liberated if we paid what is asked for stuff, and they've never earned as much money.

Well I'm near the end of this letter and I'm not at all satisfied with it, feeling as if I've bored you to tears, my apologies Peggy, hoping you had a good time and thanks a lot for taking up precious holiday time to drop me a line. I didn't mind getting alarmed! Hoping I can work these crosses off!— You alarmed?

Cheerio Yours John xxxxx

Then it started to rain and the sun baked earth turned to mud. The letter tells of a rescue by motorbike of his men under fire who had been left to die by their commanding officer. The Corporal disobeyed an order, jumped on his motorbike and saved them. Now that is real heroism.

T10704283 Dvr. John Hindle D Platt. 2076 Corps Transport Coy R.A.S.C. C.M.F. Sept 21st – 22nd

Dear Peggy,
I am writing to reply to your very welcome airmail which arrived yesterday, sent on the 19th. It's certainly great getting mail from you.

In another day or two I'll be getting a new truck, so I will have to christen it Peggy II or is it better as before? I'm sorry to lose the one I have now, she's a real good barrow. You'd be surprised how you become fond of an army vehicle, all the same I hope this is the last I have. It's no cop this weather, the last two days it's just poured down. I'll never cease to wonder at the way land turns to mud. We've had some fun out of it all the same, I'm sure the wops must think we're mad, this evening there was a hectic mudslinging match, it's good fun when you're in overalls. All the same rain is very annoying at times like this. Another couple of months should see a change in things, the news is certainly good, it may not be long before all is finished and we are all home again.

Could you take an order for a civvy suit? Or does that line not come under dressmaking? It is certainly a useful thing to learn, it takes me all my time stitching on a button, why the army don't put zip fasteners on clothes like a B.D. *(battledress)* beats me. I would sack the whole lot of girls who stitch button on our clothes if I'd my way, it's a wonder the buttons hold on at all.

By the time this letter arrives your dance will perhaps be over with, here's hoping it went down well. I bet the blokes from work will be very thankful for a bit of extra do ray me, (money).

You try and tell me you aren't doing too bad with the guides. I think it's going some thirty of you, you'll be needing a crown next. What is the next rank from captain in the guides? Finished with camping for the year? We haven't! The tents the army use for tropical weather would be ideal for home. Padded tent, white inside, blue on the outside, a good wide fly, blue inside and white on the top. Warm in winter, cool in summer. I dare you may have seen pictures of them. Maybe when the war is ended you'll be able to buy them cheap.

Harvest festival reminds me of the way the Ities celebrate it. About a month ago the countryside was lit up by bonfires. It was a pretty sight miles away across the hills and valleys with fires, every farm had one, just like an out size birthday cake.

The Mohammedans will be celebrating Ramadan about this time, fasting till the sun goes down and then as soon as the sun drops below the horizon away go all the Arabs to eat their couscous and to drink strong coffee. I've joined them at times, a dignified race in a quiet way.

I was pleased to hear you had met Harry and Olive. Mother tells me he's turned all varsity style in his talk. I was sorry to hear that. He's a good lad though. I'm looking forward to having some arguments with him, personally a lot of things about the Church I'm against, it's very narrow minded in many ways. I've no room to talk but there's too many trimmings about the core of the church, and they always seem to be in debt, raising money for organs they've bought. Never think of getting in the capital first. Whether you're R.C., C.E. or any other denomination you're never taught to do wrong, that is about the one and only part which hasn't changed since Christ's time. Churches and cathedrals are refreshing, but there again why not put a large percentage of the money needed to build modern cathedrals

216

in hospitals. I would rather give money to the Royal Infirmary than put it in a collection box to extend Blackburn's Cathedral, That is only an example. As for worshipping there's more sincerity in a voluntary church parade before or after any do's, then you will ever find in a church. The way I see it is the way a person treats its neighbour, a corporal of ours is an example.

He refused to obey an order so he could save a few of his men pinned down by a Spandau nest, he rode back and forward with a motorbike to bring his boys out. He was told it was useless to go, ordered to stay put, but he went in and out five times. That's Christianity in its finest form, everybody are not called on to do that, but you get down to the foundation of it all at times. I'd better sign off now Peggy sorry if I've bored you.

Cheerio Love Jack xxxxxx

Progress up the boot of Italy was slow, the 1944/1945 winter hampering any offensive. Bologna was a sticky target, not able to be taken until the spring of the final year of the war, so dad waited just south of this city for improved weather, releasing the final push which came quickly. The 8th Army reached the River Po on St George's day 1945 and dad crossed it on a pontoon bridge which he described as a strange sensation, his wagon bobbing up and down as he moved over each supporting boat. Quickly replaced by a Bailey bridge—an ingeniously engineered structure which could be unfolded at the river bank—dad made a few crossings of this river bringing up the troops and supplies. The ending of hostilities came 6 days after the first crossing of the Po on the 29th April when the Germans surrendered. Dad thought that both of the opposing commanders in chiefs had just said we have had enough and the fighting stopped. This is dad's desire to see the ending as not a triumph by the Allies over the Germans. It his characteristic enduring ability to forgive and search out the good in people. In reality, Germany was finished—Hitler taking the cyanide pill and gun to his head the following day on 30 April 1945.

Victory in Europe day came 8 days later, dad described it as a damp squib. It did not come as a surprise because the fighting was already over in Italy. It was celebrated with a bottle of wine which one of the lads had kept for the occasion. A short toast and handshakes all round and that was it. No dancing on the Mall; no drunken carousing. Still in service, still with jobs to do and still with danger all around. Dad described a fear that set in after the end of the war. A fear that having survived so much that death would come with the careless stepping on a land mine or driving over one. A cruel twist of fate. He was worried about booby traps and other threats that were yet to emerge which kept the 8th army ready for combat. Terrifying dangers lay all around.

One night he was driving his lorry down an Italian lane. It was time to stop for the night to get some sleep but before he did so he went on a foraging expedition. It was dark, but by the faint light of the moon he had seen tomato vines in the fields either side of his vehicle. He thought I will have some of those tomatoes fried up for my breakfast tomorrow. Fresh fruit and vegetables were not a common feature of his army rations so he went off into the fields to pick some tomatoes. He returned to the lorry and bedded down for the night. The next morning had a surprise for him. In the light of day he saw signs warning that the tomato plantations were full of mines. His tomato scrumping the night before took place in a mine field. He did say the tomatoes were delicious even though he was nearly killed picking them.

Spring saw his wagon motor northwards where he stayed just outside Venice in Mestre from where it was a short journey to explore the canals, piazzas and buildings of this incredible Italian city. After that they moved on to Treviso a short journey north of Venice where orders to go armed into the city were made because large numbers of Italian partisans were celebrating victory and the Allies were concerned that they may try and take control over the country. Dad understood why he had to carry his rifle, but he was uncomfortable in doing so probably because he wished to join in with the celebrations. He remembered that the partisans all wore colourful neckerchiefs.

These are the two letters he wrote immediately after the end of fighting. He had written other letters to mum in early 1945 where he had declared his love for her. They are very personal, emotional letters so they are not included. The young girl he had first met many years ago at Aunty Lucy's New Year's party blossomed into a bright and beautiful woman. During the war they were tentatively courting as the letter to his sister telling how Peggy hoped that dad could join her at her employer's dance in November 1942 showed. Understandably she wanted to take dad to her employer's ball as he is a fabulous dancer, despite denials in his letters to mum. He never stood on her toes. Peggy went alone or chose a different partner to accompany her to dances. Letters between them continued to find their way across the seas during dad's time away in Africa and Europe, but dad finally declared to her that she was the only one he could ever love.

T10704283 Dvr. John Hindle D Platt. 2076 Corps Transport Coy R.A.S.C. C.M.F. May 4th 1945

My Dear Peggy,

All my thanks for your very welcome letter with the good news that Ronald was out of danger. It's very nice of the matron to send you a letter as well, he would be well looked after. Let's hope there is no more bad news. Glad you twigged the answer to that riddle, maybe you've heard more about it since, Lilian won't know the answer, please tell her when you see her.

It was funny reading your letter and I came to the place where you said the news is great, "We had just heard of Jerry surrendering to us over here", it's hard to believe, Lady Astor's D Day Dodgers started first and finished first, everybody feels quite proud. The good old P.B., I have earned it. The second time a Jerry army has surrendered, it sank into their thick skulls at last who is the boss. I wouldn't like to go through it all again though, all bad things come to an end as well as good ones.

You can guess what I'm sweating on like everybody else, the quicker the ending, maybe a faster return home. It can't be long before the whole issue ends. We've even got a brand-new football today, things are looking up.

This afternoon we had an inter-platoon football match, they last half an hour, four small teams in a knockout competition, the names are drawn out of the hat to make a team. Everyone joins in, a staff sergeant had a busted nose, you ought to have heard the mock sympathy showed to him. I'm having a good time now working hard and playing hard, and sleeping like a log under canvas. It would be nice to give your company a few good tents. Maybe you've seen them, three poles hold up the roof, tent is padded keeping out the cold and heat, the fly is also twin layered, a swell tent. Living with the cook there's always tea in bed at reveille, how do you like that? The only complaint is I can't stay in bed till 10 AM when the sun is nice and warm. Then after all it is chilly washing and shaving at 7 AM, half an hour after reveille. Maybe I'm being spoilt.

You certainly would have to go a long way, as you say to find a park like our own, I've still to see one as good. It will be grand to see nice lawns and flowers again, the Italians never bother with such things as gardens. They just seem to work for bare existence, it is not a land of milk and honey as people used to think.

I don't think there is anything else to write about, maybe we will be able to send letters same as you do at home, no need for censoring. I'll be glad when there is no need to watch what you write about. Some day we will have no need to write letters, be a change.

Well I'll sign off now Peggy, hoping you've still better news of Ronald. Cheerio!

All my fondest love Jack

xxxxxxxxx

T10704283 Dvr. John Hindle D Platt. 2076 Corps Transport Coy
R.A.S.C. C.M.F. May 9th 1945

My Dear Peggy,

All my thanks for your very welcome letter which arrived yesterday V.E. day. I was reading it at 3 AM this morning, after being out rather too long for my liking, driving. This morning being a holiday I stayed in bed till twelve, tonight I'm on guard, really it's V.E. day today isn't it? Ending one minute past midnight. It's certainly grand to know it's all over with, as far as Jerry goes, but I can't believe it's true. Being in Blighty now must be smashing. Over here there were a few impromptu fireworks. Flare lights going off all over the place, what a change. A week or two ago the same things wouldn't look pretty to a lot of blokes.

Some boys at a place where I was yesterday were celebrating, fishing in ponds with dynamite, quite good fun but a wasteful way to fish, we had a good time.

It's certainly grand to hear your Ronald can now write home, Penicillin is certainly marvellous stuff.

I know the Frank Pennell family well. He used to teach me at night school years ago, he's a decent chap. As I write this letter I'm dressed in one pair of thin cotton underpants two identity discs on a piece of string and a pair of gym shoes. It's looking hot, good training for the Jap do. A nice thick ice cream sandwich would go down well now and then a tea, set out on a nice white tablecloth, with jelly, blancmange, trifle, thick cream on top, lashings of crisp lettuce, lamb and mint sauce, and pickled onions.

The finish of Harry and Olive's affair was mutual, they're both good friends.

Maybe you're right about going home to be disillusioned, I certainly hope we are not Peggy. Now it is all over it makes you feel it may not be long before we meet again. In the army it's best to build on nothing, a war ends but work doesn't and I can't help but feel it will be quite a while before I'm home again. Naturally I'm hoping that overseas service comes down to 3 years, if so that means six months more to do which will soon pass, we can only wait and see.

I'm glad you don't smoke Peggy maybe it is old-fashioned of me but I can never have patience with the girl who does. I doubt if I'll have time for a big majority of girls back home, and I'm not the only one. Phew! We do have them in the old country, a foreigner is like a red rag to a bull, they love variety. You'll properly tell me off but they're my opinions.

Well I'm at the end of the paper so I had better sign off and write two more letters before tea. Hoping everything is as grand your end is mine.

Cheerio! All my Love Jack
xxxxxxxxx

The surrender of Germany did not lead to the disbanding of the 8th Army. The Allies had occupied Europe; its future control had to be resolved and Churchill with his foresight and wisdom knew it was vital to keep his army in place should another war emerge from the one that had just ended. But dad had to face this alarming prospect of never returning permanently to civilian life but remaining a fighting soldier for an indefinite period. Leave home was an unknown. He had to keep on working.

No leave home for the soldiers of the 8th Army until the many months after the VE day ceasefire but there had been rest camps in Italy.

Dad told me about the rest camps including the one he wrote about in his letter to mum when he played football for a navy. "I went to one in Bari—no discipline in the rest camp but we had to behave outside, which we always did anyway. The next rest camp was in Florence in 1944 for a few days. Then there would be parades and other formal events in the rest camp which was a bit of palaver when all you wanted to do was to get away from military routine. I was often glad to get back to my lorry and mates. It was a free and easy life in the 8th Army, apart from when we were getting shelled or shot at, but that became part of normal life for us. It was just the way it was."

Such incredible resilience shown by him. But he was not the exception. He was not a hero. It is what everyone did. They got on with it. They were not cowed or beaten by fear or anxiety about their situation. They did not complain or moan. There was an enemy to be defeated.

Austria

The next stage of his journey ever northwards took him into the Alps to the city of Villach, in Austria. A beautiful, mountainous country, he immediately fell in love with it. Large parts of Austria had been left untouched by the scars of war. In the east of Austria Russian forces had occupied territories taking the capital Vienna in April 1945, but elsewhere there were no remnants of bloody battles, no dangerous mines or other hidden munitions. Life became more relaxed among the snowy Alpine peaks; there was less worry about dying from a random encounter with a fanatical SS soldier still intent on fighting on despite the capitulation of Germany. Dad described a day out he organised for his mates.

"When I was stationed at Villach I decided to arrange a grand day out for the lads. I researched the options by having a bit of a nosey when driving around in my 1500 weight truck, the smaller one. I saw a cable car going up the mountain by the side of Lake Ossiach. I parked up by the lower station and got on the cable car. It was the Kanzelbahn that took me to the village of Gerlizen which is a small village on top of the mountain overlooking the lake and the surrounding countryside. The villagers used the cable car as their main form of transport up and down the mountain.

"On getting back to the Unit where we were stationed a mile or two outside of Villach near the River Drau, I told my mates I will take you out for a trip out up the mountains. So they all got in my 3 ton lorry and I drove to the Kanzelbahn. They liked going up in the cable car but when we got up they weren't interested in the magnificent views. They wanted to know where the beer was!"

His pals not sharing his love of exploration of wild places, were only interested in finding the local alcohol.

"We went hunting deer in the forest, to get fresh meat. One of the lads had a hunting rifle given to him by an Austrian. We were down by the river and this lad saw a deer. He was a countryman and had spotted it. He had been brought up to shoot deer. The captain of the platoon joined us but he had brought his tommy gun which is an automatic weapon. The Captain did not have chance to shoot it so we kept well behind him. It was too dangerous—him letting off a machine

223

gun. The Captain made too much noise. He had no idea. The deer were shot by the chap who knew what he was doing.

"I skinned and gutted it. We gave it the cook house and ate fresh venison that night. At the end of war the Austrians were desperately short of food and hunted the deer themselves. Our 8th Army unit had a party for the children from our rations so the local children at least had a good meal. Having eaten the venison we had much more we could give away. The children would come and collect what we had left over to take home. We did without food ourselves many times— children would come out especially in Italy hungry and we would give them our rations. We had some German soldiers, prisoners of war who were attached to us. They said that in Denmark they had eaten good food, Danish bacon, telling us it was a great place to be stationed in."

"The German prisoners of war given to us, to do all the labouring. They just joined in with us, ate with us. We became pals, all mucked in together. Many of them were the ones who had been on the Eastern front fighting their way through Hungary from Crimea. They had had a tough time. Their guns had jammed from overheating—there were more Russians than bullets to kill them. The German soldiers we were with hated the SS because of their superior, arrogant attitude. It was free and easy in Villach. Loose discipline, after the war had ended."

Dad is a thinker and often reflected on his war experience. Of all his recollections this next one was one of the most disturbing to hear about. It originates from the ongoing fight for the peace after the end of World War II. War might not have ceased, it could have continued, but this time against the Soviet Union now enlarged through its occupation of lands to its west. The prospect of continuing war must have been so unnerving. Just when you think you and you loved ones are safe and no longer at risk of being shot at or bombed or hurt, the possibility of further war menacingly looms up. This war would have most likely have deployed atomic weapons to conquer the seemingly inexhaustible supplies of Russian soldiers who Stalin had mercilessly sent to the front line. But when dad overheard this conversation it was before the explosions of the nuclear bombs at Hiroshima and then Nagasaki. This was overheard after when working around Klagenfurt where he was then stationed.

"What shook me after the war and made me think was what I had heard when working as a driver in the 8th Army car section. It certainly made me a bit frightened about whether I would ever return home to Blackburn and England. More war was on the cards. It would have been us up against our previous Allies, the Russians. Our propaganda in the war continually reported how great the Russians were during the war; no doubt their involvement saved us. Their sacrifice which meant our survival was devastating. At the end of the war when we ended up in Austria I was in 8th Army car section—a nice little number. I was responsible for driving a staff car. I was based at Klagenfurt and my job was to drive the Colonel of the Lancashire Fusiliers. Klagenfurt was near the frontier with those various countries called the Balkans before the war. These different lands which are now separate independent countries called Slovenia, Croatia, Serbia, Montenegro had previously been united as one country—Yugoslavia by Tito. Tito had led the partisans against the Germans. He was a communist but not part of Soviet Russia. He wanted a country separate from any other power. At the end of the war the ownership of the port of Trieste which lay in Italy was a bone of contention. Tito wanted Trieste so he could have the facilities of a safe harbour. The Allies did not want to give up Trieste to Tito and there was lots of political hoo-ha about it.

"I heard my colonel briefing this other officer as I was driving them. I was a staff car driver. He said that the British and Americans did not know the situation with regard to Stalin's intentions. They were unaware whether Stalin was going to back Tito in his claim for Trieste; if he is I heard the Colonel say then the British and the American were quite prepared to go to war with the Russians. They would not relinquish Trieste to the Russians. I also heard that there was an American armoured division coming down to support the 8th Army but that we would be cut off in that part of Austria if we went to war against the Russians. I thought this is cheerful. Here I am likely to be surrounded by Russians. The Russians were in Czechoslovakia to the east of Austria and Tito was in the lands to the south of Austria with more Russian divisions not far off in the east. The General said there will be no hope for you as the Russians will just come across. The Yugoslavian partisans were in the woods nearby where we were stationed. We could see their camp fires in the forest at night. He also said that the German army captives in Italy were being reorganised into units to support the 8th Army. Nobody has spoken about this and I am still waiting for it to come out. The Allies were organising the defeated German troops into a fighting force who would have joined with us and the Yanks in fighting Stalin and Tito's partisans. This included their rearmament. The USA were also intending to send a division After the war a thousand aircraft flew down Yugoslavia on the pretext of honouring the resistance; the real reason was a show of strength. It was saying to the

Yugoslavs that if Tito was going to war over securing Trieste for himself then he would be against the massed might of the USA and UK forces. Hearing this discussion between the top brass that I was driving made me feel really fed up. Worried that I would again be at the battle front and us stationed not far from the fearless and ferocious Yugoslavian partisans on returning to camp I told my mates what I had heard. I said that we would be cut off and slaughtered. I suggested that if war was declared that we should get a motorbike to escape and get away. We would have been up against it, against the guerrilla army of Yugoslavian partisans if war had been declared without much warning. Maybe it would have been desertion. But we had defeated Hitler, we were in no mood for a war against Stalin. The British and Americans were quite prepared to go to war with Russia and enlist the support of the defeated German army. I am waiting for that to come out. It has never come out has it? Obviously Russia did not back Tito's demand for Trieste.

"It was dreadful what happened to the Russian soldiers who had fought with the Nazis. They were sent back in trains or lorries to be shot. There were many cases of them jumping out of their transport into rivers or ravines to a certain death, but preferable to the torture and firing squad executions that they knew would be their destiny meted out by the Red Army Russians. From where we were in Austria we could hear them being shot. It was awful. Even though they had been our enemies and had fought against us, at the end of the war all we wanted was peace, an end to the killing and maiming. These Russians had been part of the German army, but were not subject to the agreements of prisoners of war which we had with the Germans. They were returned to a certain death."

Dimitry Karsazky's Story

My very best friend had a father who was Russian who for a time had fought with the German army before deserting and making his own way across Europe—a marked, wanted man. He eventually ended up in the United Kingdom as a refugee after the end of the war where he married his wife, a Czechoslovakian and like him, one of the millions of displaced persons. As refugees they worked hard in the country that had offered them a home. They had a daughter, who became a dear friend—my soul mate. My friend's father had an extraordinary war time. It is a story that must be told. Like so many accounts in this book it is testament to resilience, self-reliance and resourcefulness. He survived against all odds because of these qualities, and of course that strange commodity—luck or fate and a willingness to abide by the guiding voices of his ancestors. Born in the Ukraine in the 1920s was not a lucky move. Especially if you are born into a family of Kulak's. The Kulaks were a class of small farmers who owned a bit of land, some livestock and had sufficient income from their small holding to employ farm workers. In the eyes of the Russian Communist state they were seen as capitalists, for no other reason than owning and farming small parcels of land. The response of the communist Soviet State was to collectivise the land, in other words to seize the land, the animals and the property of these farmers. The state became the owner. This wholesale nationalisation of any privately owned land was not deemed by Stalin sufficient to destroy the kulak as a class. He wanted their complete eradication which was achieved by sending them to the Gulag labour camps, relocating them to other areas or simply starving them out. Hundreds of thousands of Russian kulaks, if not millions were murdered in this way. Anna's dad lived in an area that is now on the border between the Ukraine and Russia. Today the nearest Russian main town to his birthplace is Taganrog. The nearest Ukraine town is Mariupol. At his birth in the year of 1926 he became a citizen of the Soviet Union, the Ukraine being a constituent republic of the Soviet Union. It had been part of the Russian Empire until it disintegrated through revolution and the execution of the autocratic ruling Romanov dynasty led by Tsar Nicholas II. On the collapse of the Russian empire, it left a vacuum and ethnic Ukrainians sought to set up their own Republic independent of the power of Moscow government. It was not to be as the Ukraine also succumbed to the Bolshevik communist movement and the Ukrainian Soviet Socialist Republic came into being. It had little autonomy. It was controlled from Moscow and that meant it was held in Stalin's brutal grip. History has once more repeated itself with the invasion by Russia of independent Ukraine in March 2022. Putin is another Stalin, a cruel, heartless man causing untold suffering on Ukrainians and their country. How we must always confront and squash these dictators. But we didn't. We preferred the Russian Rouble opening our borders to money that stank from the sin of corruption and greed.

Born in an area called the Donbass region named Dimitri he was a Ukrainian Russian, or a Russian Ukrainian. Starvation marked his childhood. In 1932 to 1933 a famine killed between 2 to 10 million Ukrainians. A number of causes could have resulted in the starvation of Soviet Ukraine. Handing over the farms to be run by Communist officials who were ignorant of sound farming methods, centralised government interference, criminalisation of the old age practice of picking up ears of wheat which mechanical or other harvesting had left behind on the soil or deliberate genocide, are some of the reasons for empty mouths and stomachs. What is without doubt is that the Russian regime run by Stalin from Moscow caused the famine by its policies. Understandably Ukrainians started to hate Stalin and Russians.

When Germany and Russia declared war Dimitri's parents told him to leave home and go west to avoid conscription in the Russian Army. Before long the German army had occupied the Ukraine and Dimitri joined them, thinking it would help him move away from the threat of being captured by Red Army troops loyal to Stalin. Being of Slavic origin German racial rules deemed him as totally subservient and racially impure. Not one to suffer the indignation of being treated as a lower class of human being he escaped from the German army and started an incredible walk across central Europe always going west. He lived on his wits but was helped by a guardian angel. One night when sleeping in a forest he was visited by what he described as an angel which told him he must flee and go a different way than he intended, retreating almost. He quickly gathered up his meagre possessions and headed further into the forest away from the roads that he had wished to follow. As he was pushing through the trees he heard back from where he had been camping shouts and firing—German voices. If he had stayed five minutes longer and not heeded the warning from the angel he would have been shot. His guardian angel stayed with him throughout. Sometimes he would find food left by a friendly peasant, sometimes he slept in a barn. He had to make sure that he kept making his way west to avoid capture by both the retreating German forces and the advancing Russian forces. He made it through and lived. He was not returned back to the Russians after the war as by then he was no longer a soldier of any country, just a young man who had survived by his wits and much more, including the inexplicable circumstance of being visited by an angel.

And yet like so much of history it has repeated itself in this far corner of Europe. The area of the Donbass fought over in the last war is once again, as is the whole of the Ukraine, in the deathly turmoil of a war for survival. A fight against a tyrant. No change then from the Hitlers and the Stalins. Why cannot these delivers of death bring love instead?

And back to Dad's story.

Living in Klagenfurt and Villach, dad fell in love with Austria. He learnt how the onset of a snowy winter was looked forward to because it meant that the skis could come out and the mountains explored. The proliferation of gondolas and cable cars came with the investment poured in by the Americans under the Marshall Aid plan. It allowed the reconstruction of Austria which was occupied until 1955 by the Allies. Driving a staff car dad enjoyed travelling around Austria.

"Driving the staff car I often had to go up to Vienna which like Berlin was divided between the Russians, the Yanks and us; the French also had a sector. Austria was also under the control of these four countries and I had to drive through the Soviet occupied sector from the British sector to go up to the Schoenberg palace where I sometimes stayed for a few days. In order to get through the Russian checkpoints quicker I had a cigarette ration and bribed the Russian guards. 'Hey Ivan have a few fags,' I would say and they would wave me through."

Dad was able to explore the region of Austria where he was based. He had many enjoyable days as these letters show all sent from Austria.

T10704283 Dvr. John Hindle D Platt. 2076 Corps Transport Coy R.A.S.C. C.M.F. July 21st 1945

My Dearest Peggy,

Very many thanks as always for your very welcome letter for July 16 which arrived here yesterday.

So after all the wondering whether you would be a nurse, you can't go. I can understand how disappointed you will feel, but it's probably for the best. Don't let it worry you Peggy, you tried, but missed but I think it's as good as going right through with it, and the job certainly is not one to worry

about missing it. I can't preach but you'd be feeling balked like myself, after volunteering 13 times for the Merchant Navy, once for the RAF and one has come true, but not because I volunteered. When in Scotland I put my name down for overseas service, you're the only one I've told so keep it mum, sorry I told Harry. Needless to say I feel there's been enough travelling, but looking back I wouldn't have missed it, on the other hand I certainly don't want another dose. There's nothing to say, but if I were you I wouldn't volunteer, but most likely I would. The most sensible policy is to stay at home, and that goes for your Frank as well, I bet your Ronald feels the same way. I expect Frank will be like the rest of us used to be, impatient to get in, how is he placed? It's funny I feel really sorry you couldn't satisfy your feelings, but glad because it's probably better you didn't, it's funny how to put it, maybe you can make out what I mean. A lot of things happen for our own good which we don't realise till later, don't let it bother you Peggy dear.

It's good to hear the weather kept fine on your field day last Saturday, and then dancing enough to put me out, in bed at ten every night, dancing would just about kill me. You should have been with me this afternoon, at long last I managed another trip up the Kanzlebahn on my day off. It is 3211 feet from the lakeside to the summit, I'm sure it is the queerest thing I've travelled in. You go in the booking office and then into the lift arrangement it holds about 15 people and is slung by a girder on a thick cable, six wheels run on the cable with the car slung underneath, another endless cable pulls you up the mountain. The door shuts, there is a click and away you go, the road past the station slides away underneath you, then a house here and there, seems well below, next thing you are high above the pine trees, between you and the sky are a couple of awfully thin looking cables and a good distance below there is a stream. Once your nerves settle down you can look out and enjoy the scenery, it's really marvellous, everything begins to look toy shaped and there's lakes and mountains stretching for miles. About 10 minutes you arrive at the summit and you feel it was well worth the risk, there is none really, but you feel windy at first, it's like being suspended, between the top of Pendle and the road below with the exception that you've over 3000 feet of a climb broken twice by a couple of massive pylons, the cable is hitched to them. Funnily enough I never felt dizzy, my ears seemed to fill up, as if I was blowing down my nose and holding it at the same time.

You are 6000 feet above sea level, so maybe the rapid change in altitude does it, I thoroughly enjoyed it.

I'm writing this part of the letter the day following the first part, it's Sunday afternoon 4 PM. I knocked off work one hour ago feeling like the advert for an oil change. Did nothing else today but work hard with petrol and a brush polishing up the gearbox, and the odds and ends under the truck ready for an inspection, at 14.55 I got browned off so I did my washing and then started to try and finish this letter.

Mother sent me a cutting out of a newspaper. I will pin it up on our noticeboard. A war correspondent had an interview with an army commander and he said, all those who served the continuous one and a half years in C.M.F. will have had leave by Christmas, sorry the end of the year. It is planned that next year all troops serving in Italy or Austria will be on the same basis for home leave as B.L.A. If that comes true there is only five months at the most to wait, let's hope it is right dearest. It seems to be impossible the best news I've had for a long while. I put a photo out of "Parade" in this letter. Every day almost I drive past the big signboard, two miles past that board is where I'm living. The photo on the other side will give you an idea of the country where I live, sorry the papers crumpled, but it's a bit I picked up. It's a place where every prospect pleases and man defiles, or something like that is how the saying goes.

The flies are a pest at the moment, keep hitting me as I write. I don't think there's anything else to write about. It's better now the non-frat. ban has been lifted, but I've no intention of marrying a Fräulein Peggy, I must say from what I've heard about a lot of girls at home, they wouldn't disgrace an Englishman. There's sure to be a lot of soldiers marrying them after being disillusioned by their wives and fiancés and they would do a lot better than the girls who've married the Poles and etc. There is only you for me Peggy and the thought of you means far more than anything else, it's everything over here. Well I'll better sign off and write to Mother.

Cheerio! All my love Jack,

P.S. Sorry I pulled the photo apart as I folded it up, just like me!

Xxxxxx

The B.L.A. was the British Liberation Army who fought on the Western Front following the Normandy invasions in June 1944. Dad was understandably aggrieved that soldiers who had been fighting for just over 12 months were being considered for leave home, when he had been fighting for over 2 and ½ years. From this letter it is apparent that dad is influenced by relationship breakdown that happened during the war. He had mentioned it previously in his letters home. The men fighting far away had left girlfriends, fiancés and wives. Not seeing them for years some women decided to end the relationship and met other men whom they may have gone on to marry. Dad is particularly cross about them marrying Polish men. The reason is not known. It could be that it happened to one of his friends. He also has an eye for Austrian women whatever he writes to mum, as he is pleased that the rules have been changed so that soldiers can fraternise with the local women whom he clearly finds attractive as he suggests they may make a good match for a service man. He is though, as in all his dealings and communications, utterly honest in explaining his views on relationships with the Austrian female. He also confessed to mum that he had volunteered to serve abroad when stationed in Scotland. He clearly wanted to escape the mundane and as he saw it useless efforts of making his kit white—the blancoing, and also the square bashing. He had chosen to serve abroad because he wanted different experiences from foreign cultures and places. He was always wanting to be on the road exploring new and unvisited regions.

T10704283 Dvr. John Hindle D Platt. 2076 Corps Transport Coy R.A.S.C. C.M.F. August 13th 1945

To My Dearest Peggy,
    It's now 8 PM and I'm sitting in the door of our tent writing in reply to your letter which arrived here this afternoon, always as welcome as they always are, if not a little more so with each fresh one I get, it's grand.
    There's nothing fresh to write about since I last wrote to you, everything is still the same, but time keeps passing and as you say every day is one day nearer. Now that the war has ended it is more certain we will meet sooner, as long as it will seem. I've cut a poem out of "Crusader", it's very nice and even though it is vague it may help you to see how I feel. It's almost sure to be months and months before I get leave at the present rate, but never mind sweetheart it will soon come. Most blokes who came abroad have no girl to

see, being turned over, good fortune doesn't come in it with me, it's more than that.

There is some news of what I've been doing, sorry I broke off the last paragraph so abruptly. It's beyond me how I feel dearest. Yesterday we had the whole of Sunday off from work, after lying in and a lazy morning five of us thumbed a lift to the Kanzll, admired the glorious view and came back. We then thumbed again and rode down to the lake near Klagenfurt aboard a fast moving A.F.V. and stayed the afternoon at the NAAFI lido. We drank tea and munched biscuits and listened to the band. Then we decided to be sailors, so a couple of rowing boats were hired. Before setting sail from the pier we nearly had 12 stone of Cockney overturning the boat, he just jumped about two feet into it, that was Mass as we call him, short for Massy. I rowed for a while then Mass took over. Soon we were going up a narrow winding river, talk about having a good time we hardly stopped laughing from going up to coming out. If there was a corner we'll end up on the bank for giving the wrong instructions to the oarsmen. We got stuck in the mud once, another time we collided with the other two rowing away and turned them completely round. They even managed to sail in a boat—house, we must have disturbed the Austrians in their chalets by the riverside. Phew, we did get in some mix ups, it was good fun though. After a while we managed to dock nicely, to cap it nicely the boat sailed under the landing stage as we got off. After the rowing we had our supper, mash, spam and beetroot and sliced peaches with tea. After a walk along the waterfront the five of us took the back seat in a bus running part of our way to Villach. They are run by our corps. That was also a highlight of our outing, it was the first time since leaving home that we'd had a bus ride. Leaving the bus we soon caught a truck running our way and just before 9 PM we were drinking tea in the Villach canteen. Afterwards a three mile walk across country to our location made us feel ready for bed. We had a grand outing up a mountain, down to the lake 30 miles away, we travelled by foot, cable, boat, armoured car, a bus and a three ton truck in an afternoon, it's good fun, when you can get out like that.

I am glad you are not mad at me volunteering to cross the ditch, silly as it was but when I did it, it was because I hadn't the sense to know better, but I would have been more miserable in England blancoing and stamping my feet on a parade ground. Of course there would have been regular leave, but I can't help wanting to put my nose in, or couldn't help it then. The last 2 1/2 years have learnt me more of goodness and vileness than anything else could do. I'm like the rest of us abroad, we've realised we never missed the water till the well ran dry. Even though I say I'm glad I haven't missed it, I'd never do the same again for pounds a day, well the worst parts, not the whole of it, maybe it would have been better for me to have missed it. That's what makes me wonder if it's changed me too much. Please try and allow for anything I may do out of the ordinary. It's pretty bad when I can't even dance, there hasn't been much chance to learn, I hope I don't show you up dear if we land on a ballroom floor. All the same I'm quite prepared to take the strain of remembering my P's & Q'S.

Oh! Well I think I'll sign off and hope the weather was of the Italian variety as advertised for your holidays. Then you can make good use of your swimsuit. By the way if I get skis I'm almost looking forward to this winter.

Your namesake has just had a de-coke and she's going like a bird. I won't be able to bring her home as much as I'd like to. Sounds silly but a truck becomes part of you, and you have terrific confidence in what it will do. In the last push, she travelled thousands of miles without a murmur, an order to start moving for Calais is all that is needed, four days easy, 6 to Blackburn would be quite reasonable. Now I've clear glass in my headlights so night driving is a pleasure. I like to be in a nice warm cab on a quiet road just humming along, these are the nice things.

Well I must sign off and go to bed.

So cheerio.

Your ever loving Sweetheart Jack
Xxxxxxxxxxx

T10704283 Dvr. John Hindle D Platt. 2076 Corps Transport Coy
R.A.S.C. C.M.F. August 24th 1945

My Dearest Peggy,

Many thanks for the happy letter I have just had from you today, it was grand to hear that you had a week of good weather and the war now over at the same time it's certainly grand. The next job is to bring the boys home from Burma, but they won't for a long while.

Sorry but I'm writing about leave again, we had a draw again for it two days ago. Instead of being a one in thirty chance of getting it, there was a one in six chance instead, which brings the last possible opportunity for going on leave to about 30 weeks from now. Naturally we are sweating on the next allocation being as big or larger than the last, how many weeks we've to wait I don't know. Don't you think it's a big improvement? It certainly gives us hope of leave before the end of the year. A few days ago I wrote to Mrs Castle one of our MPs and told her just what I thought and the rest about the way we are being given news? About release and leave, more so you at home. I said a statement should be made saying how long it will take to give us leave. My cousin wrote to me how mad he was about it, so I let steam off hoping it may have an effect, if same is censored I'll have had it, but I'll never agree to being kept in the dark about these things. Honest I'm as wild as anything you deserve more than anybody to know within what time I'll be home. B.L.A. were told they would have leave within six months, that was a whole war on the know nothing , but I'll be home someday and we <u>will</u> have a good time, all the same I do feel more optimistic about having a leave before the end of the year. Don't build on it dear because if I didn't manage it, we would only be very disappointed. From a 1 to 30 to a 1 in 6 chance is very good and that's why I feel more optimistic.

We haven't had any time off as yet for V.J. day, celebrations on V.J. evening we brought a piano from our H.Q. and had a singsong and all those broke the pledge. We make our own celebrations, they're very quiet in relation to those at home, but we had a grand time, we're all pals together and it's quite a party when we get down to it. From your account it certainly seems as if everyone went mad. Of course, in a country like this it is different than home, there's no comparison. When the German war ended everything was more or less the same for us. We were certainly sorry to miss the parties at home, more of a feeling of relief than anything, and then a little celebration. In northern Italy we'd to walk around armed after the end to stop the different Partisan parties from starting a battle of their own, we'd have killed every one of them we came across if they'd started. They're a nuisance these continentals, a war ends and the next thing they are ready to start again. If they had, it wouldn't have lasted long, we were in the right mood to stop them. It just shows what they are like, a red scarf round their neck and a conglomeration of armament strung around their bodies and they become saviours of Italy when we've moved in, glorified gangsters and Fascist turncoats. Sorry I'm well off the point but that was celebrations in Italy, quite a comic opera effect.

I laughed at the squaddie who'd forgotten his way to Audley, poor beggar he must have had a basin full to forget his way home. It's very likely I'll be the same way but there will be no groping about in the blackout. There's a few lights on in town but it never seems to be any different. From the tales the odd lucky ones who've been home tell us they see trains lit up and rushing through brightly lit stations, is a real eye-opener.

A few days ago I had a mild disappointment. Lilian had sent me six films for my camera and when they arrived they were a size too small, you can have films sent on when you're abroad, it's a pity she didn't hear about it sooner. Once I get the right size by the time snow is laid thick upon the ground I'll have one taken showing me on skis, if I get them.

I'd certainly be glad of the words for our song. I'm still waiting to hear it played, maybe the time is dying out if you haven't heard it.

It must have been grand fun meeting a couple of strange girls and find out they can take leg pulls in large doses, it must have been a super duper holiday, and the wrestling matches thrown in, it's good fun but not sport, you've to go for a laugh and a good boo when you feel like it. If ever you see the Condor you'll know he used to be in the same platoon as myself, he wouldn't hurt a fly, even if he has killed a few Jerries as a paratrooper on D Day and Arnhem. He used to give us a side show in Africa, bending iron bars on his arm, you could take a hefty kick in his stomach and sprain your foot, he sorted a Nissen hut which was full of squaddies out, all in fun, certainly a tough guy, but the mildest sort of chap imaginable. I hope you aren't going to start on me if it has given you ideas, peace at any price please! It isn't nice being knocked around. I'm still dizzy after a few rounds with nice thick gloves on about three weeks ago. We box among ourselves now and again, our local champ went to town on me, it was good fun though, but I never seemed to see him, the Bells of St Mary's were chiming in my ears. I did feel happy.

I'm glad you received the postcards I sent, the country round here is very beautiful but you can't appreciate it like you could do on holiday in the same place. Tomorrow Sunday I'm hoping to go and meet my cousin again, we'll probably go boating on the Worthersee, a favourite spot of the Duke of Windsor's, we believe in touring these continental society places, but not in a nice Rolls, well a three ton truck gets you along nicely so that is better than walking. If we can get about six of us to make a party up tomorrow we'll have a terrific time for the afternoon, a kind of army workmen's trip on a small scale is how I can describe it best, you'd enjoy yourselves if you came rowing with us, we have a jolly time.

Your Ronald must be having an anxious time and you at home as well, it will certainly be nice to come home and see him on his feet and fit and well again. We grouse and grumble but when you're in good health it's everything to be thankful for. Well I'll sign off now Peggy dear, this is the second day of writing, so maybe I've written too much, if I read through this letter again it would probably get torn up. I do that now and again.

Cheerio! All my love. Yours Jack

xxxxxxxxxxx

After all those years of being away Dad was still waiting for his leave home. Eventually it happened.

Dad described his journey, "We travelled over to Germany staying near Munich. Travelling on the autobahns we saw little evidence of the destruction of the war as we did not venture into the towns and cities. It was a long drive. I cannot remember all of the journey but we ended up in Calais and then were put on a boat. Disembarking at Folkestone we spent the night in a big hotel that had been taken over by the army to use as a transit camp. We travelled back to England from Calais with soldiers who had been in the D-Day invasion. The lads who had been in Europe had enjoyed home leave already. We had not been home for 3 to 4 years. The 8th Army had a tremendous bond. We did have leave after the African campaign—but in Africa in those hotels in Hammamet in Tunisia."

Mum was the first he telegraphed on his only and first leave home in September 1945. Arriving at Folkestone he immediately sent a telegram saying he would be home that Sunday evening or possibly the next day. Already signing his telegrams with "LOVE JACK" their long distance relationship had obviously deepened over the three years dad had been away from home. He had to return back to Austria. Months would pass by before he was finally demobbed home. Eastern Europe was occupied by the USSR. The possibility of another war was real. Fortunately for dad and for us now it never happened because it would have likely have resorted to nuclear weapons.

Heroes

Over the years after the war dad shared many stories from others who had served in the war. One of the most remarkable relates to an ordinary guy who did not need to use the F word in nearly every sentence to describe his heroic war history. He did not need to pose as a hard ex SAS man or aspire to be a caricature of the hard SAS or other special forces who now make money out of books and unreal reality TV programmes. People watching such programmes seem to believe what they are seeing as representative of real life in an elite fighting force. The key to an elite fighting force is that you cannot be seen or heard—that's what makes them so effective. Certainly there would be no screaming at a celebrity or other so called recruits who seemingly want to test themselves against manufactured exercises. The liberal use of the F word is ineffective as a motivation tool revealing many fault lines. If someone really wants to test themselves there are much more valid challenges—the Original Mountain Marathon held at the end of October; running the Bob Graham round twice nonstop; swimming the English Channel twice there and back without getting out the water, the Lake District Mountain Trial. So many ordinary folk choose challenges which benefit not only themselves in doing the challenge but other people, the Just Giving pages are full of them. These are the people to admire and look up to, not the self-seeking celebrity.

This is about a man who did not need to be sworn at to do something incredibly heroic—he just did it.

Dad's words:

"Ken Thorpe lived next door to us in Brighton Terrace. He had been taken prisoner in North Africa. He was in the 8th Army like me, in the Tanks Corps. He was taken by the Germans and became a prisoner of war. We had always been told just to give our name, rank and number if captured. The German Officer that interrogated him told Ken exactly which regiment he was in, where he had been trained, where he had first landed in Africa, where he had fought— the German officer told Ken the whole history of his service. There must have been spies working in the War Office for this German officer to know this.

"The Germans apologised to Ken when he was handed over to the Italian army for imprisonment. The German officer told Ken that the Italians will treat him worse than the Germans would and that was his experience. He had a tough time. He was transported over to Italy, to a prison camp, but when Italy surrendered the British prisoners of war were free, so it was a good thing that he was imprisoned in Italy and not Germany. He was told by his former prison guards that the British will be coming for you and that he could wait for them in the accommodation which had been his prison. Ken thought no they won't be coming for me. The top brass will not be thinking about rescuing him way behind German lines, half way up Italy. So he cleared off, left the prison camp and joined the Italian Partisans in the hills. He fought with them against the Germans. Ken told me one time he was attacking a group of German soldiers, shooting at them. The Germans came after them; and he had a close shave because these were very fit German paratroopers who could run fast and were gaining on Ken and his Italian partisan mates. They just got away managing to escape the Nazi paras.

"As the Allies made their way up the boot bit of Italy and becoming closer to where Ken was fighting with the partisans he realised that could re-join his 8th Army at last. He made his way through the German enemy lines back to the British forces. He could not just return to his previous fighting unit—the tank corps. As he had been a prisoner he was treated as having been out of the army. He had to leave the 8th Army and was repatriated back to Catterick Garrison. At Catterick he was treated as a new recruit which was belittling and frustrating for him considering what he had done. He ended up back in the war in Europe.

"One day he was looking over the garden wall into our back yard when we lived on Brighton Terrace. Harold Parker was visiting us from Barrow. They say it is a small world. Harold had been taken prisoner with him at the same time and they remembered their meeting in the original German prison camp in North Africa—the holding camp before prisoners were sent onwards to their permanent prison. Harold had been sent to Germany, so he was imprisoned until the end of the war. He was not released and never had the opportunity to fight with the Italian Partisans like Ken did."

Dad is a realist. He feels lucky to have born. Is it luck to be born to a soldier who had a 50% chance of being sent to the Somme but went to India instead? Luck or chance or fate, call it what you will, is cruel. It seems to prefer some people in the good fortune it brings and punishes other in the pain it hands out. That dad was lucky to be born is an understatement. 704,803 service men died in the First World War between 1914 and 1918. His father might never have come back, but he did and returned home, to get married and start a family. Dad never sees himself as having been amazingly brave, stoical and calm throughout the war. Undoubtedly Ken Thorpe's resourcefulness and self-reliance in leaving the prisoner of war camp to join the Italian partisans was incredible by today's benchmarks of what is described as an amazing personal achievement.

But there were umpteen Ken Thorpe's. Men and women who came home after the war, went back to an ordinary job and spoke with modesty of their war experiences. Those who avoided being called up were already on their particular ladder of achievement, they had the best jobs not easily displaced by those who had spent the last few years fighting. Such men and sometimes women did very well for themselves. There was no desire in those returning from the carnage of war to seek the spot light of a YouTube or Facebook or Twitter or Instagram or TikTok world; they had no need to clock up numbers of friends, likes, smiley faces. To survive there could be no following the crowd, people expressed their individuality, made their own choices, made their own judgements, made their own calculations of risk—all done when facing severe personal danger. In the 21st century there is less material poverty, more opportunity to experience and communicate with the world through the web or by travel, more possibilities than before the war, better education and health, but as ever massive inequalities in the extent to which people can take advantage of the myriad of material and social improvements. Ideas and discourse are hijacked by pressure groups; the need for rational debate and discussion quickly becomes polarised and argumentative. Unwarranted accusations are made; sides are taken, the underlying problem continues to fester and is not solved.

Take for example the NHS. For years the struggles of its junior doctors and nurses in providing a professional, reliable and caring service to patients has been known. Many doctors and others have written about how without working the hours for which they are not paid the NHS would cease to function. Not having basic facilities such as a designated space where they can make a cup of coffee or even write a discharge letter in peace, having little mental health support though working in one of the most stressful environments. The NHS is held together by very thin threads, constantly mended by NHS workers. During the height of the coronavirus pandemic every Thursday night at 8.00 pm a public clapping took place for the NHS and key workers. The clapping brought people out on their streets or balconies or to their windows to share in this mass applause. The NHS staff, the public transport workers and other who risked their lives and some who sacrificed their own precious life, would I am sure have preferred that a commitment to real change so that their lives were not put at risk, proper remuneration was provided and support from their employer was guaranteed. Clapping did nothing.

But the NHS is a political football. Spending more money may not be the solution to improvement. It may be. The political argument always centres on which party can spend the most money, not on whether patient care and treatment can be improved. Ask the people who work there with the patients; not necessarily the managers, but the front line workers. They know. They always know. Much was said that coronavirus would change us as a nation. That the NHS key staff would once again be valued and not verbally and physically abused by those who cannot have their way in the waiting room. That we would build caring communities where respect and consideration for our neighbours would take precedence over any selfish motivation. Sadly it was not to be. Hot weather and the loosening of the lock down combined with disposable cash, provided by the government without any conditions attached, resulted in herds of people trashing beaches, parks, leaving their shit and rubbish for others to clean up. Drink and drug fuelled gatherings in places like Moss Side Manchester or Brixton insulted those who had put other people first. These are poor places with poor people. No doubt the people who live in the surrounding streets would have locked their doors, but they would not have been able to lock out the noise or disturbance. Such brazen selfishness. The police were helpless. People were allowed to do what they want, breaking the law whether snorting cocaine or getting into a knife fight whether on a Bournemouth beach or in a field on the edge of Manchester. But all this behaviour has faded in the disapproval rating stakes following the disclosure of the umpteen parties in Number 10, Downing Street. Lies, trust broken, integrity absent—the British people deserved so much better having gone through so much.

So why do people not take their rubbish home with them? Why do they throw it out the car window? Why do they leave it by the river bank or on the sands? They have come by car. They have a bin at home. The answer is simple and one as a nation which we dodge around answering or confronting because it is uncomfortable. We wish to see ourselves as clapping with our neighbours, not doing the nasty, self-centred, anti-social stuff. Motorists too lazy to take their rubbish home and put it in a rubbish bin chuck it out their car. It is an act of hate directed against their home land—their spoiling and damaging of their own country. Someone else will clear it up—the government, the council, the public spirited angels who step in—we are so used to have everything provided to us that some of us, and it may only be a sizeable minority, do not care. Believing they are entitled to ruin their own beautiful land, a land that so many died for in the two world wars, entitled to please themselves, pursue personal freedom without a care for any other person, taking for granted their privileged position of first world inhabitants. It has to stop—this selfishness, this self-seeking, this demanding, this entitlement, this disregard for other peoples' needs and welfare. Otherwise the Kens of this world and millions other such as a colleague dad had worked with who was at the Bridge in Arnhem trying to stop the Germans have been betrayed. He refused to surrender and kept on fighting.

Dad talked about John Eden, a past Chairman of Silverdale Parish Council who had flown in a glider which had landed on a canal bridge in the Normandy landings. He was 19 at the time. A private in an Airborne Division he visited Normandy again in June 2019 for the 75th commemoration of the D Day landings. And Arthur Finch serving in a destroyer ship had planned like those who escaped from below deck in dad's convoy, how to escape and survive. Many more who came back to seemingly ordinary lives having already lived an extraordinary life. These were self-reliant, resourceful and resilient people and the nation was crammed full of them.

Dad did though have another call up. He was a reservist. Being a reservist meant that he could be called up at any time and he was, on this occasion to be ready to fight the communists in Korea. Sharing his thoughts about the prospect of returning to the battlefield he was his usual light-hearted self.

"I thought that was it when I was demobbed you think that's it—no more army. But I was told it was last out first in. And I was one of the last out in 1946. Rather though I think they selected us, as we were all from the 14th and 8th army. The 14th had fought in Burma and had the worse time of any British soldier in the war fighting the Japanese. The 8th Army was famous because it had been established a long time starting its life in Egypt. Its men continued fighting until Victory in Europe. The 14th Army war did not end until 2nd September 1945 when Japan officially surrendered."

Dad was first told to report for a medical to establish whether he was fighting fit. He had hurt his ankle at the weekend when in the Lake District when out walking, probably on the Fairfield Horseshoe which is his favourite hike. On the

Monday night his ankle was painful and swollen. He decided to visit his GP Dr Livesey in case it was broken. His GP thought it was a sprain, but sent in him for an x-ray at Blackburn Royal Infirmary. Dad joked to Dr Livesey that he did not want his ankle to get better by Thursday as he was due his army medical having been called up for training. Dr Livesey stared at dad, a bit flummoxed by what dad had told him. Looking very serious and sounding solemn Dr Livesey said he was also going to be at the medical on Thursday because he was the examining doctor. Dad felt a bit uncomfortable, but then Dr Livesey smiling told dad not to worry because he was examining the Ear, Nose and Throat, not the working of the legs and feet.

Dad had a fantastic time back in training. His ankle improved so he was not prevented from going and he was so glad he did. Based at Formby near Southport he said it was one laugh from the start to finish. They were all Lancashire lads, who like him had been in the army during the war. They were there for about a month, and had a break in the middle to travel home for the weekend. They all thought it was a bit of joke that they had been called up and were being trained, but one of the reservists who was there with dad, a solicitor who worked in an office, had for some reason seen all the kit bags stored in a warehouse ready to be allocated before they joined their transport to Korea. It became a deadly serious possibility that he would be leaving his newly wedded wife, Peggy and one year old baby daughter to go and fight communists in Asia.

Dad was paid whilst he was training, but a self-employed reservist could claim no financial recompense so when the brigadier came round one day and asked how this chap liked being back in the army, the brigadier received a reply that he certainly did not, as he had lost his income. That was possibly the polite version.

Dad was subsequently pleased and relieved that his services were never required by the army, staying safe and sound in Blackburn, as he met an ex-soldier, a postie back in Civvy Street who had been in the tank corps in Korea. The postie told dad that conditions had been terrible and the lads out there had had a rough time. It was very cold and the clothing provided was inadequate. Their boots rotted and they had to call on the Americans to obtain decent clothing.

Not much changes. How much do we value our men and women who put themselves on the front line for us facing death and injury? In Afghanistan the Government knew that the Land Rovers transport were hopeless at protecting driver and passengers from mines, called IEDs improvised explosive devices, when soldiers were on patrol in Taliban strongholds. Provision of boots was often inadequate requiring soldiers themselves to purchase their own suitable footwear for the changing and seasonal climate. Many other failures in equipment have been documented and it seems that procurement and supply of such essentials is not improved, lessons not learnt. People who put their lives on the line because their job description demands that should not have to make do and mend and source their own equipment.

During the first wave of the Coronavirus pandemic there were daily stories of insufficient PPE (personal protection equipment) being provided to doctors, nurses, health care workers and others whose livelihood brought them into contact with the infection. Doctors purchased snorkelling masks; nurses made their own scrubs, individuals rallied to their help in so many ways demonstrating resourcefulness, inventiveness, imagination and sheer determination to resolve the problem. The NHS responsible for providing adequate PPE to its staff struggled to fulfil this duty. The Government paid millions to their friends without ensuring the tax payer received value for money. When the Government spends money it is your money that is being spent paid for by you through the taxes you pay. Help to mend the hole in the PPE equipment supply came from many sources from vacuum cleaner entrepreneurs to dress making hobbyists. The people came to the rescue as they often do in such situations. History tells us that the state can never meet all our needs especially in time of crisis; ultimately we rely on ourselves, family, friends and communities to make the right choices and save us from peril.

So having experienced a cataclysmic change from the virus, preparations are needed to combat a much greater threat. The melting of the arctic permafrost allowing tons of carbon and methane to escape into the world's atmosphere, needs to be contemplated and demands real action now. Such a massive release will warm the planet very quickly leading to the death and destruction of life itself be it animal or vegetable. The toxicity of the oceans would rise. Food would quickly run out. The world would be uninhabitable for humans. This is a worst case scenario, but it is possible, just like a pandemic was always possible, but thought to be a remote risk to our comfortable safe lives in the UK especially as the SARs virus, which has a much higher death rate, did not reach our shores. All wishful and muddled thinking as SARs does not transmit like Covid 19. It is a sluggish beast of a virus. Thankfully Covid 19 is not as dangerous to life as

SARs, but it still caused havoc and the dreadful tragedy of many deaths; each individual death a huge loss to those left behind to mourn their loved one. Climate change is still our biggest threat, much bigger than a pandemic. And time is running out, if not already run out. Baby steps are being taken to save our planetary home. As humans we all have to accept, especially the privileged of the developed world, that our way of living must change drastically. The vast majority of us have difficulty in changing our ways. We are our biggest threat.

Priorities have changed. In 1942 it was to defeat Hitler, Mussolini and the Emperor of Japan. Now it's a half-hearted attempt to deal with the climate emergency. Half-hearted because it is obvious what can be achieved in war time when the country had to manufacture tons of fighting equipment—tanks, rifles, aeroplanes, requisition and convert hundreds of ships, train thousands of men and women into a military service, organise and ration food supplies and other essentials to name a few of what the country managed to do practically on its own, but with the obvious help then of the countries in its Empire. Even though the threat is present and obvious through flooding, fires, disappearing ice to mention a few, it does not galvanise us into immediate action because the threat comes from something we live with day in, day out, something that is as familiar as the air we breathe and the water we drink and wash ourselves in—the weather. The weather is part of everyone's lives. We all share and experience it. It is not experienced as evil or frightening or threatening unless the weather becomes an ugly force during a storm, a lightning strike, a drought, an inundation. Weather is something we live with; it changes from day to day and sometimes it has extremely problematical manifestations. The consequences of the weather are terrifying if water is rushing into your home or it is being engulfed in flames, but the sunnier summers and the warmer winters generally are welcomed by us. So this enemy of climate change that is boiling up the world will cause much more destruction than all the wars put together if left unchecked. Encountering us with the smiling warm face of a hot summer sun, it is difficult to translate such an apparently benign encounter with the growing monster that lies beneath it.

The British are obsessive about weather. And no wonder. A sunny day not only raises the temperature, but also the mood. A blue sky that stretches from East to West throughout a full day sometimes feels like a fantasy when living through days of grey clouds blocking out any hope of brightness. Clouds that may release rain or snow or stretch endlessly as an oppressive shroud. Hearing the words "high pressure", "settled", "over Britain", when said sequentially by the weather forecaster is an experience akin to hearing your raffle ticket being first called out when you have the pick of the good prizes, the bottle of fizzy wine or scotch rather than the dregs that everyone leaves—recycled from previous raffles. Those ubiquitous prizes of the large umbrella emblazoned with a corporate logo incompatible with your image, the box of toiletries dating from a post Xmas Boots sale, a wicker work donkey brought back from a Spanish holiday.

Knowing there is to be a run of guaranteed blue sky days rather than the disappointment of a forecast hedged in if's and but's is a lottery win of the first prize for all, rather than the waiting to see if your ticket is picked and the maybe's of rain or shine are all that are left to be claimed.

Unhindered sun in summer means barbecue parties can be planned and should it coincide with a big televised sporting event taking place on a Saturday or Sunday then the jackpot of a fun weekend is looking promising. A World Cup match—England playing if you are an England supporter—supermarkets south and east of the Borders sell out of beer and burgers by midday. Summer clothes stuffed at the back of the wardrobe behind dark heavy garments are dug out; sunglasses and sandals are purchased. Everything dreamed of becomes possible. Climbing that mountain, biking that road, painting the fence, planting geraniums, being nearly naked, picnic in the park, swimming outdoors, ice cold alcohol, staying cool with mates, siestas, unencumbered sweaty sex.

Joy of joys, but a long hot summer used to be a rarity apart from during exam time. The best time to book a stay vacation was in June when a hot spell was certain. GCE and A level students swatted and studied during an almost guaranteed heatwave, looking out beyond their bedroomed window to a blinding heat parching the grass and scorching skin. The aim was to get as dark skinned as possible and the best way to do that was to fry in oil. The damaging effects of the sun on skin were not known, but probably the benefits of free Vitamin D sunshine doses, without the need to take daily doses of cod liver oil, were also not widely appreciated. Any type of oil would do; the rich plastered themselves with Amber Solaire, the poorer had to hunt out vegetable oil which did not really appear on shop shelves until the mid-1960. But olive oil had the medicinal qualities of softening ear wax if dropped into a blocked ear, so there were a lot of people pretending to have hearing problems to buy a bottle of olive oil from the pharmacist. These were miniature sized bottles compared to the litre bottles now seen on shop and supermarket shelves. Our relationship with weather is complex. Suffering damp dismal days may have made us quietly appreciative of climate change until its wider implications are known. Freezing cold water pours into the Atlantic Ocean from melting Greenland glaciers. Some scientific models have shown how such an influx of icy water into the Atlantic may cut off that balmy Gulf Stream that prevents us having the sorts of winters that beset Nova Scotia. Temperatures for months below 0 degrees centigrade would have us longing for the drizzle. Mess with nature and it will mess with us and we will come off worse. Lesson learnt from coronavirus.

How quickly our comfortable lives can change through potential and forecasted threats. Look no further than the consequences of the transmission of a virus from a bat to a human being in a faraway province in China. Such a seemingly minor event caused death, economic and social chaos. For some inexplicable reason shop shelves were emptied of toilet rolls. Not bread, not vegetable or fruit or milk. Toilet rolls are not essential to life especially if you have soap and water. Unfortunately bidets have never become fashionable in the UK, people prefer the less hygienic practice of a relatively thin piece of paper between their hands and the faecal matter. Toilet rolls are not essential to life— carbohydrates, proteins, fats, and other nutrients such as vitamins and minerals are essential. But people make strange choices when under threat. How greater will be the problem if food production ceases, the oceans become toxic and water itself dries up.

But climate change was a problem for the future world in 1942. But it is our problem now just as making sure there are no more pandemics.

Unless humans do what they can be really superb at—use their brains, skill and knowledge together to find an alternative to coal, gas and oil. Wind, solar and wave are working already, but more sources of power are needed. Hydrogen is a strong contender to get the planet out of its apocalypse trajectory.

An immediate momentous, collaborative effort of all scientists, engineers, governments, investors to produce energy which is absent of carbon is imperative.

Moving On

Time for a pause. Time to reflect. Time to assess the future; just like the British public did at the end of the war when they voted in radical policies recognised by them as owed for those who had suffered the trials and tribulations of 6 years' war fare and whose determination to survive for better days had delivered them from the hell of world conflict. A free national health service available to all, an education system to provide opportunity to all, national insurance to provide for retirement pensions and financial assistance if unable to work through ill health or unemployment.

The golden years of full employment had arrived. Technology invented an ever increasing bounty of consumer goods based on a never ending supply of electricity—televisions, refrigerators, twin tub washing machines, electric kettles and toasters. All manufactured in the UK. Car owning increased. People sought to improve their homes through DIY or became the occupiers of new council houses. More manufacturing in the UK of sofas, dining tables and chairs, beds, sideboards. Nearly every item in a home was domestically made. No Made in China labels were seen.

Dad's Uncle Fred Jefferson benefitted from the growth in the desire to have a quick personal means of transport, protected from the elements, a space away from other travellers—the car. Uncle Fred was his mother's younger brother:

Dad described his exploits as follows

"Uncle Fred Jefferson went to Canada at a guess around 1929. He did that because of the slump. Lack of work in Blackburn I assume; I remember him just before he went to Canada. Not at lot I remember about him, his image is very faint. He came back just before the war because in Peterborough, Ontario where he lived they had an annual fair. Each shop in the town gave out tickets to its customers according to the amount of money spent in the shop by the person over the year. Uncle Fred did not have a lot of money so had not spent a lot in these shops, so did not have a lot of tickets. The tickets gave entry into a competition, the winning prize of which was a car. It was at the annual fair that the winning ticket was drawn. Fred had the winning ticket. He won the car and then sold it right away. He had married a Canadian woman called Nora. They went on to have three children called Jack, Laurie and Joan. He decided that now he had some money he wanted to return to England. On his return he worked at Barrow in Furness as an engineer at Vickers armament works. He was then called up joining the RAF. I think he had signed up in the "mugs militia"; a nick name given to people who had put their name down to join one of the services before the war. You could put your name down and join one of the services and got money when war broke out. Anyone on the "mugs militia" was called up as was uncle Fred, but he got out because he was an engineer in a reserved occupation at a works in Blackburn. Because he had worked during the war, he was able to save up money to buy a garage in Mellor Brook after the war. He prospered as those who weren't in the forces, usually did. The garage grew and he bought the big house behind. A sound businessman who did really well for his family."

War ended. Rationing of food and other essentials continued for a while but as shown by his Uncle Fred's story the slow increase in living standards, together with health, social and education reforms started to change British lives slowly.

Like many men coming back from the war, settling down and marrying the love of their lives was a priority, as well as finding a job. Dad was fortunate in that he had a job as a butcher in the family business waiting for him when he was demobbed.

Dad and mum's romance continued to blossom even after he had to return to Austria following his brief leave home in September 1945. Youth Hostelling trips to the Yorkshire Dales on bikes and by foot, tennis playing in the Corporation Park, dances, family parties, visits to the seaside cemented their post war relationship. Leisure time was a luxury after the deprivations and restrictions of the previous 6 years. They were married on 03 April 1948 at 2.00 pm in St James' Church in Blackburn. Mum's dress was made of white satin. She had two bridesmaids, Lilian dad's sister and Gwen her cousin. Both bridesmaids' dresses were made out of a silk crepe chiffon in different colours. Gwen wore pink and Lilian blue. White carnations adorned both bouquets and button holes. Photographs and a film of the wedding was taken. The women guests wore double breasted wool coats with sturdy, clumpy shoes. On their heads were even doughtier hats. The war had meant that clothes bought or made had to be practical and last. Materials were difficult to obtain because of continuing rationing so seeking out a new fashionable outfit for a wedding was not possible, unless exceptionally wealthy.

The choice of music was predictable. Mum on the arm of Grandad Stratford (the wrongly maligned malingerer) walked down the aisle to meet dad to the sounds of Wagner's wedding march from Richard Wagner's opera "Lohengrin", most commonly known as "Here comes the bride". Sometimes a second line of "60 inches wide" is added by mischievous or perhaps bored children waiting to escape the church and enjoy the party. Two hymns were chosen—"Love divine all loves excelling" which dad has asked to be played at his celebratory memorial service when he passes on to that Heavenly kingdom. His spirit will be there, but not his body which he has donated to Liverpool Medical School to help future doctors develop their knowledge of anatomy. The second hymn sang was "O perfect love, all human thought transcending." The couple processed out of the church again to the old favourite of the Mendelssohn's Wedding March. Interesting, but irrelevant that the music that started and ended their nuptials is written by Germans, one adored by Hitler, the other hated.

Mum was a Girl Guide Captain. On leaving the church porch after their marriage the happy couple walked through an arch made by all the guides holding up tent poles over their Guide Captain and her new husband. Lots of photographs were taken, the guests looking happy and almost relieved to be doing something as normal as celebrating a marriage, after the years of war uncertainty.

The wedding car was a Rolls Royce which took them down the steep hill of Shear Brow into the town centre. The reception was held at the Adelphi Hotel on Railway Road overlooking the boulevard and train station. Dutton's brewery where mum worked was built next to the Adelphi. It was the hostelry which showcased Dutton's products beer and other products, owned and managed by the brewery. Her employer sent a telegram to the Adelphi Hotel, a short walk away down the street. It would have been quicker and easier to deliver the message by hand, rather than going to the Post Office much further away on Darwen Street.

Llandudno was the honeymoon destination, but no children were conceived there, their first child a daughter being born in March 1950.

All their savings had been used to purchase their first home, a small two up, two down terraced house just about big enough for themselves and the baby. When the second child was born, the family moved into a terraced house with three bedrooms, two receptions, a kitchen, outhouses, a back and front garden and an attic. Evidence of improvement in living standards. Children were healthy given free orange juice, and at school a bottle of milk in the morning. There was never any left. Children valued the food they were given. A hot school dinner— a main meal and a pudding—cooked on the school premises from raw and fresh ingredients was provided free to all school children, until such universal entitlement was removed by Margaret Thatcher. Play was in streets empty of cars and other vehicles. Health and Safety was unknown. Risks were taken— playing on the top of old air raid shelters, jumping off buildings, climbing onto roofs and up trees, going off into the park with friends unaware of stranger danger. Whooping cough (technical name pertussis) and poliomyelitis (polio) vaccines were introduced for children in the 1950s, meaning the risks of severe disablement or death from these conditions vanished. It was a good time to be born because everything was getting better. Penicillin heralded the era of antibiotics which kill killing diseases. There was no vandalism, property was respected and people left their doors unlocked. Educational opportunities for all opened up.

Gradually the town changed from cotton mill chimney dominance to a more mixed industrial landscape. Different kinds of industry moved in or existing factories modernised to make new products or provide parts for the growing desire to own labour saving domestic appliances and a television.

Immigrants mainly from the Punjab part of India and Pakistan and also from Bangladesh were encouraged to come to Blackburn to work in the mills after the war because of the shortage of workers.

Knowledge of immigration into the UK over the 20th century is not well known. When did people arrive? Where did they come from? Why did they leave their homes in what to us as tourists may seem inviting climates and exotic cultures, arriving in a damp, dark, unfriendly Britain, recovering after the war? Much is discussed about the consequences of immigration, but not the reasons for immigrants coming. Myths, misunderstandings and sheer wilful ignorance has produced totally erroneous beliefs. One such is that the Windrush brought the first African Caribbean people to the United Kingdom. There is a belief that before that time there were only negligible numbers of persons with a skin colour that was not white in the UK. That might have had some credence in places including Blackburn removed from the capital and slave trading ports of Liverpool and Bristol. Dad remembers there being only one person of probably African Caribbean descent who lived in Blackburn before the war. Dad remembers he lived down Addison Street and worked in a factory. He was a customer at what they called their "Bottom shop". (Given the name—bottom as it was in the bottom of the river valley that runs through Blackburn.) There have been black people in Great Britain since at least the Roman invasion. But we should not perceive many black and south Asian or anyone who came from the former colonies or whose families were seized and then owned by British slave traders and plantation owners as immigrants, as others, as not us. They have been part of a wider British community under the power of the Empire and before, some of their ancestors' bodies owned by the slave owners or the East India

Trading Company. They are part of this country because they are part of its, looking back now—sometimes unfortunate history, certainly judged by our standards.

Many families from immigrants originated from beyond the shores of the British Isles. Millions persecuted just as Scottish crofters, Irish peasants, Lancashire hand loom weavers and all others whose land was stolen and then fenced off by powerful landowners. Dispossessed of their rights to even a home. There has always been migration from the rural to the urban for many centuries even predating the Industrial Revolution. Many crossed the Irish Sea to this island driven by starvation. The iniquities of the previous centuries committed by those who had the power to commit such offences against humanity resonate still in many ways and forms. We must know this history, we must know our collective heritage, that this history of struggle against oppression, against hunger, against homelessness, against persecution, against systematic murder and annihilation of certain peoples unites us regardless of the colour of our skin, the texture of our hair and the shape of our eyes or mouths.

So many from the Empire went and fought for this country. In the Second World War as dad's experiences testify, but also in the First World War and in all other conflicts. Black men who were volunteers from the West Indies left their Caribbean islands to die at the Somme. Such sacrifice, such devotion to mother Britannia. Now we are multicultural and multi ethnic because of the shrinking of the world through travel, an ever expanding world wide web, educational opportunities and the dominance of English as the earth's most common language.

The long peace in Europe and co-operation between its nations has assisted economic development and consequential prosperity. A huge success story for Europeans, the term meaning all those who live in Europe not just those who live in the European Union. It includes us in the United Kingdom. All have enjoyed increased standards of living and continue to do so compared to the times before the Second World War. But as then, inequalities remain between the haves and the haves not. Blackburn lost its traditional industries, as did so many other places.

The Empire Pride, the ship that transported dad to Africa originally specified to be a cargo ship, was changed to that of a troop carrier. It was built in 1941 at a shipyard at Whiteinch on the River Clyde in Glasgow by Barclay, Curle and Company. It became a scruffy industrial estate with shuttered low lying buildings and barbed wire topped fencing. As with the Lancashire Mills the industries which provided trade, employment, training for apprentices, skilled work have gone. Disappeared in dad's lifetime. But it was not by accident, more like design, there are many reasons for the deindustrialisation. One of the main reasons was the deliberate abolition of traditional industries such as coal mining, steel manufacture, ship building, heavy engineering—the making of things, other than food stuffs to sell. These industries were located mainly in the West Midlands, the north of England, South Wales and the central belt of Scotland. They were systematically killed off or helped to their destruction by Government policies particularly in the 1980s in favour of service and financial industries located primarily in the south. Those areas that suffered deindustrialisation have never recovered. The bothersome working class being supressed in the process.

There were other reasons for the death of making things. Intransigent unions which were reluctant to embrace new working practices or which sought to battle it out, in the case of the miners, with poor strategies. Who would start a miner's strike at the end of winter when coal stocks were high? Margaret Thatcher was a more formidable adversary than Ted Heath. She made plans, she implemented them and won. Coal mines closed. The UK became reliant on imported coal, gas and home grown nuclear energy sources. But stuff and things could be made cheaper abroad. Try and find clothes that are still manufactured in the UK. You may have to travel up to the Isle of Harris or to the Scottish Borders to find home spun cloth. Try and find anything made in the UK in shops or on line. Look at the labels, look at all those piles of imports from abroad—mostly from undemocratic, despotic China. China has concentration camps, it imprisons its citizens without trial. Do you really want to buy from such a place when your beloved ancestors fought Hitler to rid the world of his horrible dictatorship?

The Man with More Lives than a Cat

Dad survived coronavirus by isolating, like lots of people. He has survived so many near-death events. Why?

Impulsive and always seeking a new adventure, dad's escapades have brought him close to death on a few occasions. In later life he has survived numerous illnesses, including an operation where his heart stopped and he had to be brought back to life through shocking his heart. Regularly confronted by the extreme personal danger in the war by the bombing, torpedoing and machine gunning by the enemy he sometimes put himself in danger by wandering off and exploring around where he was stationed. He has a wanderlust which nearly took him into enemy territory when he saw a hill top village in Italy which he thought looked interesting. It was occupied by the Germans so never reached his destination.

Before the days of YouTube videos providing visual and talking advice and instruction on carrying out any DIY job, repairs and refurbishments were very much done on a try and see it basis. Dad and mum noticed one day that the coal fires in the downstairs living room and kitchen were not burning as they should. He discovered the reason. Water was coming down the chimney onto the coals from the chimney stack which was leaking. Dad decided that repointing the bricks on the stack would solve the problem. Enterprising as ever he decided he would be the Fred Dibnah of Lynwood Road where they then lived and mend the stack himself. He climbed out of the attic window pulling himself up to the roof ridge line which lay just below the stack. He pointed one side of the stack using an oily mastic and that was to be his near undoing as he started a slide down the roof as he attempted to move round to one of the other four sides of the square chimney. The oily mastic had made the slates slippery. He managed to stop himself by digging his feet in the gutter that bordered the end of the roof. He then crawled along to a part of the roof unaffected by the oil that had come from the mastic and inched his way back up. Undaunted and undeterred by his near collision with the yard below he did not then decide to employ a work man to finish off the pointing the chimney stack, but undeterred found a rope, tied it around his waist, anchoring the other end on a roof beam in the attic and climbed out again onto the roof to finish what he had started, succeeding in making the chimney waterproof.

Dad probably undertook this job on a day when there was some big occasion that he needed to attend with shoes shined (which they always were), shirt and suit pressed, hair smoothed into place with the ubiquitous Brylcreem, all tidy and present, to go on parade. Not an army parade but a church anniversary parade. The adrenaline of doing things at the very last minute fuelled his buoyant personality. The local St Silas's Church anniversary saw a huge processing through the streets around the parish of hundreds of worshippers and different groups associated with the church such as the Sunday School, the uniformed children's organisations of Scouts, Guides, Cubs and Brownies, the Mother's Union, the Billiard club (men only then of course) and many others which made up the local community. A similar celebration to the Whitsuntide Walks, banners were held high. Their embossed or woven pictures announcing the organisation whose members processed behind their own particular banner. Streamers flowing out from the banner would be held usually by a child or young woman. Children wore new white frocks, socks and shoes, and flower garlands in their hair or straw bonnets. A brass band played, behind which the white vestments of the church choir, the verger, the vicar and other church officials billowed out in the sweet May breeze. And yes it never rained and the sun always shone for the Church Anniversary. Church was entered singing "Onward Christian Soldiers." The church full. All the pews taken, people stood in the aisles and at the back around the font. A huge combined choir of hundreds of voices relished in singing some of the most rousing and moving words and music ever written for Christian worship. The Battle of Hymn of the Republic was a favourite with its words of triumph of good over evil. Born out of the American Civil War it was originally composed to remember the anti-slavery campaigner—John Brown. This hymn came to the cotton towns of Lancashire during the American Civil War when the workers in solidarity with those seeking to end slavery sang it then as they sang it a century later—in defiance of any authority that seeks to limit the freedom of mankind.

> Mine eyes have seen the glory of the coming of the Lord;
> He is trampling out the vintage where the grapes of wrath are stored;
> He hath loosed the fateful lightning of His terrible swift sword;
> His truth is marching on.

Glory! Glory! Hallelujah!
Glory! Glory! Hallelujah!
Glory! Glory! Hallelujah!
His truth is marching on.
I have seen Him in the watch fires of a hundred circling camps;
They have built Him an altar in the evening dews and damps;
I can read His righteous sentence by the dim and flaring lamps,
His day is marching on.
I have read His fiery gospel writ in rows of burnished steel!
"As ye deal with my condemners, so with you My grace shall deal!
Let the Hero, born of woman, crush the serpent with his heel."
Since God is marching on.
He has sounded forth the trumpet that shall never call retreat;
He is sifting out the hearts of men before His judgment seat;
Oh, be swift, my soul, to answer Him; be jubilant, my feet!
Our God is marching on.
In the beauty of the lilies Christ was born across the sea,
With a glory in His bosom that transfigures you and me;
As He died to make men holy, let us die to make men free!
While God is marching on.

Let us die to make men free. That's what the adults of this congregation sang. Because that is what they had done.

The hymn brought to mind all those in that church who had 15 years ago come through the war. Their voices raised heavenwards remembered all those many men and women known to each of them who had died to make women and men free. Other hymns being that perfect traditional Welsh anthem—Guide me O Thou Great Redeemer, I vow to thee my country and Jerusalem were also part of essentially a Thanksgiving Service. This community singing released emotions of anxiety, fear and sadness. Singing together such music and words brought immense happiness. Now this mass experience of singing Christian songs comes only at Christmas when carols are sung in concert halls and town squares.

There are many miserable, unhappy people in the United Kingdom, their sadness medicalised as depression for which a talking therapy or a pill is prescribed when really the root cause of their suffering needs to be dug out and dealt with. Even though a return to a Christian faith or other religious faith, providing it is not obsessive and damaging which many faith practices are, can offer an emotional support network. Islam, Christianity and Judaism gives access to a knowledge of God. This knowledge will not solve the problems of poverty, poor housing, abusive controlling relationships, ill health, but it may offer some benefits. It has certainly helped dad to thrive and enjoy life to its utmost over the years. But then dad did not have all those deprivations just itemised. He came from a relatively prosperous family, he was fit, he had a sunny disposition and people warmed to him, a house then was a home, not an investment to make money from. Jesus Christ said that we must love our neighbours as ourselves. If we did there would be no inequality or unfairness. Other women and men down the ages from different religious and secular creeds and beliefs preach compassion, respect and understanding between people. It can be such a tough task for people to put other people before themselves for all sorts of reasons, but many do as has been seen by the selflessness and devotion to caring for others witnessed in hospitals and care homes not only throughout the pandemic, but at all other times when a person comes for healing, treatment and care. A lot of self-interest derives from the rights and privileges that have been accorded to the individual at the cost of the common good. Rights without responsibilities means that a culture of the individual's needs and wants thrives at the expense of a wholesome and sharing society.

Dad's belief in God and forces beyond the current perception of science may seem to some irrational and without any logical foundation. A lot of the way that we understand the world around us is through our experiences, which admittedly may give some conscious and unconscious bias to favour a particular view point.

Spirituality is in decline as people seek secular forms of thinking about themselves and the world about us in practices such as mindfulness. Access to other universes, other forms of life may have become imperceptible to those who deny their existence and so are not tuned into experiencing the seemingly inexplicable.

Growing up in a household that pursued rational thought and discussion, it was accepted that there were such phenomena that could not be explained by conventional knowledge. The only explanation lay in the presence and activities of a poltergeist, a ghost, a spirit or a branch of quantum physics yet to be identified or explained. This willingness to being open to the unknown, the incomprehensible, the possibility of the existence of other forms, worlds and beings was by no means seen solely as the province of the deluded. Friends, families and work colleagues accepted the presence and workings of the unusual as being a usual part of life. The seemingly inexplicable sometimes had a potentially valid explanation.

A group of six men all working in the same office, one of who was dad, decided to test the theory of life after death, that the one who died first would come back to the office and give a sign of their continued existence. Not such a macabre pact then that present day sensibilities may so assess. Not many years out of the war every man in that office had during the war witnessed many deaths. Dying was accepted as part of living. Death is inevitable. There is no escape. Here is dad's account of the return of one of his work colleagues after he had died.

"The first to go was Len West. He was my boss, tall and not an ounce of fat on him. Very brainy. Len was staying up near Keswick with his family. My cousin Harry happened to be in the area, part of a Blackburn Naturalist society trip to Keswick. They had been walking over Cat Bells and coming back down they saw this tall man running down some fields with his children. All of a sudden he fell down—just dropped down and did not move. Harry ran to some nearby cottages and knocked on the door for help. It was too late. He was dead. A few days later we were sat in the office and all of a sudden there was this mighty crash as a picture hung on the wall came hurtling across the office like it had been thrown. It did not just drop down if the picture hook had failed. It came across the room. We all said it was Len who had come to visit us and show us there is life after death by throwing that picture at us."

Other accounts abounded during the 1950s and 1960s, an oral tradition of incomprehensible events witnessed and experienced, but not captured on film or sound recorder. Only the attestation of the spectator as proof of the fact. That water came flooding through the ceiling in a friend's house; an occurrence sporadic and beyond the technical ability and knowledge of water engineers, architects and plumbers to explain. A total mystery. A dog its hair on end, growling into a corner of a room which the occupant of the house later established was a priest hole, now bricked over, but once the hiding place of a Roman Catholic clergyman, no doubt discovered by a Roundhead and put to the sword.

One more account of a sprit. This time it appeared in the house in which lived the Hindle family.

There were four of us which could, if mum was still alive, give sworn evidence of the events in the late 1960s of a very strange night in our terraced house in Blackburn.

It is the visitation of a poltergeist. A spirit so not amenable to being captured on film. The knocking sounds could have been recorded. Not any old poltergeist. Not angry, but friendly to warn of a silent gas escape that could have blown the house and all its occupants to high heaven and beyond as they lay sleeping like the dead in their beds. And then a persistent knocking was heard. Not by the teenage children in the house, whose dreams were buried coffins, never to be opened. A parent's sleep can be addled by the birth of children. The waking ear forever and ever listening for threats to the wellbeing and safety of their offspring. So it was the parents who heard it woken by a relentless drumming coming from behind their bed head. The bathroom was the next room adjacent to their bedroom wall. There was no one in there when the father of the family started to search for the source of the knocking.

What was it? Who could it be? The attic was also searched. Teenager's dreams were disturbed as parents thought that a boyfriend had been smuggled into a daughter's bedroom—super charged imagination took over—had a drainpipe been climbed and a window opened to let in the intruder—there was no one else there, not in the bedrooms, in the bathroom, in the kitchen, in the back lounge, in the hall. The back door and front door were checked but they were securely locked. There had been no physical imprint on the house that could explain the knocking.

But one room was not checked. The front room. This was a room common in many homes until the modernising '60s and '70s produced houses built with one downstairs living room running the whole length of the house. The front room was a hallowed space in most homes. It would be cluttered with glass cabinets, pianos, coffee tables, upright and untouched three piece suites covered with small hand embroidered cloths over the backs and arms of settees and chairs. Such cloths are called "antimacassars". A fascinating word. The front room was a place only to be entered on special occasions, usually when visitors came. It should have been entered that night as the reason for the poltergeist's warning was in that room.

In the morning all became nearly catastrophic on entering that not entered room. The front room was full of gas. The pilot light to the gas fire had gone out. It was the time when pilot lights were on constantly and if extinguished there was no safety mechanism to shut off the pilot light so a stream of gas, although only tiny started to escape gradually filling up the room in silence. If anyone had entered the front room in the morning switched on the light not only would all of the contents of that room—the piano, the sideboard with the best china and crystal, the posh three piece suite that accommodated visitors and various and successive boyfriends of the elder teenager, the "Crossley Sultana all wool" carpet bought at one of Howarth's sales ("definitely a posh shop") located in Darwen Street Blackburn, whose thick pile had allowed no further escape through the door into the hall and house beyond. The imperceptible gas seepage over many hours gathered and thickened in the room. Bought at one of the monthly knock down sales, this precious carpet, the leftover from a bigger roll that had carpeted a fancy Manchester hotel, would have been blown to bits together with all those four people living in the third terraced house from the top of the road, if the light had been switched on. Fortunately there was no light switch in the hall outside the room. If there had have been a switch outside or if the mother of the house who opened the front door room in the morning had been a smoker with a lit cigarette in her mouth this story would never have become a memory and retold. I would not be writing this now. Luck, fate, chance does play such a big role in the ability to live a long and contented life. And it did and does in the life of this man.

So who was knocking, a persistent loud knocking that sounded as though the wooden mahogany bed head itself was being battered. It was not an animal or bird. The wall behind the bed totally solid allowing no trapped creature to tap out a forlorn plea for rescue; the noise was louder than a tap in any event. It was not a referred sound. No mystery here. A lady who had lived in the house before was knocking to keep her home and its present bodily occupants in one piece. It was Mrs Robinson the former owner. She had died in the house and wanted to protect her home in which she was obviously still living as a spirit or ghost. Maybe she had scant interest in the present occupants and just wanted to ensure that her home was not blown to high heaven where she had not yet managed to move on to. Deceased from this world, but living in the next or in another universe or dimension. A helpful visitation indeed. She did not actually succeed in altering the household to the gas escape as the now 99 year old never went in to the front room—a strange omission which he cannot explain to this day. Probably because it was the space in the house that shall not be entered unless dressed in Sunday best, probably including a hat of some description for the ladies, a room reserved for entertaining aged aunts, uncles, cousins, and others needing to be impressed by the quality of the carpet and ornaments. Elder sister like all 1960s teenagers broke the rule—the room was not a show off space—it was for kissing and cuddling a member of the opposite sex.

Dad walked past the door when checking the house in the middle of the night. Not a place to be disturbed in daily household routine he left it alone. So the house could have been blown up and all the Hindles could have joined Mrs Robinson in another place. Who are these helpful intruders? Some may call them spirits; some may call them ghosts. Some may say the explanation is a load of nonsense. That there is no such things as ghosts or spirits or poltergeist. When you are dead, you are dead. But perhaps not. Nothing is as it seems.

This is a memory, not imagined, but pure in its reality. A memory verifiable by those four people who lived through the experience—two of which were like most teenagers—sceptical of adult utterances. The mother who never believed in poltergeists or ghosts was converted and the knowledge she gained that there was definitely some form of existence after death, not just the promise of it claimed by many religions, made her own passing easier. We were blessed to have survived and live on.

Mass education has led to a welcome decrease of superstition. Ignorance is the bedfellow of the bigot and the savage. Enlightenment in so many ways has been brought to so many people through so many advancements and discoveries in science, technology and the arts. Women no longer have to rely on old wives tales to navigate their periods and conception. Everyone has access to all genres of music. People can choose or manufacture their own persona and identity. Religion provides hope of a life after death, an escape from complete separation from loved ones who we leave behind. The promise of everlasting life meaning we will be reunited with those who have gone before us and those who will follow us. A lifeline for some believers.

And considering dad's many escapes from that final end of earthly existence he has extremely good fortune or a direct line to his maker. God though is not a Harry Potter. His powers are not magic. S/He works a lot through people. More likely dad has cheated death so many times because he just loves being alive so much and never sees a bad outcome to anything that assails him.

This includes the numerous times he has been rushed into hospital because of a medical condition that he has ignored. His favourite saying being "I'm fine" regardless of whether he cannot breathe, his legs have gone from under him or his heart has stopped.

An enlarged prostate which made him feel sick was put down to an upset stomach. Treated by a family remedy always given in different doses for a bad tummy, fever or pain, was Indian Brandy. He became so sick that he could not eat or urinate. He was in his 60s and suffering from a condition which affects many men. Males certainly from dad's generation, are not as tuned in the workings of their bodies as women, do not hear or listen to the red flags their body may be waving at them. Eventually and reluctantly a GP was called by mum who had him admitted to hospital immediately where a surgeon excised a large amount of the offending gland that was squeezing the outlet tube from his bladder. Fortunately it was not cancerous.

He did though in his 80s have a severe infection of his liver which caused an abscess. It led to blood poisoning requiring intravenous antibiotics before the abscess was drained. During this procedure, dad's heart stopped. He was brought back to life and transferred to the cardiac unit where he astonished doctors by getting up within 24 hours to use the toilet and shower. He has always took pride in his personal cleanliness and has hated anyone doing any personal care tasks for him. He never gives up, he always fights for independence in all he does.

Within twelve months dad had to be admitted to hospital again of all days— New Year's day when flu was raging in Lancashire and he was placed on a vascular ward where the cleanliness was appalling. Blood stained the floor. It needed a good mopping with bleach or other disinfectant. He had turned yellow. A scan found a blockage in his bile duct. Gall stones had accumulated there. A tube down his throat manoeuvred by the fantastic gastroenterologist doctor placed a stent mechanism which permanently opened up his bile duct to allow the stones to escape and enable the free running of this bodily digestive fluid once more.

Another time in hospital was in his 90s when the GP sent dad for an endoscopy—yet another tube down the throat. His GP was concerned at his low red blood cells count. Wondering whether he could be bleeding internally, the diagnostic test of pushing a camera down the throat to the stomach was recommended. Going down his throat the front of the tube pierced his throat. The clinician abandoned the investigation thinking that there was some kind of blockage preventing the tube going any further, when the real reason was that it had become stuck in the flesh that makes up the oesophagus. An offer to keep him in overnight because he was having difficulty drinking fluid and the nurses thought his throat may be swollen or bruised was declined with the usual refrain. "I'm fine." He went home and in his usual conviction that there was nothing much wrong with him did not become alarmed when he was unable to eat or drink much without coughing. Having a hole in the throat is not conducive to passing food down into the stomach. He became dehydrated and weak. Eventually the Out of Hours doctor was called who immediately sent him to hospital. He was admitted and eventually given a scan which identified the offending hole. Immediately a white sign was affixed to his bed saying "Nil by mouth." Food and drink and saliva could enter into his body through the hole with a very high risk of giving him an infection and sepsis. His grandson, a doctor working abroad at that time, was alarmed at his chances of survival. Antibiotics were pumped into him and he was fed intravenously. Miraculously he had no ill effects. Puncturing the oesophagus has a high risk of eventual fatality. He did not need an operation to sew up the hole. It healed itself. He enjoyed his two weeks in hospital as he did not feel ill and once he knew what was happening his usual positive self kicked in. He started enjoying himself chatting to other patients and the overworked NHS wonderful staff. The state of a person's physical health is so determined by their mood and personality. Because dad is so unshaken and undoubting in his belief that life is a gift to be enjoyed every second of the day regardless of the adversity he survives to live for many more days.

There have been one or two excursions to A and E for passing problems like bladder infections when he could not urinate, the last time left him off his legs and he had to be admitted.

But he has also had a couple of accidents in later years which again may have killed someone else but not him. In his early 90s driving down to Hawes from Ribblehead en route to visit his daughter in Yorkshire, a sudden hail storm covered the road in ice. Being an expert driver for many years with no accidents he immediately changed gear down and braked. The braking was enough to send the car skidding and into a roll. The car landed on its roof on the verge next to a stone wall. He was dangling upside down with his seat belt on. He unbuckled his seat belt and landed on the roof. The driver's door would not open so he crawled over to the passenger door and opened it to get out of his car. As he did so he was greeted by the words "Don't move." A local GP was driving up the road and saw dad's upside down car. An ambulance was called, he was checked over by the GP. There were no injuries. When asked if he wanted to go to hospital for a further check over he replied as usual. "I'm fine." The police totally stunned at this 90 plus year old's resilience and toughness drove him onward to his destination so that he could enjoy his time with his daughter.

Losing count of how many encounters with the door which says "death", there are more.

Highland cattle are not keen on having their photos taken. Once on holiday in Scotland dad was foolish enough to decide to go into a field with highland cattle to take a photograph of the cow. As he was doing so, the cow not surprisingly deciding he did not want his photograph taken by a human, went for him. Dad looking through the camera lens saw the beast's big horns and head first. Dad just managed to scramble away in time, jumping over the gate to safety. A lesson learnt—cows do not like paparazzi.

In Spain, not many years ago at all he hired an electric scooter. The problem was the controls. He was used to riding a bike. The accelerator attached to the handle was like the brake control on a bicycle. He squeezed the accelerator thinking it was a brake with the consequence that he scooter launched off over a large step. His injuries were confined to a nasty scraping of skin down his arm. No bones broken, no bruising. Again a lucky man.

This is the last letter dad wrote to mum after his leave home in September 1945. Still there in Austria he was a happy man, not just because the snows had come, but because his future truly was golden.

Feb 8th 1946

My Dearest Peggy,

Hello! again dear I'm writing this letter in front of a red-hot stove in the canteen waiting for a concert to start given by the boys in the barracks here, it's an impromptu affair but it passes an evening on nicely, phew it's hot, I'll take my jacket off.

Now it's Saturday night and I've copied the first part of this letter off last nights to keep up the sequence, the other paper got dirty in the pocket of my second-best B.D. trousers. What happened last night was a quicker turn-off of the light than I expected for the concert. Now it is Saturday evening and its five minutes to our hour dear. I've not been farther than this canteen all the evenings of this week. Outside the snow has thawed and

there's nothing else but mud and water around these barracks. It's not at all tempting to go to the pictures. Tomorrow night there's boxing in the ENSA theatre for the championship of this part of Austria. The province we're in is called Kärnten, so all the Army units are completing. Boxing on a Sunday! It will give all my great aunts a blue fit once they hear of it, do you believe in Sunday entertainment? To a certain extent I do, but not for outdoor sports like football etc. or the cinema, six days of the week should be enough for that in my opinion. I've seen the continental Sunday and can honestly say I prefer our own style. If people can't entertain themselves for one day of the week, I certainly feel sorry for them, let it be quiet I say. The argument about having wars on Sundays doesn't mean anything to me, two wrongs don't make a right. Sunday is best kept as a quiet day in my opinion, there's generally enough hurry and bustle the previous six days to last me anyway.

There's more stiff times ahead for all of you at home according to the paper. Austria is short of food, but I went in a butcher's shop here the other day and also behind-the-scenes. The meat he had hung up was first-class, home killed and there was good stuff going in the sausages as well. Our cookhouse use this butcher's bacon slicer for slicing the bacon used here for the morning's breakfast. Then we have kids coming round begging for what we throw away. A chap in our room says Australian tinned butters are sold in the shops, people are definitely short, in fact seriously short of food, but as yet I can't see any collapsing for lack of it. Maybe Austria is better placed than other countries as bad as it is. I believe Greece is in a bad way, or was. Italy is a hungry place, especially in the towns. When people are hungry they show it by losing self-respect, and everything deteriorates. In Austria very few indeed have tried to beg, borrow or steal off me. As for the latter there is very little stealing. I think Africa was the place where I saw more people hungry, followed by Italy. With the worst place there was Naples, I wouldn't like to be stationed there. I only hope there'll be a change for the better before long, the new food minister has got off to a bad start. He should never have promised normal rations when there was hardly any chance of that coming off. A lot of people are going to crack up if they don't watch out, everything is at its lowest.

It's now Sunday evening 21:30 hours and I'm writing this letter to you in bed. I landed back here at 8 PM after being out all day. Seeing as it was

Sunday, I dressed up to go driving, the lads laughed at me when I told them I was going motoring for a change. I went to Villach and in the afternoon ran round to a football match with the boys I'd to bring back. Then we went to the Kanzelbahn and made our way back to Klagenfurt in the evening calling in at a restaurant in one of the villages by the Worthersee, in fact we had a good time. I arrived back here in the barracks and to put the perfect end to a happy day a letter from you was waiting for me on my bed. It's grand darling if I couldn't see you tonight, I found the next best thing, a letter. Maybe I'd better try and reply to it before going any further or is it farther?

Oh! Oh! You've been industrious impossible when you get out of bed at 10 AM why half the day's gone then, you're a queer sort of cook letting the needle get stuck and then the currants turn out grand! So I wouldn't need a hammer and chisel to break 'em, would they break a pneumatic drill? Heavy sarcasm! Seeing as I'm a connoisseur at currant cake eating. I'll risk one when I'm home dear. It certainly sounds as if you've been kept busy, surprising what a lot of places need cleaning in a house isn't it? Arab style is the best? Loose stone walls, a thatched roof, if you're posh a separate room for the goat and pig, a mat or two for sleeping and sitting on, a few earthenware jars and plates, a doorless door and there's your house—no need to use a vacuum cleaner, the hens clear the breadcrumbs, how would you like that as a house? In fact, it is quite awful. Enough of poverty stricken Arab houses. I still think houses with doors and windows is better if not as simple.

I really enjoyed reading your account of Marion's wedding, Jack must have been in a sweat waiting for over half an hour. She is one girl I really would have liked to see married, she would look well in a white dress. I don't like weddings in costumes and uniform. From accounts she certainly had a good send off, if you've to make a speech after being married I'm not going to get wed. Peggy dear you'd have to prompt me then, please excuse the inevitable, (when I come home). Sorry dear we'll have to have a rehearsal. Jump on me sweetheart if this is wrong of me but next time, I want to put an engagement ring on your finger darling and if things are better we'll be able to de mob mother's cupboard and throw a party after it. You can perhaps see my feelings dearest, but there's just our two selves, but it would be grand to make others happy as well. As you say here's to all our tomorrows. I'm willing to chance what they bring, we could laugh at joys and troubles together and enter the tomorrows gaily. It's just how I feel dear, but another part of me says don't have a care. If it was only myself , I wouldn't bother about what the future is. Now I just want to make things as fool proof as I can. I've piles of confidence, but I've to watch myself or I do hare-brained things. Whenever you think I'm liable to do something foolish tell me dear. If you think I'll steady up with a word from you dear, I'll be sure of doing well. I just feel it darling, we'd make an unbeatable side.

Well, it's time I went to sleep, dear, and with the thoughts of you, it's a lovely comforting feeling going to sleep thinking of you every night, it's glorious, darling.

So goodnight and God Bless,

Yours always

with all my love

Jack

xxxxxxxxxxxxx

Venison for the troops and hungry Austrians

Dad's "Mr Wu" wash day

Mum and dad's wedding day

Post war peacetime courting

Italy – dad's tented home

Dad in his army lorry named after his beloved future wife – Peggy